Leadership in a Changing China

LEADERSHIP IN A CHANGING CHINA

Weixing Chen
and
Yang Zhong

First published in 2005 by
PALGRAVE MACMILLAN™
175 Fifth Avenue, New York, N.Y. 10010 and
Houndmills, Basingstoke, Hampshire, England RG21 6XS
Companies and representatives throughout the world.

PALGRAVE MACMILLAN is the global academic imprint of the Palgrave Macmillan division of St. Martin's Press, LLC and of Palgrave Macmillan Ltd. Macmillan® is a registered trademark in the United States, United Kingdom and other countries. Palgrave is a registered trademark in the European Union and other countries.

ISBN 1–4039–6734–2

Library of Congress Cataloging-in-Publication Data

Leadership in a changing China / [edited by] Weixing Chen, Yang Zhong.
     p. cm.
Includes bibliographical references and index.
ISBN 1–4039–6734–2
     1. Political leadership—China. 2. China—Politics and government—1976–
I. Chen, Weixing, 1957– II. Zhong, Yang.

JC330.3.L445 2005
320.951—dc22   2004050762

A catalogue record for this book is available from the British Library.

Design by Newgen Imaging Systems (P) Ltd., Chennai, India.

First edition: January 2005

10 9 8 7 6 5 4 3 2 1

Printed in the United States of America.

Contents

ACKNOWLEDGMENTS

Leadership in a Changing China is a collection of papers selected from an international symposium organized by the Association of Chinese Political Studies (ACPS) on April 3, 2003 at the University of Tennessee-Knoxville and sponsored by Chiang Ching-kuo Foundation for International Scholarly Exchange and the University of Tennessee.

The 16th National Congress of the Chinese Communist Party (CCP) convened in Beijing on November 8–14, 2002 marked the first ever smooth and peaceful transition of power since the CCP was founded 80 years ago. It is a good occasion to reflect upon a changing China. Realizing that "leadership in a changing China" is not a small task and requires collective wisdom, we invited experts in their own fields from China, Singapore, and the United States to share their insights with us and shed lights on the subject. This book is the result. We would like to thank all the contributors for their participation and Chiang Ching-kuo Foundation for International Scholarly Exchange and the University of Tennessee-Knoxville for their financial support. We would also like to thank Ms. Debby McCauley, Ms. Ping Zhuang, and Ms. Xiaoyang Hou for editorial assistance. Weixing Chen would like to acknowledge and thank the Office of Research & Sponsored Programs at East Tennessee State University for its support for his research and research activities.

EDITORS AND CONTRIBUTORS

Weixing Chen is professor of political science at East Tennessee State University (coeditor).

Yang Zhong is professor of political science at the University of Tennessee (coeditor).

Shulong Chu is professor of international relations and director of the Center for Strategic Studies at Tsinghua University in Beijing, China.

John Fuh-sheng Hsieh is professor of government and international studies and director of the Center for Asian Studies Center at University of South Carolina.

Youxing Lang is associate professor of politics in the Institute of Comparative Politics and Public Policy of College of Law at Zhejiang University in Hangzhou, Zhejiang, China.

Gang Lin is program associate at Woodrow Wilson Center for International Scholars in Washington, DC.

Guoli Liu is associate professor of political science at College of Charleston.

Xinning Song is professor and executive associate dean in the School of International Studies at Renmin University of China in Beijing, China.

Yongnian Zheng is senior research fellow in the East Asian Institute at National University of Singapore in Singapore.

PART I

INTRODUCTION

CHAPTER 1

INTRODUCTION: LEADERSHIP IN A CHANGING CHINA

Weixing Chen and Yang Zhong

Change is probably the most operative word in political science. Indeed it can be argued that political science studies center around differences or variance (to use a social science jargon). Two major questions concerning political and social changes are how and when they will occur. Over 20 years ago Valerie Bunce published a provocative book entitled *Do New Leaders Make a Difference? Executive Succession and Public Policy under Capitalism and Socialism*. In the book she studied the impact of leadership succession on changes in public policies through a comparison of the United States and former Soviet bloc countries. Bunce found remarkable similarities between the two systems with regard to policy changes resulting from leadership changes. Bunce argued that

> In both systems succession involves ambition, conflict, the airing of issues, the eventual victory of one candidate over another, and policy change once the honeymoon interacts with the campaign experience. The essence of the process—its impact and its logic—would seem to be very similar, East and West.[1]

Specifically, Bunce found that new leaders in both socialist countries and Western democracies do matter. She also found that the pattern of change is also similar between the two systems. In both systems innovative changes will occur early under the new administration, but the changes tend to slow down and the leadership settles into routines until the next leadership change.[2]

It is probably not so difficult to conclude that new leaders do make a difference in communist countries. Had Chairman Mao lived another 10 years, the Chinese Communist Party (CCP) would not have adopted the new reform policies in the late 1970s, and the dramatic changes in the former Soviet Union in the late 1980s would be hard to imagine without Mikhail Gorbachev. A much more difficult question to answer is the nature or parameters of the changes that resulted from leadership succession in communist countries. The type of changes under a new leadership depends on a number of subjective as well as objective factors such as individual attributes of the new leaders, socioeconomic and political conditions in the country, institutional constraints, a crisis situation, and timing. Unfortunately, political scientists are still incapable of making precise predictions on the nature or parameters of changes caused by leadership succession.

There was a leadership succession at the 16th National Congress of the CCP convened in November 2002. Hu Jintao succeeded Jiang Zemin as the new party secretary of the CCP, Wen Jiabao replaced Zhu Rongji as the new premier of the State Council and a new Politburo was born, even though Jiang Zemin retained the pivotal position of the chairmanship of Central Military Affairs Committee. One remarkable aspect of this leadership succession is the fact that it was the first time that leadership succession occurred peacefully and institutionally in the history of the People's Republic of China since 1949. The questions that observers of Chinese politics have been asking and trying to find the answers for since the fall of 2002 are whether this new leadership will be different from the last one and what kind of changes will occur under the Hu-Wen administration. The following chapters of the book attempt to provide preliminary answers to these questions by focusing on policy changes, institution building, and new foreign policy orientations. This book provides both timely information about a changing China and fresh perspective for understanding a changing China.

Noticeable changes have occurred since the leadership succession in 2002. Hu Jintao and Wen Jiabao have brought a pragmatic leadership style into the new administration. For example, the Hu-Wen administration canceled Politburo's annual summer retreat at Beidaihe, a seaside city in northeast China, and shortened the length of the annual session of the National People's Congress (NPC). A much publicized change during the new Hu-Wen administration is their "putting people first" orientation. Exhibits of this new orientation include more frequent visits to rural and poor regions of China, shifting focus to the rusting industrial base in northeast China, adjusting government policies toward rural China, and bowing to the public, which was rarely done by Chinese leaders. How meaningful and long-lasting are these changes going to be and what other changes will be introduced by the Hu-Wen administration? Answers to these questions depend on whether the new leadership is able to break the institutional constraints and engage in building new institutions at home and making China a more responsible player abroad.[3]

The process of economic reform is one of liberalization. China's economic reform started with Deng Xiaoping's assuming power as the second generation of Chinese leadership after the death of Mao Zedong. The implementation of the Household Responsibility Systems in 1979 in rural China began the Deng's era and the endorsement of capitalism in China's economic development by the CCP Politburo in 1992 after Deng Xiaoping's *nanxun* (tour of the South) marked the end of his era. Promoting economic growth and introducing market-oriented reform in China involved depoliticizing the Chinese polity, economy, and culture. The essence of Deng's effort to depoliticize the Chinese polity, economy, and culture was to transform China's planned economy into market-oriented economy through getting institutions right. If excessive centralization was to blame for the economic stagnation before the reform, it became necessary to encourage local initiatives and innovations in policy and organizational terms. Promoting economic growth was, after all, a local endeavor as nobody could depend on higher Party authorities for their own prosperity and revenues. Deng's reform therefore acted to strengthen the regions at the expense of the center and to solidify the political importance of economic capital and market position. Transforming China's planned economy into market-oriented economy through depoliticizing Chinese polity, economy, and culture was to endorse capitalist practice in China's economic development. Institution building under Deng served to compromise economic liberalism and political authoritarianism, but the contradiction from the combination of one-Party state socialism with competitive capitalism was not resolved. New institution building continued in post-Deng China.

Unlike Mao or Deng, Chinese leaders after Deng Xiaoping are no longer revolutionaries but technocrats. If the legitimacy of the CCP was, to a large extent, based on Communist ideology and the charisma of CCP revolutionaries like Mao Zedong and Deng Xiaoping, the era of Communist ideology and charismatic leaders came to an end with the death of Deng Xiaoping. For technocrats, performance has become the new criterion of legitimacy. To perform is to maintain sustained economic growth, and to maintain sustained economic growth requires further reforming China's economic system and reducing the state's regulatory power through decentralization and privatization, which requires further institutional liberalization. As the performance criterion of legitimacy concerns the survival, power, and leadership of the CCP in post-Deng China, institution building is both a result of and motivation for performance for the third generation of Chinese leadership under Jiang Zemin and fourth generation of Chinese leadership under Hu Jintao.

The reality in post-Deng China was that the CCP must try to attune itself to the new conditions of the reform. Jiang Zemin's effort was encapsulated in the "Three Stresses" (stressing politics, political study, and political moral spirit) and "Three Represents" (the CCP represents advanced culture, advanced forces of production, and the interest of the majority of Chinese population). Jiang's "Three Represents" were written into the CCP Constitution at the 16th Party Congress. Jiang under the new conditions of reform in post-Deng China went one step further in terms of institution building. Jiang tried to broaden China's social base to include the capitalist class in China's political order and put forward his vision of a *xiaokang shehui* (a well-off society), both of which were driven by the performance criterion. His vision of *xiaokang shehui* and "Three Represents" emphasize even development in China between the costal and inland provinces and between urban and rural areas and *xiaokang* for majority of Chinese instead of the Western concept of "middle class" to distinguish China's development path from the Western development path.

Even though China's leaderships and institutions have shown some capacity to cope with the rapid pace of socioeconomic change and address new issues and challenges in the past, much needs to be done institutionally for the fourth generation leadership. The current political institutions are seriously inadequate to cope with the totally new economic and social realities of China. China's economic reform and openness have created conditions for the development of personal difference, opening up spheres of action that are not subject to collective control. Many of the economic challenges (such as maintaining sustained economic growth and narrowing the wealth gap) that the fourth generation leadership faces can only be resolved with political solutions along the lines of democratization within the CCP and in the society at large. In addition, economic performance alone, which has its limits, may not provide adequate legitimacy for the fourth generation of Chinese leadership. Indeed, the real challenge and opportunity for the fourth generation of Chinese leadership are how to veer China toward the path of democracy. The new leadership also faces international challenges that have direct impacts on the new leadership's achievement of domestic goals and political legitimacy. The Taiwan issue and peaceful relations with neighboring countries are probably the two most crucial international issues facing the new leadership. It should be recognized that there are two major constraints for the new Hu-Wen administration in policy innovation: the shadow of Jiang Zemin in his capacity as the chairman of the Central Military Affairs Committee[4] and the fact that Jiang put several of his closest allies on the new Politburo's Standing Committee. With these two constraints it is hard to imagine major breakthrough in policy innovation will occur under the Hu-Wen administration in the near future even though incremental institutional changes are more likely.

Looking at changes and continuities in perspective, this book is divided into two parts: (1) Leadership change and institution building (chapters 2 through 5) and (2) leadership change and new foreign policy orientations (chapters 6 through 10), both of which convey the likelihood that China is moving toward an institutionally more responsible polity, internally as well as externally. Yongnian Zheng opens the book with a very detailed, but concise summary of the 16th Party Congress, and the subsequence of the chapters by Gang Lin, Weixing Chen, and Guoli Liu, Yang Zhong and Youxing Lang that follow Zheng's chapter runs from the central level to the most rudimentary level. Shulong Chu starts the second part with a concise and insightful discussion of significant departures of Chinese foreign policy at the 16th Party Congress, and the subsequence of chapters by Xinning Song, Guoli Liu, and John F. Hsieh cover the internal factors that affect Chinese foreign policymaking, the transformation of Chinese foreign policy, and cross-Taiwan Strait relations after the 16th Party Congress.

In chapter 2 Yongnian Zheng examines the degree of institutionalization of power succession from two perspectives: the outcomes of the 16th CCP National Congress and the politics behind it and ahead. Zheng notes that the mandatory age 70 for retirement applied to everybody including Jiang Zemin when it came to who should step down from the CCP Politburo and the trend of electing younger and better-educated leaders also continued as reflected in the new CCP Central Committee. In line with decentralization, provinces were better represented in the CCP Politburo and Central Committee, and in the meantime, *taizidang* (offsprings of Party elders) were also better represented in the CCP Politburo and Central Committee. The political process regarding power succession went rather smooth, judged by these outcomes despite the fact that personnel reshuffling at the top level was largely determined by politics behind the scene. The expansion of the CCP Politburo Standing Committee from seven to nine indicated that the leadership line-up outcome reflected factional political institutionalization though it, understandably, favored Jiang's faction. Factional struggle certainly continued, and Hu must meticulously toe the line set by his predecessor after the Party Congress. Nevertheless, the outcomes of the 16th Party Congress have provided some positive indication of the institutionalization of political succession in China. It is after all the first ever peaceful leadership transition in the history of the CCP. The scale of change among the top leadership is also unprecedented as characterized by the greater number of younger and better educated leaders. Hu is certainly confronted with the challenge of consolidating his power. His success in the fight against SARS did help him in creating an image of a new leader, but there is no indication that he will be his own man very soon. A bigger challenge for Hu is political reform. How Hu can make the Party and government more transparent, accountable, and democratic is the key to meeting the aspirations of the Chinese population while consolidating his own power and maintaining the Party's grip on power. Zheng's background check on the new leadership is very informative.

In his chapter Gang Lin discusses institution building in three areas: (1) leadership transition in terms of rule making and path dependency, such as age and term limits, grace period for CCP senior leaders, as well as anchoring Party leadership to the government, (2) Party building in terms of "Three Represents," two vanguards and one developmental Party, and (3) intra-Party Democracy in terms of institutional innovations and constraints. The PRC presidency, NPC chairmanship and State Council premiership have been constitutionally subject to the two-term limit since 1982 and a mandatory retirement age of 65 was applied to ministerial and provincial officials over the last decade though no such age and term limits were specified as a formal rule for national Party leaders. However, at the 15th CCP National Congress in 1997, an informal age limit (70) was applied to the election of CCP Politburo members, and it was again applied to the election of CCP

Politburo members at the 16th CCP National Congress. Lin argues that the practice of age and term limits for Party and government officials from lower level to upper level reflects a clear path dependency. That is, leadership transition is constrained by past choice of rules to end the life-tenure system. Lin also discusses the two norms of anchoring Party leadership to the government and separating the Party from the government, both of which follow the regime's general principle of one party rule. Intra-Party democracy, the institutional dimension of Party building, has always been associated with different leaderships' theoretical innovations, such as "Three Represents," collective leadership in terms of power sharing among the Party elite, division of power within the Party, and introducing electoral mechanisms into the Party. In developing intra-Party democracy, the Chinese leaders have adopted the strategy of improving existing institutions within the Party's traditional system of democratic centralism, but the democratic aspect of centralism has developed from one leadership to another in the reform era.

In the following chapter Weixing Chen and Guoli Liu argue that building a new political order in post-Jiang China represents the new direction in Chinese politics. Building a new political order in China involves the transformation of the CCP, the establishment of institutional petition access to power for the Chinese, and rule of law. The CCP has been transformed over the course of China's economic reform ideologically and institutionally. Ideologically, the CCP has rejected the communist ideology in China's economic reform, which has lost its appeal to both its members and Chinese citizens. Institutionally, the power of the Party has been shifted from the center to the locales and the Party's political control over its members and the Chinese has been greatly weakened. The CCP as a political party has decayed. As a result of its transformation, the CCP has since the economic reform tried to provide institutional access for the people, because what is at stake is the power and legitimacy of the CCP and the social and political stability of China. Avenues of institutional access that have either been established or strengthened since the economic reform include village elections in the rural area, the People's Congress system, *xinfangban* (office of correspondence), and hot-line centers. A critical aspect of building a new political order in China and link of political and economic reforms is the rule of law in the Chinese political context. In China, the Party's legitimacy derives from its successful leadership and commitment to economic development, and the rule of the Party is increasingly associated with the rule of law, because the rule of law is critical to a viable framework of social and political stability and sustainable economic development. Constitutionalism is a key to rule of law, and market economy must be a legal economy. This perceived logical relationship between the requirements of market economy and the rule of law, to a large extent, underlined the advocacy on the rule of law by the central leadership since late 1992 when the construction of a socialist market economy was made the target of future reform and development. In addition, to establish the authority of law is also critical to solving the growing problem of corruption in China. Ultimately, in the search for solutions to China's social, economic, and political problems, the organized force of the state may have to meet the unorganized and transformed citizen-masses halfway, either through institutions or on the street.

In chapter 5 Yang Zhong takes an institutionalist approach to study local politics. Focusing on the institutional arrangements of Chinese village authorities and their relations with higher state authorities, Zhong analyzes two different approaches to the mounting problems in China's rural areas: muddling through and institutional changes. Rural China has been a trouble spot for the Chinese government since the late 1980s. Rural problems are often summarized as *san nong wenti* (three rural issues: peasants, agriculture, and rural areas). The peasant problem refers to the peasants' declining income, poor living conditions, and low education level. The agricultural problem involves the low profitability of Chinese agricultural products, scarce agricultural land use, low agricultural technology levels, and the vulnerability of Chinese agricultural economy in world competition after China's accession to the World Trade Organization (WTO). These two problems lead to the overall rural problems of instability and potential chaos in the Chinese countryside. We all know that Chinese revolution was a peasant revolution. Chinese government has taken a cautious and reactive muddling approach in addressing the *san nong wenti*. The introduction of village elections should be understood in this context. Zhong cautions that Chinese peasantry may well be a contributing factor to China's crisis if no serious institutional changes will take place at Chinese local levels soon. Paradoxically, the ultimate solution to China's *san nong wenti* may lie in the reorientation of state policies and democratization of the political structure at higher levels, which is the focus of Youxing Lang's analysis in chapter 6.

Youxing Lang examines the roles and functions of national political elites in the process of village elections and illustrates the importance of elite network and its strategies. He examines the rationale of national political elites for promoting village election and the process of the passage of the Organic Law of Villagers' Committees in 1987 by the NPC, which is one of the critical aspects of elites' crafting. He also discusses how officials at the Ministry of Civil Affairs promoted village elections through building a sound macroenvironment, designing laws, rules and regulations, making institutional arrangements, and three cooperative projects. Lang, in his detailed documentation of the process, identifies and analyzes three kinds of resources in building up the momentum for village elections and forcing the issue onto the local agencies: expectations and pressures from peasants, the pursuit of their own interests, and the support of top leaders.

As the process of institution-building proceeds at home, China also faces international challenges that may derail its internal development, especially after joining WTO. China has been trying to be a responsible player internationally. A central theme in the new leadership's international strategy is its emphasis on peaceful rise of China as an international power to pacify the potential fear on the part of the rest of the world for a stronger China. In chapter 7 Shulong Chu discusses the major shift in China's foreign policy at the 16th CCP National Congress from "opposing hegemony" to "maintaining international peace and promoting common development." The change in language reflects a shift in attitude from a negative and confrontational one to a positive and cooperative one toward international affairs and China's relations with the United States. This new change has been manifested in China's policies toward U.S. invasion of Iraq and in the Korean peninsula. Specifically, unlike France and Russia, two permanent members of the UN Security Council who strongly opposed U.S. invasion of Iraq, China, also a UN Security Council member, noticeably kept a low key on the Iraq issue. China also modified its position on the North Korea nuclear issue. As Chu points out, China prior to the 16th Party Congress had always shown sympathy with North Korea and avoided criticizing North Korea in public. Since October 2002, however, China has openly stated that China supports non-nuclearization of the Korean peninsula, which is tantamount to say that China opposes North Korea's nuclear programs. In addition, China has put pressure on North Korea to come back to the multilateral negotiation table.

Chu further explains the rationale behind the shift and its significance. He argues that one of the main reasons explaining the shift in foreign policy attitude is the fact that China has integrated its economy in the global economy and become the fifth largest trade power after more than 20 years of reform and openness. In other words, China has much stake in maintaining the current global economic structure and international peace as anybody else in the world. In addition, Chinese people have become much more confident in dealing with the outside world after China has in recent years scored some major victories in the international arena such as winning the bid in hosting 2008 Olympics and being admitted into WTO in 2001. With these diplomatic victories Chinese people are shedding away their "victim" mentality acquired since the mid-nineteenth century (after the Opium War) and their deep-rooted suspicions of the West. Chu also notes that these trends will continue under the new leadership in China.

In his chapter Xinning Song also argues that China is adopting a more cooperative and constructive approach in its foreign policy and analyzes the interaction between key elements of Chinese domestic politics and its foreign policies. Song focuses on several domestic factors and their impact on China's new foreign policy orientations. The key factor is declining legitimacy of the CCP in the last 20 years. Economic development has become the sole basis for the legitimacy of the CCP and therefore the most urgent issue facing any leadership of the CCP. Any country's foreign policy is the extension of its domestic politics. China is no exception. Since economic development is so crucial to the legitimacy of the CCP, CCPs foreign policy agenda has to serve the central task of continued economic growth in China. That is why China has opted to join WTO despite of the risks, to establish cooperative relationship with the West and to maintain peaceful relations with neighboring countries.

In chapter 9 Guoli Liu offers a general description of continuities and changes in Chinese foreign policy orientation. He notes that one aspect of the new foreign policy orientation is that it is even more pragmatic and less ideological than the one before the new leadership succession. This new pragmatic foreign policy orientation is even reflected in the diplomatic formalities of the new leaders' official visits to foreign countries. For example, the Hu-Wen administration has decided to reduce the entourage accompanying top leaders' foreign trips and simplify the send-off and welcoming-back ceremonies for national leaders' foreign visits. This new foreign policy style has something to do with their *pingmin* (common people) background and their new "putting people first" domestic agenda. Like Shulong Chu and Xinning Song, Guoli Liu also makes the note that the new leadership in China is no longer "anti" something but "for" something in its foreign policy orientation and economic development continues to be the center of the leadership's foreign policy orientation.

In chapter 10 John Fu-sheng Hsieh examines potentially the most explosive issue in China's foreign policy: the issue of Taiwan. Hsieh argues that China's policy toward Taiwan has been fairly consistent over the years, which is the peaceful unification of China under the "one country, two systems" formula and the use of force against Taiwan if the latter declares formal independence. According to Hsieh, the fourth generation of leadership in China will continue this policy toward Taiwan. However the uncertainty in cross-Taiwan Straits relations comes from Taiwan given the volatile nature of Taiwanese politics and the divergent views on the national identity issue among the people in Taiwan. Therefore the key factor that is likely to affect cross-Straits relations lies in the internal political dynamics in Taiwan. In this context the March 2004 presidential election in Taiwan was an important event to watch. Hsieh's article was written before the election. Now the Democratic Progressive Party (DPP) has won that controversial election and it looks like the fourth generation leadership in mainland China has a major problem on its hands with four more years of the DPP government in power. Any misstep on either side may cause a serious crisis between the Taiwan Straits and regional instability in East Asia.

NOTES

1. Valerie Bunce, *Do New Leaders Make a Difference? Executive Succession and Public Policy under Capitalism and Socialism* (Princeton, NJ: Princeton University Press, 1981), p. 240.
2. Ibid., 223.
3. New institutionalism has been fairly popular among political scientists in recent years. For a complete discussion of the various versions of new institutional theories in political science, see B. Guy Peters, *New Institutional Theories in Political Science: The 'New Institutionalism'* (New York: Printer, 1999).
4. In a recent session of NPC held in March 2004, Jiang Zemin still walked in front of Hu Jintao when top leaders filed into the conference auditorium, which means either that Jiang is still in control of the CCP or that Hu still shows deference to Jiang. In either case, it suggests that constraints are still there for Hu to become his own man.

PART II

LEADERSHIP CHANGE AND INSTITUTION BUILDING

CHAPTER 2

THE 16TH NATIONAL CONGRESS OF THE CHINESE COMMUNIST PARTY: INSTITUTIONALIZATION OF SUCCESSION POLITICS

*Yongnian Zheng**

The 16th Congress of the Chinese Communist Party (CCP), convened in Beijing on November 8–14, 2002, marked the first ever smooth and peaceful transition of power since the Party was founded more than 80 years ago. Neither Mao Zedong nor Deng Xiaoping, despite their impeccable revolutionary credentials, successfully transferred power to their chosen successors. The originally appointed successors, Lin Biao, Liu Shaoqi, Hu Yaobang, and Zhao Zhiyang, all fell by the wayside. The fact that Jiang Zemin, a technocrat whom detractors dismissed as no more than a mere seat-warmer in 1989, has presided over such an unprecedented transition is all the more significant, as Hu Jintao was not even Jiang's preferred successor.

Although the 16th Party Congress ended, the outcomes of the Congress continue to grip the attention of China watchers, including government leaders and officials, academicians and businessmen. They remain interested in the key personnel changes, new power configurations, amendments to the Party Constitution and their implications. The political succession institutionalization is among a few of the most important issues in Chinese politics. I argue that China's succession politics has been greatly institutionalized under the third generation leadership. This chapter attempts to examine the degree of power succession institutionalization from two perspectives: The outcomes of the 16th Party Congress, and the politics behind it. Institutionalization, first of all, can be judged by outcomes. Nevertheless, without an understanding of the political processes that produce these outcomes, it is difficult to grasp the essence of China's power succession.

This chapter is therefore divided into three parts. The first part discusses the major political outcomes of the 16th Party Congress. The second part examines the context of Chinese politics prior to the Congress and the major outcomes in relation to the context. The third part addresses the issue of ensuring power succession in China.

CHANGES IN THE LEADERSHIP STRUCTURE

All six of the previous seven-member Political Bureau Standing Committees, other than Hu Jintao, stepped down as they reached or went beyond the mandatory retirement age of 70. Jiang forced Li Ruihuan to retire at the age of 68 only. Table 2.1 shows members of the Political Bureau and its Standing Committee. The 16th Party Congress witnessed the continued trend of electing younger and better-educated leaders. In. the expanded Political Bureau Standing Committee, eight of its nine members are new. Within the Political Bureau, fifteen out of its sixteen members (excluding its Standing Committee) are new. Only Madam Wu Yi moved up as an alternate member

Table 2.1   The Political Bureau and its Standing Committee at the 16th Party Congress (2002)

	Name	Age	Education
Members of Standing Committee	Hu Jintao	60	Qinghua University
	Wu Bangguo*	61	Qinghua University
	Wen Jiabao*	60	Beijing Geology Institute
	Jia Qinglin*	62	Hebei Engineering Institute
Average age: 62.1	Zeng Qinghong*	63	Beijing Engineering Institute
	Huang Ju*	64	Qinghua University
	Wu Guanzheng*	64	Qinghua University
	Li Changchun*	58	Ha'erbin Industrial University
	Luo Gan*	67	Beijing Steel Institute
Members of Political Bureau (excluding Standing Committee)	Wang Lequan*	58	Central Party School
	Wang Zhaoguo*	61	Ha'erbin University
	Hui Liangyu*	58	Jilin Provincial Party School
	Liu Qi*	60	Beijing Steel Institute
	Liu Yunshan*	55	Central Party School
	Wu Yi	64	Beijing Petroleum Institute
	Zhang Lichang*	64	Beijing Economic Institute
	Zhang Dejiang*	56	(North) Korea University
	Chen Liangyu*	56	PLA Military Engineering School
Average age: 59.8	Zhou Yongkang*	60	Beijing Petroleum Institute
	Yu Zhengsheng*	55	Ha'erbin Military Engineering Institute
	He Guoqiang*	59	Beijing Chemistry Engineering Institute
	Guo Boxiong*	60	PLA Military School
	Cao Gangchuan*	67	Soviet Union military school
	Zeng Beiyan*	64	Qinghua University
	Wang Gang* (alternate)	60	Jilin University

* Newly recruited members.

in the last Political Bureau to become a full member in the present Political Bureau. The average age of all Political Bureau members is 60.6, compared with the average age of 63 for the 15th Congress, 62 for the 14th, 64 for the 13th, and 72 for the 12th.

All Political Bureau members have a college education. The trend toward a technocratic leadership has continued unabated. Like the last Political Bureau, the present majority Political Bureau members have engineering background. All members on the Political Bureau Standing Committee are engineers, a contrast to the last Political Bureau Standing Committee where Li Ruihuan and Li Lanqing did not have an engineering background. Another important difference is that, unlike Jiang Zemin, Li Peng, Wei Jianxing, and Li Lanqing who studied overseas (such as in the then-Soviet Union), the current crop of Political Bureau Standing Committee members received their education in China. In other words, they have no overseas educational experience compared to their predecessors.

Within the Political Bureau, there are three members with social sciences and Central Party School backgrounds. Wang Gang, an alternate Political Bureau member, is a graduate from the Philosophy Department of Jilin University. Wang Lequan and Liu Yunshan graduated from the Central Party School. Their appointment does not signify that the Party will depart from its predominance by technocrats.

In the Central Committee, 180 of its 356 members or 50.6 percent are new entrants. Such a rejuvenation scale is large by recent standards. Table 2.2 shows the average age of the Central Committee member is 55.4, compared with 56, 56, 55, and 62, respectively, in the four preceding congresses. There is also a progressively younger crop of leaders in the Political Bureau and its Standing Committee.

Table 2.2 also shows that in terms of education, the percentage of Central Committee members having a college education is 98.6, compared with 92 for the 15th Congress, 84 for the 14th, 73 for the 13th, and 55 for the 12th. It appears from the above that promotion to the Central Committee and Political Bureau is increasingly based on education and performance, although this is not the sole deciding criterion.

Table 2.2 Changes in average age of members of the CCP leadership, 1982–2002 (including education level of Central Committee members)

Congress/Year	Members of Central Committee		Members of Political Bureau Standing Committee	Members of Political Bureau
	Age	With college and above education (%)		
12th (1982)	62	55.4	73.8	71.8
13th (1987)	55.2	73.3	63.6	64
14th (1992)	56.3	83.7	63.4	61.9
15th (1997)	55.9	92.4	65.4	62.9
16th (2002)	55.4	98.6	62.1	60.6

Distribution of Power

Although Hu Jintao ranks highest in the Political Bureau Standing Committee, he lacks factional support. There is virtually no one in the Political Bureau Standing Committee whom he can count on for obvious support. Wen Jiabao appears to be much like a loner in the Political Bureau. In his political career, Wen has been careful to shun factional politics, contributing to his political longevity. Known as the "humpty dumpty" in China's political circles, Wen has outlasted three of his mentors namely Hu Yaobang, Zhao Zhiyang, and Jiang Zemin. Like Zhu Rongji, Wen is expected to focus his energy on tackling serious challenges confronting the economy rather than engaging in factional politicking.

In contrast, Jiang, even though he relinquished his senior Party post, can count on six supporters among the nine members of the Political Bureau Standing Committee. They include Wu Bangguo, Jia Qinglin, Zeng Qinghong, Huang Ju, Wu Guanzheng, and Li Changchun. Another factor in Jiang's favor is the disappearance of the Qiao Shi faction in the Political Bureau Standing Committee.

Although Jiang succeeded in forcing Qiao Shi to step down from the Political Bureau at the 1997 15th Party Congress, he still had to contend with Qiao's supporters, Wei Jianxing and Tian Jiyun. With both stepping down, Jiang's faction has even greater room to maneuver. Given the influence Jiang still wields, it is not surprising that the media has portrayed Hu as a hapless leader under Jiang's shadow, with headlines such as "Hu's in Charge?,"[1] "Hu pledges to confer with Jiang on issues,"[2] "The Shanghai faction consolidates its grip on power,"[3] and "Is Hu going to be lame-duck leader?"[4]

Jiang's faction, however, may not be monolithic, mainly due to factions among his own men, which will make it difficult for them to work together as a unit. There are essentially two groups. The first, the Shanghai Gang, comprises Wu Bangguo (NPC Chairman), Zeng Qinghong (Vice State President, President of the Central Party School), and Huang Ju (Vice Premier). The second group, Jiang's loyalists, comprises Jia Qinglin (CPPCC Chairman), Li Changchun (in charge of propaganda), and Wu Guangzheng (in-charge of General Discipline Inspection Commission).

There could be even factions within the two groups. For instance, Huang Ju is reputed to be calculating and may not be able to get along with Zeng Qinghong. Also, as Jiang's men hold key positions in different party and government organizations, they may ultimately have to be more accountable to the institutions that they represent. Furthermore, one cannot rule out the possibility of one or two Jiang's men trying to get close to Hu to ensure their long-term political survival. Such intrigue will get more intense as Jiang gets more advanced in years.

Greater Provincial and "*Taizidang*" Representation

An interesting outcome of the 16th Party Congress is the greater representation of the provinces in the Political Bureau. In the Political Bureau

Table 2.3 Growing provincial representation

	Name	Local base*
Standing Committee	Jia Qinglin	Beijing
	Huang Ju	Shanghai
	Wu Guanzheng	Shandong
	Li Changchun	Guangdong
Political Bureau	Wang Liquan	Xinjiang
	Hui Liangyu	Jiangsu
	Liu Qi	Beijing
	Zhang Lichang	Tianjin
	Zhang Dejiang	Zhejiang (Guangdong)
	Chen Liangyu	Shanghai
	Zhou Yongkang	Sichuan
	Yu Zhengsheng	Hubei
	He Guoqiang	Chongqing

* Local base at the time of the 16th Party Congress. There have been some changes since then. For instance, Hui Liangyu is now the Vice Premier; Zhang Dejiang the Party Secretary of Gungdong; Zhou Yongkang the State Councilor and Minister of Public Security; and He Guoqiang the Head of the Party's Central Organization Department.

Standing Committee, there is now a relative balance between representation of Beijing and that of the provinces. Table 2.3 shows that four out of the nine members, namely Jia Qinglin (Beijing), Huang Ju (Shanghai), Wu Guanzheng (Shangdong), and Li Changchun (Guangdong) are from the provinces and cities. Looking at the Political Bureau as a whole, the balance is in favor of provincial representation. Thirteen out of the twenty-four Political Bureau members (or 54.2 percent) come from the provinces. Such a heavy representation of the provinces in the highest leadership has never taken place in previous party congresses where most leaders came from central bureaucracies.

Table 2.4 shows that the bias is toward the coastal provinces among the thirteen provincial leaders, namely Beijing, Shanghai, Shandong, Guangdong, Jiangsu, Tianjin, and Zhejiang. This is due to the Party's recognition of the importance the coastal provinces have played and will continue to play in China's economic development and its willingness to allow these provinces to have a greater say in the Party's highest decision-making body. Also, the support of the coastal provinces is crucial in effectively carrying out the Western development strategy, Hu's key focus.

There are only four inland provinces represented in the Political Bureau, namely Xinjiang, Sichuan, Hubei, and Chongqing. Although the figure is more than the previous Political Bureau, the inland provinces representation is still symbolic. One could surmise the leadership wants to show it attaches importance in spreading wealth to the inland provinces. Xinjiang's inclusion in the Political Bureau for the first time indicates the Party's commitment not only in bringing economic progress and prosperity to the province but also its determination to contain separatist movements there, especially in an age of global antiterrorism.

Table 2.4   Representation of coastal and inland provinces

	Name	Province
Coastal	Jia Qinglin	Beijing
	Huang Ju	Shanghai
	Wu Guanzheng	Shandong
	Li Changchun	Guangdong
	Hui Liangyu	Jiangsu
	Liu Qi	Beijing
	Zhang Lichang	Tianjin
	Zhang Dejiang	Zhejiang (Guangdong)
	Chen Liangyu	Shanghai
Inland	Wang Lequan	Xinjiang
	Zhou Yongkang	Sichuan
	Yu Zhengsheng	Hubei
	He Guoqiang	Chongqing

Table 2.5   The rise of *taizidang*

Name	Present position	Family background
Zeng Qinghong	Political Bureau Standing Committee Member	Son of Zeng Shan, Minister of Internal Affairs
Yu Zhengsheng	Party Secretary, Hubei	Son of Huang Jin, Mayor of Tianjin
Xi Jinping	Party Secretary, Zhejiang	Son of Xi Zhongxiong, PLA General
Bai Keming	Party Secretary, Hebei	Son of Bai Jian, Deputy Minister of First Mechanical Industry
Wang Qishan	Party Secretary, Hainan	Son-in-law of Yao Yilin, Political Bureau Standing Committee member
Bo Xilai	Governor, Liaoning	Son of Bo Yibo, Political Bureau member
Hong Hu	Governor, Jilin	Son of Hong Xiuzhi, PLA general

Yet another significant outcome of the 16th Party Congress is the emergence of so-called "*taizidang*" (or offspring) of Party elders. This group had been deliberately sidelined for at least the past 10 years. Deng Xiaoping had denied them access to power for fear of evoking ill-will among the people.[5] Memories of the 1989 Tiananmen incident, under Deng, where students called on the Party to rid itself of political favoritism and nepotism were still vivid. Being associated with a *taizidang* at that time was more a political liability than an asset.

In contrast, the 16th Party Congress saw much greater prominence accorded to *taizidang* in the power hierarchy. Table 2.5 shows several who have recently risen to prominence. Foremost among them is Zeng Qinghong, member of the Political Bureau Standing Committee and son of

Table 2.6 The Central Military Commission

	Previous members	Present members
Chairman	Jiang Zemin (1926)	Jiang Zemin (1926)
Vice Chairmen	Hu Jintao (1942)	Hu Jintao (1942)
	Zhang Wannian (1928)	Guo Boxiong (1942)
	Chi Haotian (1929)	Cao Gangchuan (1935)
CMC Members	Fu Quanyou (1930)	Xu Caihuo
	Wang Ke (1931)	Liang Gaunglie (1940)
	Yu Yongbo (1931)	Liao Xilong (1940)
	Wang Ruilin (1929)	Li Jinai (1942)
	Guo Boxiong (1942)	
	Xu Caihuo (1943)	
	Cao Gangchuan (1935)	

Zeng Shan, former Minister of Internal Affairs. Others include Yu Zhengsheng (Party Secretary, Hubei), Xi Jinping (Party Secretary, Zhejiang), Bai Keming (Party Secretary, Hebei), Wang Qishan (Party Secretary, Hainan), Bo Xilai (Governor, Liaoning), and Hong Hu (Governor, Jilin).

The emergence of *taizidang* can be attributed to the following three reasons: First, they are considered by the Party to be reliable and loyal, particularly at a time when the Party faces many daunting challenges. Second, a number of *taizidang* have proven themselves to be capable and deserving of the posts they currently occupy. In other words, meritocracy also applies to the *taizidang*. Third, unlike the Deng period, where it was politically sensitive to promote the sons of Party elders still alive, now there is less need for such caution as many of these elders are no longer around.

Party Still Controls the Gun

The 16th Party Congress once again reaffirms that the Party remains in control militarily. In line with the tradition set at the 15th Party Congress, no military man is appointed to the Political Bureau Standing Committee. Also in accordance with previous practice, two representatives of the military, Guo Boxiong and Cao Gangchuan, are appointed to the Political Bureau. Table 2.6 shows that Guo Boxiong and Cao Gangchuan are also concurrently Vice Chairmen of the Central Military Commission (CMC).

Jiang Zemin, a civilian and non-CCP Central Committee member, remains in control of the PLA (People's Liberation Army) as CMC (Central Military Committee) Chairman. He appears to be following in Deng's footsteps as CMC Chairman from 1987 to 1989 even though not a Central Committee member. It is, however, unclear how long Jiang intends to hold on to this position. Some analysts have speculated that Jiang is likely to step down from his CMC post in March 2003 when he will have to relinquish his post as President. Others predict that he will stay on for a bit longer. An article in the *Asian Wall Street Journal* even suggests that Jiang could stay on for at least 3 years, quoting Jiang's aide who revealed what Jiang told foreign dignitaries calling on him.[6]

Within the CMC, other than Jiang Zemin and Hu Jintao, six out of its nine generals have stepped down. There are three significant points about the CMC setup. First, with the exception of Jiang Zemin (76) and Cao Gangchuan (67), the rest of the members are around 60 years of age. This places them among the fourth generation of leaders and contemporaries to Hu. Second, only three of the six vacated military spots have been replaced. They are by Liang Guanglie (62, Chief, PLA General Staff), Liao Xilong (62, Director, General Logistics Department), and Li Jinai (60, Chief, General Armaments Department). The main reason for not filling all vacated positions is perhaps leaving room for Hu to make his own appointments.

Third, like the Political Bureau Standing Committee, some sort of factional balance has been achieved in the CMC. The two retired generals, Zhang Wannian, former Vice Chairman of CMC, and Fu Quanyou, former Chief of General Staff, have ensured that their own men have assumed positions in the CMC.

Table 2.7 shows the background of the CMC members. Zhang Wannian's supporters in the CMC include Guo Boxiong (who served under Zhang as Deputy Commander, Beijing Military Region), Li Jinai (who served under Zhang when he was Commander, Jinan Military Region) and Xu Caihou (who takes over from Zhang as the key go-between for the Party and the PLA nerve centers). Fu Quanyou's supporters in the CMC include Liao Xilong who fought in the Vietnam War in 1979 and with Fu, helped enforce martial law in March 1989 in Lhasa. Interestingly, that was also the time when Hu Jintao was Party Secretary of Tibet. Liao Xilong is reported to be Hu's ally.

The question arises as to whether Hu can command the military as effectively as Jiang. This is crucial if Hu is to succeed in consolidating power.

Table 2.7 Background of CMC members of the 16th Party Congress

Name	Background
Jiang Zemin	Chairman, CMC
Hu Jintao	Vice Chairman, CMC
Guo Boxiong	Executive Deputy Chief, General Staff Headquarters; Commander, Lanzhou Military Region and Deputy Commander, Beijing Military Region
Cao Gangchuan	Director, General Armament Department; Deputy Commander, Vietnam War
Xu Caihou	Executive Deputy Director, General Political Department; Political Commissar, Jinan Military Region
Liang Guanglie	Commander, Nanjing Military Region. Also served in Jinan Military Region and Beijing Military Region
Liao Xilong	Commander, Chengdu Military Region
Li Jinai	Political Commissar, General Armament Department; Political Commissar, Commission of Science, Technology and Industry for National Defence

Hu can hope to build on Jiang's success to some extent in institutionalizing Party–military relations. Some of Jiang's initiatives included creating a more professional PLA; promoting generals to key positions in the military; promulgating the National Defence Law of 1997 that established the Party's legal control over the military; de-linking the military from business, and; increasing the military's defense spending at double-digit rates every year since 1989. Other than institutional means (and perhaps more important), Hu will have to win over the trust and confidence of the PLA. This will take time.

Jiang's Legacy

Jiang has secured his place alongside China's two great leaders, Mao Zedong and Deng Xiaoping. This was partly because of Jiang's success in managing the Chinese economy and elevating China's international status. China is now a World Trade Organisation (WTO) member and will host the 2008 Olympics. It is also a constructive player in the U.S. war on terrorism. China is arguably the only successful and most powerful remaining communist bastion.

Closer to home, Jiang has strengthened the basis for the Party's continued monopoly on power, possibly for many more years to come. The inclusion of the "Three Represents" theory into the Party Constitution marks the culmination of years of efforts by Jiang to widen the social base of the Party by admitting capitalists as well as to ensure that it stays relevant. The preamble of the Party Constitution was also changed to reflect the CCP as the vanguard not only of the working class, but also of the Chinese nation and Chinese people. This is a significant move by the Party to distance itself from any distinct social class and move toward a political entity that will represent and coordinate the interests of various social classes. Nevertheless, what kind of political entity the Party will ultimately evolve into remains to be seen.

Most attention in the Western media has focused primarily on the "Three Represents" theory and its significance, but does not fully explain Jiang's legacy. Equally important, if not more so, is Jiang's vision to transform China into a *xiaokang shehui* (comfortable society), which was the title of his political report to the 16th Party Congress. The goal is to lay a firm foundation for achieving full-scale modernization by 2050. According to Jiang, China has already accomplished the first of the two steps toward modernization set by Deng 20 years ago.[7] Building on previous successes, Jiang has set the target of quadrupling China's GDP by 2020 with 2000 as the base year.[8]

POLITICAL PROCESSES ENSURING POWER SUCCESSION

Everything seems to be rather smooth, judged by the outcomes. Progress has been made and China's power succession is expected to go beyond the law of jungle stage. Nevertheless, to what degree power succession has been institutionalized has also to be evaluated by the process that produces these outcomes. They undoubtedly produced a long political process among major leaders. An examination of China's politics in 2002 will help us understand the problems that continue to trouble power succession.

The singular event that dominated China's political landscape in 2002 was the 16th Party Congress. Virtually all work on the political front for the entire year was related to or geared toward this major event. Political maneuverings intensified as incumbents jostled to secure the best possible outcomes for themselves and their supporters.

Prior to the Congress, the Party and government placed particular emphasis on setting the right tone for the Congress. Maintaining nationwide stability and ensuring minimal disruption to preparations for the Congress assumed urgency in light of a spate of workers' unrest in various parts of China (Heilongjiang, Liaoning, Jilin, Gansu, Guizhou, and even Beijing). Instead of new major initiatives, the Party and government concentrated on fine-tuning existing policies (such as sustaining high economic growth), or focusing on issues of concern to the people (tackling unemployment or reducing the burden on farmers).

The Party's propaganda machinery went into overdrive extolling achievements of the Party since the last Congress and in particular Jiang's contributions. A book entitled "Jiang Zemin on Socialism with Chinese Characteristics" containing important reports, speeches, articles, letters, and written instructions by Jiang over a 13-year period was published. Jiang's pictures appeared alongside Mao Zedong and Deng Xiaoping in public. The *People's Daily* highlighted the overwhelming nationwide support for the Congress. Also, the successful damming of the Three Gorges Dam was deliberately timed a day before the start of the Congress to drum up the celebrative mood.[9]

Party discipline was tightened. Wu Bangguo exhorted cadres not to start or spread political rumours or say anything to tarnish the image of the Party or country. He further called on cadres not to publicly contradict the policies or strategies decided by the Party but internally channel their opinions.[10] Luo Gan separately called on the Party and government to be vigilant against disruptive elements (e.g. terrorism, ethnic separatism, religious extremism, internal and external threats, and the Falungong movement).[11]

A tighter reign was simultaneously exerted by the Party and government on the print and electronics media. In June, the Party's Central Propaganda Department issued a directive listing 32 areas where the media should either exercise extreme caution when reporting (e.g. impact of WTO entry on various economic sectors in China) or refrain from doing (e.g. sensationalization of news).[12] In an unprecedented move, eight government bodies[13] came together to launch a nationwide campaign to curb the spread of undesirable information on the domestic Internet network, which could affect national security and social stability.[14]

The stress on ensuring a conducive environment for the Congress was not confined to the domestic arena. The authorities continued to raise China's international profile on foreign policy, and build relations with other countries while downplaying disputes. Most significantly, greater efforts were made to stabilize China–U.S. relations through high level visits and resumption of bilateral military ties.[15] China's relations with Taiwan were also a low key. China did not overreact when Chen Shui-bian described Taiwan's relations with China as "one country on each side" of the Taiwan Straits. China further consolidated relations with its southern neighbors by signing a framework agreement with Association of Southeast Asian Nations (ASEAN) to establish a China–ASEAN Free Trade Zone by 2010.

Key Personnel Arrangements

The jostling for power among top leadership intensified. While Zhu Rongji had indicated earlier he would be relinquishing his senior party post at the Congress and giving up his premiership in March 2003, neither Jiang nor Li Ruihuan ever stated their intention in such unequivocal terms. Li Ruihuan at 68 was below mandatory retirement age limit (70) for Political Bureau members and technically, could still remain on the Political Bureau Standing Committee. It was expected that Li Ruihuan would be the most senior and experienced member in the Political Bureau Standing Committee whom Hu Jintao would have to work closely with should Jiang, Li Peng, and Zhu Rongji step down.

Much speculation was rife in that Jiang would either fully retire or surrender only his Party and government positions while retaining the top military post. Up till the eve of the Congress it was not altogether clear what the final outcome would be. Jiang kept his future plans close to his chest and used it as a bargaining chip to secure positions of influence for himself and his supporters. Incessant calls by Jiang's supporters urging him to stay on or exhorting others to rally under his leadership added to the uncertainty. In a speech at the Guangdong Party School in July, Li Changchun, Party Secretary, urged the Guangdong Party cadres at all levels to keep in line with the leadership, with Jiang at the core.[16]

The PLA, in particular, was one of Jiang's ardent advocates. On separate occasions in January and June, General Fu Quanyou, former Chief of General Staff, called on the Chinese military to obey the Party core and military leadership led by Jiang "no matter when and under whatever circumstances."[17] General Chi Haotian, Defence Minister, echoed the same message in June.[18] These statements were strong pledges of allegiance to a person, not an office. Jiang himself fueled speculation that he would retain his military authority after the Congress when he promoted seven PLA officers to the rank of full general in June.

China's top leaders gather at the Beidaihe meeting in July for their annual retreat and failed to finalize the leadership line-up for the Congress. The subsequent announcement that the Congress would be held in November, rather than September as earlier speculated, fueled talks of intense wrangling among the top leaders. Opposition to Jiang's staying on came from two main quarters within the Party. First, Li Ruihuan had apparently offered to step down from the Political Bureau Standing Committee, though not required to do so, to exert pressure on Jiang. Second, discordant notes were sounded by Wei Jianxing from Qiao Shi's faction, decrying Jiang's unwillingness to relinquish power. Jiang was portrayed as reneging on his pledge to make room for a new generation of leaders when he forced Qiao Shi retirement in 1997.

Jiang mounted an ideological offensive to counter these challenges by enunciating the "New Three Talks" with its stresses on "Solidarity, the Big Picture and Stability." Although the "New Three Talks" was first mentioned in Jiang's May 31st speech, it gained greater prominence when the *People's Daily* gave front page coverage to an article on this topic.[19] The article appeared to be directed at containing unwarranted rumours originating from Party cadres on personnel arrangements at the highest level as well as the unhealthy jostling for power among them. This was Jiang's message to his political supporters and foes alike to rally to the Party and the nation's cause and not upset Jiang's orchestration of the leadership transition.

The reshuffling of key positions in Beijing and at the provincial level until the eve of the Congress gave some indication who would be among the leadership line-up. More significantly, the majority of those reshuffled were Jiang's men. Zeng Qinghong relinquished his post in October as Head of the Party's Organization Department, indicating that he would finally be elevated to the Political Bureau Standing Committee, a position which had eluded him for years. He Guoqiang, Chongqing Party Secretary, replaced Zeng as Head of the Organization Department. Also, Liu Yunshan was appointed Head of the Central Propaganda Department[20] at the same time that Jia Qinglin, Beijing Party Secretary, and Huang Ju, Shanghai Party Secretary, were moved to Party Central.[21] All five of them subsequently either became members of the Political Bureau or its Standing Committee.

Jiang, however, did not completely have his way in deciding the leadership line-up. The expansion of the Political Bureau Standing Committee from seven to nine showed the compromise that was struck among the various factions in the Party and government. To some extent, the leadership line-up outcome is a reflection of factional political institutionalization, albeit one predominantly in favor of Jiang's faction.

Final Ideological Preparations

Meticulous preparation went into the drafting of Jiang's political report to the Congress. The Political Bureau Standing Committee decided to form the political report drafting committee in October 2001, which was chaired by Hu Jintao and included Zeng Qinghong and Wen Jiabao. Teng Wensheng, head of the Party's Policy Research Office and Jiang's ally, was responsible for the actual drafting. The drafting committee was to come up with a report that would guide China to further the goal of building socialism with Chinese characteristics.

In order to come up with a comprehensive report, the drafting committee collated input from relevant government departments and Party organizations as well as conducted site visits to various provinces. As early as August 2001, the relevant Party organizations formed 14 discussion groups to examine issues such as Party building, the overall situation in the country, the development of advanced productive forces and culture, and distribution of income. Hu Jintao chaired meetings to collate the views of these discussion groups. Also, the drafting committee formed eight groups to conduct site visits to 16 locations throughout the country including Guangdong, Jiangsu, Shanghai, Heilongjiang, and Gansu. During the site visits, a total of 80 seminars were held which involved 914 people.[22]

Even though Hu Jintao was chairman of the drafting committee, Jiang closely supervised its work and intervened to ensure that it was on the right track. In a meeting with the drafting committee in January 2002, Jiang set political report theme which was to hold high the banner of the Deng Xiaoping Theory, fully absorb the thinking behind the "Three Represents" theory and construct a full fledged *xiaokang shehui*. Following this meeting, the drafting committee came up with the framework of the report and submitted it first to Jiang and then the Political Bureau Standing Committee for approval in February. After several revisions, a draft was ready in May, again submitted to the Political Bureau Standing Committee for deliberation.

Jiang's May 31st speech at the Central Party School, traditionally a platform for important pronouncements, gave the first public indication of the key elements that would be included in the political report.[23] Jiang elaborated on the theme he had stated in January. Most significantly, Jiang's speech showed that opposition to his "Three Represents" theory had waned and that there was now more support than when it was first enunciated in February 2000. Jiang's speech also indicated that there was an emerging consensus that admission of capitalist and private entrepreneurs was necessary for the Party's survival.

Not surprisingly, Hu Jintao was one of the staunchest supporters of Jiang's "Three Represents" theory. Hu address the Central Party School in September, extolling the "Three Represents" theory and called on Party officials to back Jiang's political vision.[24] More significantly, Hu unveiled in July new regulations on the selection and naming of Party and government leaders. According to Hu, these regulations were aimed at evaluating new leaders based on how they absorbed and implemented Jiang's "Three Represents" theory. Cadres who embraced the important ideology of the "Three Represents" were to be promoted.[25]

There were, however, dissenting voices from pro-reform liberals and hard-line communists criticizing Jiang's record, although they not seriously enough to upset his plans. In a scathing attack on Jiang's "Three Represents" theory, Bao Tong, a former aide to purged party leader Zhao Ziyang and liberal de facto spokesman in China's political elite, asserted that the Party has abandoned the workers and peasants and become an authoritarian party representing the rich and powerful. Rather than heralding the onset of democracy with the theory, Bao Tong contends that the Party is on the demise.[26] Aside from Bao Tong, two letters written by conservative critics accused Jiang of abandoning the Party ideals by welcoming capitalists into its ranks. The writer of one letter is believed to have ties to party elder Song Ping, known to be critical of Jiang.[27]

Jiang's name was eventually not included next to the "Three Represents" theory in the Party Constitution, an astute concession by Jiang not to appear overbearing and, as a political trade-off, to assign more of his men to key positions in the Party. In any case, Jiang scored a personal victory and sealed his legacy by having the theory included in the Party Constitution. The theory has entered the pantheon of Chinese revolutionary thought, sharing a status on par with Marxism–Leninism, Mao Zedong Thought, and Deng Xiaoping Theory.

Xiaokang Shehui

Jiang's vision to transform the whole of China into a *xiaokang shehui* (comfortable society) is as important, if not more so than his "Three Represents" theory although it has received comparatively less attention in the Western media. The importance the Party attaches to this vision was underscored by the use of *xiaokang shehui* as Jiang's political report title.[28]

The vision to transform the entire country into a *xiaokang shehui* has significant economic implications. It reflects a need to change China's pattern of economic growth. The emphasis, hitherto, has largely been on unbridled economic growth, with wealth concentrated in the coastal provinces and cities while pockets of poverty remain scattered around the country, especially inland provinces and rural areas. Jiang's vision aims to address this lopsided development by redistributing wealth to a larger population. This does not imply that China is turning its back on the market economy but rather increased attention will be placed on redistributing wealth through growth and stepping up economic development in the backward hinterland. This is a gradual and long-term strategy.

The term *xiaokang shehui* is also politically significant for the following reasons. First, in ideological terms, it is not only a rejection of the "middle class" concept used in the West but is also by extension a denouncement of the Western notion of liberal democracy. In the West, the development of the middle class is inextricably linked to the onset of democracy. Although detractors may argue that *xiaokang shehui* is nothing but communist jargon for the middle class, in reality the significance extends beyond a mere change of term. The Party is telling the whole country and the rest of the world that it intends to chart its own political development path. It is no coincidence that, in the same political report, Jiang rejected China developing along the Western liberal democracy path.

Second, *xiaokang shehui* is not only intellectually appealing to the Chinese people, many still yearning for a better life, but also politically sound because it propounds the attractive notion that everybody could eventually attain at least a comfortable standard of living.

CONTINUED POLITICAL UNCERTAINTIES

Ensuing Power Succession

While a fresh and younger team under Hu's leadership is now at the helm, Jiang still wields influence on the conduct of politics in the country. Although Hu is the highest office holder in the Party, it is not altogether clear whether he has the final say on important issues that affect the Party and country. Most glaringly, Hu has yet to be referred to as the "core" of the fourth generation leadership. Also, Jiang is still active on the political stage in his capacity as Chairman of the CMC.

The Chinese military, for one, continues to pledge allegiance to Jiang. In the December 2002 issue of the Party's magazine, *Qiushi*, Lieutenant General Zhu Qi, a PLA officer incharge of the security of Beijing, said that the retention of Jiang in the top military post was "an important political choice made by the Party."[29]

Jiang himself does not appear contented to take a back seat. At the height of the Severe Acute Respiratory Syndrome (SARS) outbreak, Jiang signed an order in April 2003 as Chairman of the CMC to mobilize over 1,000 military doctors to staff the Xiaotangshan Hospital specially built in the outskirts of Beijing to deal with SARS patients.[30] In May 2003, it was again Jiang who issued a condolence message to the families and relatives of the 70 officers and soldiers who perished when the Chinese Ming-class submarine they were on encountered a mechanical failure while on a regular training exercise.[31] Also, Jiang continues to receive front-page coverage in the national dailies either at important functions or when he receives calls by foreign dignitaries in his capacity as Chairman of the CMC.[32]

Uncertainty also prevails over the kind of working relationship that will unfold among the triumvirate of Hu Jintao, Zeng Qinghong, and Wen Jiabao although they appear to work well together.[33] Most noticeably, Hu and Wen have made a conscious effort to distinguish their leadership style from that of their predecessors by focusing more on the masses and less privileged. Hu's first domestic tour after being elected as General Secretary was to Xibaipo, the Party's legendary headquarters in northern Hebei province.[34] The intended message was that the Party would not forget its origin, that it was a Party founded to champion the interests of the suffering masses.

Wen, even before his appointment as Premier, had stressed the importance of accelerating agriculture and rural reform to raise the living standards of farmers and reduce their financial burdens at a Central Conference on Work in Rural Areas in January 2003.[35] Echoing the views of the top leadership, Li Changchun, a member of the Political Bureau Standing Committee in-charge-of ideology and propaganda, as well as Jiang's erstwhile ally, had on a number of occasions this year called on party organs and officials working in the media industry to stay in close touch with the people and pay more attention to the issues that affect their lives.[36]

As for Zeng Qinghong, he is keeping a low profile and appears to be supportive of the Hu-Wen leadership. Most recently, Zeng had rallied under the

Hu-Wen leadership in their efforts to contain the SARS outbreak.[37] With his mentor Jiang expected to be on the way out in a few years, Zeng would have realized that the best way to safeguard his political future is to build on his relationship with Hu and Wen. But it is unknown to what extent Zeng will be willing to defer to Hu in the long haul despite his public profession of support for Hu.

The SARS outbreak in China and efforts to contain it provide some indication of the continued jostling for power between Hu and Jiang's factions. Worth highlighting here is the simultaneous sacking of Health Minister Zhang Wenkang and Beijing Mayor Meng Xuenong in April 2003.[38] Zhang was regarded as belonging to Jiang's camp, while Meng was perceived to be Hu's protégé. While the sacking of Zhang was expected because of his blatant misinformation on the extent of the SARS outbreak and his failure to institute effective measures to prevent its spread, Meng's removal caught some China observers by surprise. This was all the more so when Meng was only appointed Beijing Mayor only three months ago, in January 2003.[39]

There is a perception that Meng Xuenong was made a sacrificial lamb by Hu to make it politically palatable for Jiang and his supporters to accept the political demise of Zhang Wenkang.[40] Most significantly, the removal of two senior government officials was Hu's strategy of confining the political fallout for the mishandling of the SARS situation to the government bureaucracy so as to protect the interests of the Party. It is worthwhile to note that Beijing's Party Secretary and Political Bureau member Liu Qi, another Jiang ally, was let off with a public apology and remains in his current position. If he had also been removed, it would most certainly have elicited a backlash from Jiang's camp and would have weakened Hu's efforts at consolidating power.

Most interestingly, a week after the sacking of Zhang Wenkang and Meng Xuenong, Hu chaired a regular Political Bureau meeting to discuss the launching of a new round of study of Jiang's "Three Represents" theory.[41] But why did Hu hold a seemingly unrelated meeting at the height of the SARS outbreak? How could the "Three Represents" theory provide an effective guide to the party leadership to combat SARS? At first glance, it is hard to see any correlation between the two. But seen from the political perspective, Hu's gesture is of some significance. Hu was making use of the "Three Represents" theory to reach out to Jiang's faction and to allay any concern that a political witch-hunt was in the offing. Hu wanted to show that he was for continuity and was willing to work with Jiang's faction to combat SARS.[42]

In fact, there was a closing of party ranks to deal with the spread of SARS. Major figures in Jiang's faction including Wu Bangguo,[43] Huang Ju,[44] Jia Qinglin,[45] and Zeng Qinghong[46] publicly exhort various sections of the Party, government, and society to work together to fight SARS. But the closing of party ranks does not necessarily mean that Hu's leadership of the Party has been strengthened. It can only be surmised that Jiang's faction has chosen for the moment to work together to face a common threat. Hu will have to continue to tread carefully if he wants to consolidate power.

Hu Jintao Remains Cautious

Hu has been careful not to appear to upstage or be seen to be disrespectful of Jiang. Since he was elevated to the Political Bureau Standing Committee in 1992, Hu has assumed such a low profile that the foreign media has often portrayed him as a political enigma.[47] Even after he was named the General Secretary, Hu pledged that on important matters he would seek instructions from and listen to the views of his predecessor.[48] Hu has even stated that he will continue with Jiang's policies.

To be sure, Hu has consciously set out to establish his own distinctive leadership style, one that is more mass-oriented. But in terms of substance, Hu has essentially not deviated much from the policies and directions set by his predecessor. At a three-day symposium to mark the eighty-second Anniversary of the founding of the Party on July 1, 2003, Hu called on the Party and the whole nation to launch a new wave of study on the "Three Represents."[49] Contrary to the views of some China observers that the SARS episode had provided an unprecedented opportunity for Hu to embark on political reforms in China, Hu completely avoided this topic in his speech.

Likewise at a Political Bureau meeting in August 2003, Hu stated that Deng Xiaoping theory and "Three Represents" should serve as guidelines for improving the socialist market economic system and revising China's Constitution, two key agenda items that would be discussed at the third Plenum of the 16th Party Congress in October 2003.[50] Hu is meticulously toeing the line set by his predecessor.

Yet under the broad framework of the "Three Represents," Hu is subtly trying to introduce some of his own interpretations. For instance, in his address at the "Three Represents" symposium in July 2003, Hu said that the essence of the "Three Represents" theory was that the Party should be established for the interests of the public and govern in the people's interests (*lidang weigong, zhizheng weimin*). This marks a shift in the Party's orientation from Jiang's focus on the role that private entrepreneurs and capitalists could play in building socialism with Chinese characteristics to one that stresses on the importance of addressing the expectations and needs of the masses. It would be difficult for Hu's political opponents to fault him on this small innovation to Jiang's "Three Represents" theory. More of such innovations can be expected in the future given the theory's broad reference.

To a great degree, Hu is in a better position than Jiang when the latter was thrust into the limelight in 1989. Unlike Jiang, Hu has successfully weathered a 10-year apprenticeship at the pinnacle of power. This is no mean achievement and is testimony to Hu's intelligence, political astuteness, and tenacity in the face of adversity. He can also tap on his network of supporters in the Communist Youth League, Qinghua University, and Central Party School, but he is likely to do so without unduly alarming the other Political Bureau Standing Committee members whose support he needs.

Conclusion

The outcomes of the 16th Party Congress have provided some positive indication of the institutionalization of political succession in China. It is the first ever peaceful leadership transition. Also, the scale of change among the top leadership is unprecedented as characterized by the greater number of younger and better educated leaders at the helm.

These improvements, however, should be set in context as the conduct of politics in China is still very much based on the rule of man. At most, the institutionalization manifested at the Congress has somewhat conditioned the conduct of political succession but has not displaced the predominant yet informal nature of politics in China. This is obvious from Jiang's success in leaving his imprint on history by getting his "Three Represents" theory included in the Party's Constitution. Also, Jiang played an instrumental role in putting his men in positions of influence in the Party and government.[51]

Hu is now confronted with the challenge of consolidating power. In the initial years at least, he will have difficulty being his own man, given the predominance of Jiang and his faction. In addition, there is Jiang's likely continued involvement in some key decision-making areas particularly on military affairs. Not only has Hu not secured Jiang's unequivocal support but also he is hemmed in by Jiang's supporters in key party and government organizations. It is too early to speculate if Hu would be a one-term Party Secretary; but what is certain is that he would have to live with Jiang's presence for a while.

Notes

* The Author would like to thank Weixing Chen for his comments on the draft and Lye Liang Fook for his research assistance.
1. *Time (Asia)*, November 25, 2002.
2. *International Herald Tribune*, November 21, 2002.
3. *South China Morning Post*, November 16, 2002.
4. *The Sunday Times*, November 17, 2002.
5. *Straits Times*, August 3, 2001.
6. *The Asian Wall Street Journal*, November 28, 2002.
7. Deng mapped out a three-stage growth strategy in 1979 as part of his plan to kick-start China's moribund economy. The first step envisaged by Deng was the doubling of the 1980 GDP by the year 1990. The goal then was to achieve a state of *wenbao* or a state where the people were well-fed and clothed. The second step envisaged by Deng was a doubling of the 1990 GDP by 2000. The goal was to achieve a well-off state or *xiaokang*. Deng's third step was to achieve full-scale modernization by 2050 although he did not spell out any targets.
8. *People's Daily*, November 9, 2002.
9. *People's Daily*, November 7, 2002.
10. *Qiushi*, April 16, 2002.
11. *Ming Pao*, April 10, 2002.
12. *Ming Pao*, June 21, 2002.

13. The eight government bodies were the Ministry of Public Security, Ministry of Education, Ministry of State Security, Ministry of Information Industry, Ministry of Culture, State Administration for Industry and Commerce, State Council Information Office, and State Bureau of Secrecy.

14. *Ming Pao*, May 3, 2002. An attempt was also made to block access by locals to log on to the internationally renowned search engine *Google* but to no avail. It is widely believed that this move was prompted by *Google*'s ability to lead Chinese users to sites considered undesirable by the authorities.

15. In his address to Qinghua University students during his visit to China in February 2002, Bush welcomed the emergence of a "strong, peaceful, and prosperous China," a much more conciliatory tone compared to the start of his administration. Hu Jintao was virtually accorded Head of State treatment when he visited the United States in April. Jiang also met Bush at his Texas ranch in October, an invitation extended only to close friends of the U.S. President.

16. *South China Morning Post*, July 29, 2002.

17. *People's Liberation Army Daily*, January 9, 2002 and June 29, 2002.

18. *People's Liberation Army Daily*, June 25, 2002.

19. *People's Daily*, July 22, 2002.

20. *Xinhua News Agency*, October 24, 2002.

21. The posts vacated by Jia Qinglin and Huang Ju were filled by Liu Qi and Chen Liangyu respectively, both of whom were politically acceptable to Jiang.

22. See <http://news.xinhuanet.com/newscentre/2002-11/20/content_634795.htm> for background to the drafting of the political report to the 16th Party Congress.

23. *People's Daily*, June 1, 2002.

24. *South China Morning Post*, September 3, 2002.

25. *People's Daily*, July 23, 2002.

26. Bao Tong wrote a 15-page essay which was reviewed by *The Wall Street Journal*. Excerpts of it were reproduced in "China's Unrepresentative Communists," *Asian Wall Street Journal*, August 28, 2002.

27. *Asian Wall Street Journal*, August 28, 2002.

28. Jiang has set the target of quadrupling China's GDP by 2020 with 2000 as base year. According to Dr. Li Jinwen, one of the drafters of China's tenth Five-Year Plan (2001–2005), this would mean achieving a GDP of around US$4 trillion by 2020 with a per capital income of US$3,100. See *The Sunday Times*, November 10, 2002.

29. *Qiushi*, "Jiji tuijin guofang he jundui jianshe—renzhen guanche luoshi shiliuda jingshen" (Actively push forward with defence and army construction—seriously imbibe and fulfill the spirit of the 16th Party Congress), December 1, 2002.

30. *Xinhuanet*, "Xinwen beijing: xiaotangshan yiyuan huifang" (Background News: Chronology of Xiaotangshan Hospital), June 20, 2003 <http://big5.xinhuanet.com/gate/big5/news.xinhuanet.com/newscenter/2003-06/20/content_929286.htm>. See also *Chinesenewsnet*, "Jiefangjun xiaotangshan yuan yuanzhang Zhang Yanling huigu xiaotangshan kangji feidian gongjianzhan" (The PLA Head of the Xiaotangshan Hospital Zhang Yanling recalls the uphill battle against SARS), July 29, 2003 <http://www1.chinesenewsnet.com/gb/MainNews/SocDigest/ Health/072920031149L:424299385.htm>.

31. *Xinhua News Agency*, "Jiang Zemin fa yandian aidao 361hao qianting yunan guanbin weiwen qinshu" (Jiang issues condolence message to the relatives of officers and soldiers of the 361 submarine mishap), May 2, 2003 <http://www.chinanews.com.cn/n/2003-05-02/26/299688.html>. See also *South China Morning Post*, "Seventy crew killed in submarine accident," *China Daily*, May 3, 2003 and "Suffocation killed 70 on sub, says report," May 5, 2003.

32. Front-page photos of Jiang have appeared in the following dailies: *Renmin ribao*, "Jiang Zemin shaking hands with the families and relatives of the victims of the Ming-class submarine mishap," May 6, 2003; *Jiefang ribao*, "Jiang Zemin and Hu Jintao meeting separately with Indian Prime Minister Shri Atal Bihari Vajpayee," June 25, 2003; *Renmin ribao*, "Jiang Zemin and Hu Jintao appearing at the wake of former Vice Premier, State Councilor and Defence Minister Zhang Aiping," July 13, 2003; *Renmin ribao*, "Jiang Zemin leading members of the CMC to meet participants at the fourteenth Work Conference of Military Officers," July 21, 2002; and, *Jiefangjun bao*, "Jiang Zemin and Hu Jintao meeting separately with British Prime Minister Tony Blair," July 22, 2003.

33. *Far Eastern Economic Review*, "China: The New Leadership—A Power Crisis Looms," December 26, 2002.

34. *Xinhua News Agency*, "Hu Jintao visits revolutionary base," December 7, 2002. It was in Xibaipo, on the eve of the Party's victory over Chiang Kai-shek's regime, that Mao Zedong had urged each and every cadre to avoid complacency and preserve the revolutionary spirit of "plain and living struggle."

35. *Xinhua News Agency*, "Stable rural policy stressed by central conference," January 8, 2003. See also *Xinhua News Agency*, "Profile—Wen Jiabao, Premier of State Council (4)," March 15, 2003.

36. *Xinhua News Agency*, "CPC leader calls on publicity officials to improve work," April 15, 2003. See also *Xinhua News Agency*, "Senior CPC leader calls for studies of 16th CPC National Congress guidelines," February 12, 2003 and *Xinhua News Agency*, "Ranking CPC official underlines publicity work," January 8, 2003.

37. *Xinhua News Agency*, "Vice-President inspects newly-designated SARS patient reception hospital," April 30, 2003.

38. They were both first stripped of their communist party posts on April 20, 2003 and subsequently removed from their official positions.

39. In contrast, Zhang Wenkang was appointed Health Minister in 1998.

40. *The New York Times*, "Hu's political future may hinge on SARS," *International Herald Tribune*, April 25, 2003. See also "SARS battle puts new Chinese leader to the test," April 26, 2003 and *South China Morning Post*, "Pair sacked over handling of outbreak," April 21, 2003.

41. *Xinhua News Agency*, "CPC to launch new round of study of 'Three Represents' theory," April 28, 2003. *Renmin ribao*, "Yanjiu zai quandang xingqi xuexi guanche sangedaibiao zhongyao sixiang xingaochao deng gongzuo" (Study within the Party on reviving the learning and imbibing of the important thoughts of "Three Represents" to a new height and its related work), April 29, 2003.

42. It is no coincidence that the same Politburo meeting discussed how to handle the relationship between economic work and the fight against SARS. The

meeting also called on all localities and departments to continuously move forward with economic work while going all out to combat SARS.

43. At the second meeting of the 10th NPC Standing Committee on April 26, 2003, Wu Bangguo called on all lawmakers to work closely with the central government to fight SARS with the joint effort of all sectors. See *Renmin ribao*, "Wu Bangguo: ba xixiang he xingdong tongyi dao zhongyang de jingshen shanglai qixin xieli di zuohao feidianxingfeiyan fangzhi gongzuo" (Wu Bangguo: Combine thoughts and actions with the spirit held by the central and work wholeheartedly together to carry out SARS prevention work), April 27, 2003.

44. During an industrial tour in Beijing on May 2, 2003, Huang Ju stressed the importance of producing adequate SARS-related medical supplies and uninterrupted power supply to SARS-related hospitals and quarantined areas. See *Xinhua News Agency*, "Vice-Premier urges greater efforts to provide supplies for SARS fight," May 2, 2003. See also *Renmin ribao*, "Huang Ju: quanli yifu quebao gongying zhongzhi chengcheng kangji feidian" (Huang Ju: wholeheartedly ensure adequate supplies and strong public morale to curb SARS), May 3, 2003.

45. At a SARS workshop in Beijing on April 30, 2003, Jia Qinglin called for multiparty cooperation by urging noncommunist parties and individuals to devote themselves to the anti-SARS campaign. See *Xinhua News Agency*, "Non-communist parties asked to help fight SARS," *Xinhua News Agency*, April 30, 2003. See also "Jia Qinglin: tongyi zhanxian yaowei duoqu kangji feidian douzheng de shengli xianji chuli" (Jia Qinglin: A united-front to ensure efforts toward a successful outcome in the battle against SARS), May 1, 2003.

46. When Zeng Qinghong visited the Sino-Japanese Hospital (a hospital designated to receive SARS patients) on April 30, 2003, he praised the medical staff who were at the front-line of the fight against SARS and urged Party members among the medical staff to play a leading role in the campaign. See *Xinhua News Agency*, "Vice-President inspects newly-designated SARS patient reception hospital," April 30, 2003. See also *Xinhua News Agency*, "CPC members urged to play a leading role in fighting SARS, boosting economy," May 21, 2003.

47. The adjective "enigmatic" was used to describe Hu in an article in *Far Eastern Economic Review*. See *Far Eastern Economic Review*, "Hu was Here," May 16, 2002. See also *South China Morning Post*, "Cadre with the wrong background who always steered clear of trouble," April 22, 2002; *Asian Wall Street Journal*, "Meet Mr Hu—or should it be Mr who?," April 30, 2002; *Straits Times*, "The Mystery—Who's Hu?," April 30, 2003; and, *Straits Times*, "Hu reveals little but gets what he wanted," May 4, 2002.

48. *International Herald Tribune*, "Hu pledges to confer with Jiang on issues," November 21, 2002. See also *Asian Wall Street Journal*, "Hu speaks softly for quiet reform," November 18, 2002.

49. *Xinhuanet*, "Hu Jintao zai yantaohui zuo zhongyao tanhua: zhenxin xue sangedaibiao lidang weigong zhizheng weimin shi biaozhi" (Hu's important speech at the symposium: whole-heartedly study the "Three Represents," follow the guidelines of establishing the Party for the interests of the public and governing in the people's interests), July 1, 2003. See also *Xinhua*

News Agency, "Hu Jintao urges greater effort in implementating the 'Three Represents' (1)," July 1, 2003.

50. *Xinhuanet*, "Shiliujie sanzhong quanhui shiyue zhaokai" (The third Plenum of the 16th Party Congress will convene in October), August 11, 2003. See also *Ming pao*, "Sanzhong quanhui taolun jinggai xiuxian" (The third Plenum will discuss economic reforms and amendments to the Constitution), August 12, 2003 and *China Daily*, "October Party Meeting focuses on amending Constitution," August 12, 2003.

51. At the 10th NPC in March 2003, a couple of Jiang's men secured key positions in the government. Among his key supporters, Zeng Qinghong is Vice President; Wu Bangguo is Chairman of the National People's Congress; Huang Ju is Vice Premier; Zeng Peiyan is also Vice Premier; Jia Qinglin is Chairman of the Chinese People's Political Consultative Committee; Chen Zhili is State Councilor and Zhou Yongkang is Minister of Public Security. Zhou's appointment marks the first time a Political Bureau member has been made public security minister since the end of the Cultural Revolution.

CHAPTER 3

LEADERSHIP TRANSITION, INTRA-PARTY DEMOCRACY, AND INSTITUTION BUILDING IN CHINA

*Gang Lin**

The world's most populous nation has a new leader, Hu Jintao. His election in November 2002 as Chinese Communist Party (CCP) general secretary and in March 2003 as Chinese president was the first smooth power transfer in the history of the People's Republic of China (PRC) that was not prompted by natural death or political crisis. However, the reelection of former Party and state leader Jiang Zemin as Party Central Military Commission (CMC) chairman, and his continued influence in Chinese politics, has fomented outsiders' speculation as to who is actually at the core, if any, of China's new leadership. Many speculate that Jiang still utters a strong voice on critical policy issues through informal channels, following the codes of conduct established by China's former leader Deng Xiaoping, who gradually transferred power to younger leaders over several years. It is safe to say that leadership transition in China is far from sharply defined—or complete—in the absence of free and competitive elections.

Prior to the 16th Party Congress held in November 2002, China's leaders had started "searching aggressively for a new set of principles and policies" to ensure its survival amid an increasingly market-oriented pluralistic society and a mounting identity crisis.[1] Consequently, the "institutionalization, formalization, and procedural routinization (*zhiduhua, guifanhua, chengxuhua*) of socialist democracy" have become the watchwords of China's new leaders in their long journey toward institution building (*zhidu Jianshe*).[2] The new leadership apparently seeks to develop "intra-Party democracy" (*dangnei minzhu*) without overhauling the existing one-Party system. The leaders believe that "intra-Party democracy is the life of the Party and plays an important exemplary and leading role in people's democracy."[3] China's ongoing institution building and political reform, therefore, are contingent on the path of socialist democracy taken by the CCP several decades ago.

This article examines China's institution building from the perspective of path dependency. Following Douglass North, the term "institutions" is used to refer to the "rules of the game" in society, which include current laws and jurisprudence, accepted habits, and formal or informal codes of conduct.[4] The concept of "path dependency," as used by Robin Cowan and Philip Gunby, emphasizes the impact of past choice of rules on current institution building.[5] Using leadership transition and the development of intra-Party democracy as two cases for study, this article attempts to demonstrate China's progress and difficulties in institution building. The questions to be examined include: What are the formal or informal rules guiding China's leadership transition? Are they changing all the time? What would be the new rules, if any, governing intra-Party politics? Has intra-Party democracy become a top priority in the new leaders' agenda for political reform? Will the Party resolve the tension between the principle of majority rule and that of democratic centralism (*minzhu jizhongzhi*)? What are the constraints of the old system on China's institution building and political reform?

LEADERSHIP TRANSITION AND RULE MAKING

The catastrophic 1966–76 Cultural Revolution and the resultant social chaos prompted the Chinese political elite to work to resolve the problem of over-concentration of power in one elderly person. Since the end of the Cultural Revolution, China's reformers, led by Deng Xiaoping, who was purged twice (1966 and 1976) by Mao Zedong but came back to power when he was 73 years old, have tried to abolish the life-tenure system for Party leaders. Consequently, adoption of age and term limits for Party and state officials, and reliance on knowledge and expertise as criteria for selecting cadres, have been practiced, incrementally, in areas from the periphery to the upper level of power. At the center of power, Deng became China's de facto paramount leader, while Hua Guofeng, Hu Yaobang, Zhao Ziyang, and Jiang Zemin served consecutively as the nominal top leader of the Party, with the title of chairman or general secretary. In contrast to Deng's dominance of Chinese politics for nearly two decades, none of the others—except for Jiang—finished his *full* term.[6] It was only after Deng gradually faded from the center stage of Chinese politics in 1994 that Jiang consolidated his authority and closed the gap between formal and informal power.[7] During the Deng era, political succession did not involve a life-or-death struggle among the Party elite, and ideological and policy disputes were much less fierce than those during the Mao era. These preexisting rules of the game established a set of parameters for leadership transition from Jiang Zemin to Hu Jintao, providing both constraints and opportunities for political actors in the new round of the power game.

Age and Term Limits: Formal and Informal Rules

The question of whether Jiang would retire from the general secretaryship after his two full terms of service (1992–2002, discounting the 3-year transition period from 1989 to 1992) stimulated speculation among overseas China watchers prior to the 16th Congress. Although the PRC presidency, the National People's Congress (NPC) chairmanship, and the State Council premiership have been constitutionally subject to the two-term limit since 1982, and a mandatory retirement age of 65 has been applied to ministerial and provincial officials during the past decade, no such age and term limits were specified as a *formal* rule for national Party leaders. At the 15th Party Congress in 1997, an *informal* age limit of 70 was applied to the election of Politburo members when Qiao Shi (71), Liu Huaqing (81), Yang Baibing (77), and Zou Jiahua (71) retired from the Politburo, with the only exception for Jiang, who was then 71. No term limit for Politburo members was implemented at the Party Congress, however. Li Peng managed to stay on the Politburo Standing Committee for his third term, and Tian Jiyun and Li Tieying were also exempted from retirement after their two full terms on the Politburo.

There is some reason to believe that *both* age and term limits were informally applied to the leadership transition at the 16th Congress. Hu Jintao's succession as Party general secretary and PRC president thereafter indicated that the general secretaryship, the highest Party position that has been attached to the state presidency since 1993, was inaudibly subjected to both age and two-term limits for the first time in PRC history. Moreover, all incumbent Politburo members who were over 70 retired from the Politburo without exception, including Jiang Zemin (76), Li Peng (74), Zhu Rongji (74), Wei Jianxing (71), Li Lanqing (70), Ding Guangen (73), Tian Jiyun (73), Chi Haotian (73), Zhang Wannian (74), Jiang Chunyun (72), and Qian Qichen (74). In addition, Li Ruihuan (68) and Li Tieying (66) also retired, even though they were under 70. Some China watchers interpreted Li Ruihuan's retirement as the result of a power showdown between him and Jiang; a more likely reason is that Li had served on the Politburo Standing Committee for two full terms. Likewise, while Li Tieying seemed not to have reached the informal age limit, he left the Politburo, apparently because of the term limit.

Evidently, the informal two-term limit was not applicable to Politburo members who would be promoted into higher ranks. For example, Hu Jintao became general secretary after serving on the Politburo Standing Committee for two full terms. Likewise, Wu Bangguo and Wen Jiabao joined the Politburo at the 14th Congress (Wu as a full member, Wen as an alternate), and were promoted into the Politburo Standing Committee after serving two full terms. Six other members of the new Politburo Standing Committee (Jia Qinglin, Zeng Qinghong, Huang Ju, Wu Guangzheng, Li Changchun, and Luo Gan) had been on the Politburo for one full term before they were promoted. All nine members, except for Luo Gan (67), were under 65 years old when they were elected or reelected to the Politburo Standing Committee, and are likely to serve for two terms, as they will be less than 70 at the 17th Party Congress scheduled for 2007.

While the age limit for national Party leaders—which refers to Politburo members (including regular members and Standing Committee

members)—is 70, members of the Central Committee are generally not supposed to be over 65. While there are a few exceptions on the new 16th Central
Committee, all of them concurrently served as state leaders (as vice chairman
of the NPC, or vice chairman of the Chinese People's Political Consultative
Conference (CPPCC)), thus extending the age limit to 70. In other words, the
age limit is more generous for national Party leaders and state leaders than for
provincial and ministerial officials, but informal rules of the game do exist.

The incremental practice of age and term limits for Party and government
officials from lower levels to upper levels reflected a clear path dependency—
leadership transition is constrained by past choice of rules to end the life-
tenure system. This does not suggest that political actors have to follow
historical precedent without modification. They can still make special cases
or reinterpret the rules under certain circumstances, resulting in a mixture of
institutional formalization and political personalization. For example, abolishing the life-tenure system was a rule chosen by the reform elite led by
Deng, but Deng enjoyed considerable leeway to play with the rule. Although
Deng, at the age of over 70, did not take the Party chairmanship, he could
still exert supreme power in different capacities, such as Party vice chairman
(1977–82), Politburo Standing Committee member (1982–87), Central
Advisory Commission director (1982–87), and CMC chairman (1981–89).
When Deng retired from the Politburo Standing Committee and the Central
Committee at the 13th Congress in 1987, an internal regulation was stipulated, giving Deng the final say on critical issues. After Deng officially retired
from the CMC chairmanship in 1989, he still wielded informal influence for
several years, spotlighted by his 1992 trip around southern China. However,
the basic rules of abolishing the life-tenure system, as well as those of age and
term limits, are compelling and point to the direction of future development.

A "Grace Period" for the Retiring Jiang

Except for the CMC chairmanship, informal age and term limits were also
applied to military leadership selection at the 16th Congress. Among eight
CMC members, Jiang Zemin, aged 76, maintained his chairmanship after
two full terms of service, enjoying a grace period prior to his full retirement,
apparently overdue. Hu Jintao continued to serve as CMC vice chairman
(starting in 1999). Cao Gangchuan (67) and Guo Boxiong (66), who joined
the CMC in 1998 and 1999, respectively, acquired vice chairmanships.
Xu Caihou (58), who joined the CMC in 1999 as well, retained his mem-
bership. In addition, three new faces were added to the CMC: Liang
Guanglie, Liao Xilong, and Li Jinai. At the same time, Xu, Liang, Liao, and
Li, respectively, took charge of the PLAs four headquarters—the General
Political Department, the General Staff Department, the General Logistics
Department, and the General Armaments Department.

Jiang's retention of the CMC chairmanship while giving up the general
secretaryship suggests that it is more difficult to transfer supreme military
power in China from one supreme leader to another. Although the Chinese

military is not directly involved in Party and government affairs under normal circumstances, it usually plays a key role in case of emergency, or under unique conditions.[8] For example, Mao Zedong successfully mobilized military support before initiating the Cultural Revolution, which was stopped 10 years later, ironically by military intervention and the arrest of the "Gang of Four," a radical faction headed by Mao's wife, Jiang Qing. Following past experience that "power comes from the barrel of a gun" and the principle of "the Party commands the gun," China's supreme leaders understand very well that control of the military is the most important means for power. Because the CMC is the source of great power, those who have this power—Mao, Deng, and Jiang—have all been reluctant to give it up. During the Mao era, the CMC chairmanship was closely attached to the Party chairmanship; in fact, Mao gained military leadership as early as 1935, even before he became the Party's top leader. After Deng became China's paramount leader, he took the CMC chairmanship from Mao's designated successor Hua Guofeng in 1981, arranging for Hu Yaobang to succeed Hua as the Party leader. Although Deng retired from other Party positions in 1987, he retained the CMC chairmanship for two more years and remained China's de facto military as well as civil leader between 1989 and 1994.

Deng's patriarchal reign over China from the CMC chairmanship (as well as from the Central Advisory Commission directorship) in the 1980s has far-reaching implications for China's leadership transition and Party–military relations. First, the traditional principle of "the Party commands the gun" no longer requires that the de jure Party leader concurrently serve as military chief. Second, a relevant regulation in the Party constitution was revised so that the CMC chairman does not need to be a member of the Politburo Standing Committee, the Politburo, or the Central Committee. Third, because of Deng's paramount status in the Party, military leadership is perceived as the core of political power in China. Consequently, Deng's detaching of the CMC chairmanship from the Party headship not only provided an institutional precedent for Jiang to follow, but also helped create the image that Jiang is still China's paramount leader. Although Jiang's retirement as general secretary enhanced the informal rule of subjecting Party leaders to age and term limits, his retention of the CMC chairmanship has highlighted the uniqueness of military power transfer in China. While other CMC members who were over the age of 70 obediently retired at the 16th Congress, routinizing the existing informal rules, Jiang's clinging to power has eclipsed any such institutionalized process of leadership transition in the military.

Civil–military relations in China are far from being clearly sorted out. According to the 1982 constitution, the State CMC directs the armed forces of the country, and the State CMC chairman, elected by the NPC, is responsible to the NPC and its Standing Committee. At the same time, the Party Constitution shows that the Party's CMC is the highest military leading organ. In fact, the two CMCs are different institutions in name, but have the same personnel. This design is a mix of the Party's intention to maintain "absolute control of the army" and its attempts to rule military affairs through legal procedures and state organs. However, neither chairmanship of the two institutions is subject to the term limit.

The CMC organizational structure is less formalized as well. Assignment of personnel to the Party's CMC is decided (*jueding*) by the Central Committee, presumably by affirmative hand raising—rather than secret voting—by the Central Committee members. At the 14th Congress, the Central Committee approved seven members for the CMC, with Jiang Zemin as its chairman, Generals Liu Huaqing and Zhang Zheng as two vice chairmen, and Chi Haotian (minister for national defense), General Zhang Wannian, Yu Yongbo (director of the General Political Department), and Fu Quanyou (chief of General Staff Department) as other members. Three years later, the 14th Central Committee, at its fifth Plenum, decided to promote Chi and Zhang as vice chairmen, and added Wang Ke (director of the General Logistics Department) and General Wang Ruilin to the CMC, for a total of nine members. The number of CMC members approved by the 15th Central Committee in 1997 was reduced to seven, resulting from the retirement of Liu Huaqing and Zhang Zheng, but increased to eleven only 2 years later. Adding new faces to the CMC *between* two party congresses may have served as a buffer to slow the leadership transition in the army *during* the congress period, but it also reveals the difficulty of a straightforward power transfer in the military.

It is unclear how long Jiang will keep the CMC chairmanship. The unusual even number (eight) of CMC members suggests that Jiang may serve as a transitional figure.[9] If Deng's precedent is instructive, Jiang's grace period may not last more than 2 years. China watchers cannot help but wonder, during this transition, who in fact will prove to be China's supreme leader, Jiang or Hu. Such speculation was encouraged by the fact that various official Chinese media ranked China's new leaders inconsistently right after the 16th Congress. While most official media, including the *People's Daily* and the Chinese website of Xinhua News Agency, still ranked Jiang as China's number one leader, Xinhua's English website placed Hu Jintao and the other eight members of the Politburo Standing Committee on the top list of Who's Who of Party Leadership, followed by members of the Politburo and the CMC, and secretaries of the Central Discipline Inspection Commission.[10]

This inconsistency vividly demonstrates China's incomplete progress toward formalization of its leadership transition. Formally, the Politburo and its Standing Committee, ritually elected by the Party's Central Committee, exert the authority of the latter (meeting only several days yearly) when it is not in session. Members of the Politburo and its Standing Committee therefore are considered to be China's top leaders, according to the Party's institutional design. Informally, the retiring Jiang is perceived as China's most senior leader—his seminal idea of "Three Represents" (*sange daibiao*, which means that the CCP should "always represent the developmental requirement of China's advanced productive forces, represent the developing orientation of China's advanced culture, and represent the fundamental interests of the overwhelming majority of the Chinese people.") has been enshrined in the Party Constitution, and several of his protégés have taken strategic posts within the Politburo Standing Committee.[11] Reportedly, in a secret acceptance speech after being appointed Party's boss, Hu pledged that he would "seek instruction and listen to the views" of Jiang on important matters, similar to what the Party did for Deng at the 13th Congress.[12]

Such an arrangement has rekindled China watchers' memory that Deng, 2 years after he left the Politburo Standing Committee but kept the CMC chairmanship, played a critical role during the 1989 Tiananmen incident that forced the dismissal of his successor, Zhao Ziyang. Despite the similarities of political arrangements in 1987 and 2002, leadership transition in general, and Party–military relations in particular, are less personalized today than 15 years ago. First, Deng's prestige within the military came from his long-time revolutionary experience. By contrast, Jiang's connections with the army began only when he assumed the CMC chairmanship after he became Party general secretary. As Party general secretary, Hu can legitimately take leadership over the military. According to official media, the Politburo convened a meeting in summer 2003, discussing military affairs without Jiang's attendance. This suggests that Party–military relations have been reshaped along the predetermined principle of "the Party commands the gun." Second, Deng's tremendous influence in Chinese politics was enhanced by a group of members of the "Old Guard."[13] On the contrary, Jiang's power base is limited to the CMC, and his protégés on the Politburo Standing Committee seem to work with Hu more cooperatively than competitively.[14] Third, Hu's formal power, not only as general secretary but also as PRC president, has not only given him great visibility in dealing with foreign and domestic affairs (SARS in particular), but also has helped him maintain a good working relationship with Premier Wen Jiabo. This distinguishes Hu from Zhao Ziyang, whose political showdown with Premier Li Peng was partly attributable to the practice of "separating the Party from the government" (*dangzheng fenkai*) in the 1980s, to which this essay will now turn. In brief, Jiang's grace period is unlikely to be accompanied by a fierce power struggle among the Party elite at the juncture of leadership transition.

Anchoring Party Leadership to the Government

Another unwritten norm adopted in the recent leadership transition is the so-called "*jiandang yuzheng*"(anchoring Party leadership to the government).[15] This norm was applied visibly at the 8th NPC in 1993, when General Secretary Jiang Zemin assumed the PRC presidency and the other three key members of the Politburo Standing Committee, Li Peng, Qiao Shi, and Li Ruihuan, took office respectively as premier, NPC chairman, and CPPCC chairman.[16] The 9th NPC in 1998 and 10th NPC in 2003 followed this rule, with top Party leaders currently holding the key government positions. Meanwhile, in 24 of China's 31 provinces, municipalities, and autonomous regions, the Party secretary concurrently serves as chairman of the Standing Committee of the Provincial People's Congress.[17] In most ministries of the government's State Council, the head of the Party Group (*dangzu*) concurrently serves as minister.

This norm is consistent with the Party's tradition and ruling principle. After the establishment of the PRC, Party Chairman Mao Zedong concurrently served as state head between 1949 and 1959, Party Vice Chairman Liu Shaoqi served as NPC chairman from 1954 to 1959, and Zhou Enlai, another vice chairman, retained the premiership until he died in 1976. One of the most dramatic institutional changes in the history of the PRC was the abolition of the state presidency during the Cultural Revolution. While the state presidency was reinstated in 1983, it did not resume its supreme status until 1993, when it was institutionally reattached to the Party's top leadership.

"Separating the Party from the government" was another practice associated with the principle of one-Party rule, which can be traced to 1959, when Mao gave the PRC presidency to Liu Shaoqi and kept the Party and CMC chairmanships for himself. With this arrangement, Mao remained the paramount leader on the "second front," while Liu, as the Party's number two leader and state president, took care of day-to-day state affairs on the "first front." The "first front," according to Mao, refers to the sphere where policies are implemented, and the "second front" refers to the area where important policy guidelines are decided. However, the institutional tension between the Party chairmanship and PRC presidency quickly resulted in Liu's dismissal and abolition of the state presidency. Mao's second designated successor, Lin Biao, attempted to restore the presidency during the Cultural Revolution, but this only made Mao suspicious of him, and contributed to Lin's sudden downfall in 1971. After the Cultural Revolution, Deng tried to separate the Party's role from that of the government. However, functional ambiguity between the general secretaryship and premiership created power conflicts and institutional friction throughout the 1980s; this has been considerably reduced since the state presidency was attached to the Party general secretaryship.

Both practices of "anchoring Party leadership to the government" and "separating the Party from the government" follow the Chinese regime's general principle of one-Party rule. Their alternating appearance in PRC history reveals the political elite's capability for developing different practices from the same principle. During the Mao era, there were no term limits for Party chairman, state president, or premier. Under these circumstances, separating the Party from the government between 1959 and 1966 could help dilute Mao's radical ideas and his absolute dominance of Chinese politics.[18] Mao's manipulation of power and his radicalism, however, resulted in the chaotic Cultural Revolution, when the Party greatly enhanced its unitary leadership (*yiyuanhua lingdao*) and the government simply became the Party's instrument for political campaigns, propaganda, and popular mobilization. After Mao, the state presidency and premiership are subject to two-term limits according to the 1982 Constitution. However, no term limits for

Party leaders have ever been written into the Party Constitution. Interestingly, owing to the political ups-and-downs throughout the 1980s, the three formal Party leaders, Hua Guofeng (1976–81), Hu Yaobang (1981–87), and Zhao Ziyang (1987–89), all failed to finish their full terms. Zhao Ziyang yielded his premiership to Li Peng in 1988, whereas the state presidency was transferred from Li Xiannian (1983–88) to Yang Shangkun (1988–93). Because of political tranquility among the leadership in the 1990s, Jiang Zemin finished his two full terms as both Party general secretary (1992–2002) and state president (1993–2003). Had the general secretaryship not been attached to the state presidency, Jiang might have been able to keep his position as Party boss. From the perspective of leadership transition, "anchoring Party leadership to the government" has informally subjected the Party leader to the two-term limit, first formalized in the governmental sphere in the 1982 Constitution. Furthermore, while "anchoring Party leadership to the government" in the 1950s served to enhance Mao's monopoly over Chinese politics, its resurrection in the 1990s helped to domesticate the Party to gradually routinized state procedures demanded by a growing market economy. For example, since the 16th Congress, China's official media has frequently reported issues discussed at the regular Politburo meetings, as well as activities of Party leadership small groups that were once unavailable to outsiders.

To summarize, while Mao exerted both formal and informal supreme power of the Party to the end of his life, Deng succeeded Mao as China's paramount leader without taking the nominal number-one position of the Party. With Deng's endorsement, Jiang acquired both the formal number-one position (starting from 1989) and informal supreme power (starting from 1994), retaining them until his retirement from the Party general secretaryship and state presidency. However, Jiang's retention of political influence through the CMC chairmanship, following Deng's precedent in 1987, recreated a gap between formal and informal power that was closed about 10 years ago. The abolition of the life-tenure system for Party leaders started from the sphere of formal power, but failed to move on in the area of informal power characterized by personal manipulation. Without a multi-party system allowing for electoral competition for government positions, leadership transition in China is less transparent than that in liberal democracies. While the PRC Constitution does stipulate the two-term limit for key government positions, the informal rules of age and term limits for Party leaders are yet to be formalized and written into the Party Constitution, and military-power transfer is even less predictable. For the same reason, the problems of the Party's dominance over government and the overlapping of the functions of the Party with those of the government cannot be really resolved. Under such an institutional framework, China's future development inexorably hinges on the Party's ruling style and capability. Thus, it is reasonable to keep a close watch on China's ongoing "Party-building" program, which is aimed at redefining the Party's identity and enhancing its ruling capability through marginal political reform.

INTRA-PARTY DEMOCRACY: INSTITUTIONAL INNOVATIONS AND CONSTRAINTS

Three Represents, Two Vanguards, and One Developmental Party

Intra-Party democracy, the institutional dimension of Party building, is closely associated with the Party's theoretical innovations regarding the concept of the "Three Represents." In response to the current wave of global economic interdependence and political democratization, the CCP has tried to "keep pace with the times" and perpetuate its lifespan by transforming itself from a revolutionary party into a ruling party, or what I call "a developmental party." It attempts to accumulate credit from building a "well-off" society by directly managing government affairs, in what I would conceptualize as "governmentalization of the Party" (*zhengdang zhengfu hua*), and also seeks to increase its ruling capability by developing intra-Party democracy. First, in its search for new ruling legitimacy, the Party claims its credentials in representing "the advanced productive forces," promoting China's economic development, and rejuvenating the Chinese nation. Moreover, to expand its ruling constituencies, the Party redefines itself as not only a vanguard of the working class, but also a vanguard of the Chinese people and the Chinese nation. By juxtaposing "two vanguards" that are not mutually exclusive concepts, the Party has actually diluted its identification with the working class and moved itself in the direction of a "party of all the people" (*quanmindang*).[19] Further, to find a theoretical justification for promoting intra-Party democracy in particular and people's democracy in general, the concept of "political civilization" has been fashioned, after the existing "two civilizations" in CCP terminology, "material civilization," and "spiritual civilization."[20]

These theoretical innovations can also be explored from the perspective of path dependency, which has been applied in the field of social sciences not so much to ideological development as to institution building and historical evolution. Ideological evolution in China, however, is also constrained by past choice of pattern in theoretic discourse. Despite Beijing's de-emphasis on communist doctrine for day-to-day policymaking for more than two decades, communism is still held by the Party as a remote ideal. The impact of the preexisting ideological framework on current theoretical modifications is unavoidable. First, "advanced productive forces" and "advanced productive relations" are a pair of concepts in Marxist political economics. During the Mao era, advanced productive relations were conceptually equal to the state ownership that was assumed to be the best means for economic development. By using Marxist terminology but shifting their theoretical focus from productive relations to productive forces, the reform elite after Mao attempted to accommodate different ownership systems while maintaining the "sacred" Marxist doctrine on the surface. Second, the CCP, in the past, was defined as the vanguard of the working class, which is part of the Chinese people. The usage of the "two vanguards" exactly reflects the Party's dilemma between retaining its traditional identity and developing new ruling constituencies. Third, while "political civilization" is a new concept created by the reform elite, one can still find conceptual linkage between political civilization and material and spiritual civilizations. Some Chinese scholars even point out the linkage between "Three Represents" and "three civilizations"—material civilization related to China's advanced productive forces, spiritual civilization related to China's advanced culture, and political civilization related to the fundamental interests of the overwhelming majority of the Chinese people.

In brief, the "Three Represents" campaign constitutes a theoretical dimension of ongoing Party building. If the idea of "two vanguards" has moved the CCP toward the direction of a developmental party for the whole people, the new concept of "political civilization" is revealing Beijing's flexibility and bottom line in its search for intra-Party democracy.

Institutional Innovations

Chinese reformers realize that as the CCP has been transformed from a revolutionary party of the proletariat into a developmental party for the whole of the Chinese people, the Party must change its ruling style and enhance its governing capability. The growing diversification of Party membership, as well as of Chinese society, calls for interest coordination and integration within the Party and poses a new challenge to the post-Jiang leadership's ruling style that is guided by Leninist democratic centralism. Constrained by the past choice of rules, the Party elite is apparently searching for institutional innovations without overhauling the existing one-Party system. Intra-Party democracy has thus become the Party's priority in its institution building. Some Party officials, including leading members at the Central Party School, have started to search for mechanisms to promote intra-Party "democracy," even extolling the virtues of a so-called "Third Way"—an institutional compromise between single-party authoritarianism and multiparty democracy.[21] Major measures being adopted or under consideration include expanding power-sharing among the Party elite, developing a division of power within the Party, and allowing limited intra-Party electoral competition.[22]

Power Sharing among the Party Elite

Collective leadership has been one of the important principles of the Party. Both Mao and Deng emphasized that the first secretary of any Party committee should not have a final say on important policy issues, which should be decided by all committee members according to the principle of democratic centralism.[23] Nevertheless, both men ended up as patriarchal leaders who together dominated Chinese politics for half a century because they failed to institutionalize Party committees as policymaking organs through developing sufficient meeting regulations and operational procedures. The Central Committee has functioned only symbolically throughout PRC history. Real decisions are made by the Politburo, particularly its Standing

Committee, headed by the core leader.[24] Similarly, Standing Committee members (*changwei*) of Party committees at the local level, especially Party secretaries, are the real decision-makers in their domains. In view of the political corruption resulting from power concentration in only a few hands, the Party has chosen some local Party committees as test sites for improvement of policymaking mechanisms. Measures include increasing meeting time periods and leaving important decisions to the full membership of these Party committees, rather than solely to the "standing members" (*changwei*) or secretaries. For example, in April 2002, the Guangdong Provincial Party Committee selected three Party leaders at the municipal level by a secret vote among all committee members, and in December 2002, the Shandong Provincial Party Committee also selected 17 municipal Party leaders by vote.[25] However, it is difficult to transform the Central Committee into a real policymaking institution, as most of its members are scattered nationwide, serving as local Party or government leaders. This membership structure, following precedent norms, does not suggest that the Central Committee will improve its function significantly in the foreseeable future.

Another institutional innovation regarding power sharing among the Party elite is to improve the functions of party congresses, which have been theoretically defined as the highest power organ of the Party. Chinese political scientists such as Liao Gailong and Gao Fang advocated as early as the 1980s that the National Party Congress return to an earlier CCP norm by convening its annual meetings.[26] In the late 1980s, counties under the jurisdiction of Jiaojiang city in Zhejiang province convened annual meetings of local party congresses.[27] Prior to the 16th National Party Congress, some scholars and experts at the Central Party School and other universities also proposed that party congresses at all levels should convene once a year (*lianhuizhi*). Their main arguments were: (1) the Party Congress system should be as essential to the Party as the NPC system is to the state; (2) party congresses should convene annual meetings, and operating procedures and regulations must be improved to ensure good discussion; and (3) at any given level, party congresses are the most important political bodies, with power to decide crucial issues and supervise other Party organizations.[28] Other scholars believe that the main function of party congresses is to elect Party committees. The priority on strengthening party congresses is therefore designed to improve their electoral functions by providing more candidates than positions to Party Congress delegates, so that delegates can have free choice in electing committee members. As a compromise, the Party decided at its 16th Congress to try out the system of party congresses with regular annual meetings in more cities and counties and to "explore ways to give play to the role of delegates when party congresses are not in session."[29] It remains to be seen how the Party will redefine the functions of party congresses in the years to come.

Division of Power within the Party
Historically, the CCPs ruling system was designed according to the Marxist–Leninist principle of "combining legislative and executive into one

organ" (*yixing heyi*) to ensure power concentration and political efficiency. Prior to the 16th Congress, some experts in China proposed discarding the idea of "*yixing heyi*" and establishing check-and-balance mechanisms among the Party committee, Party executive committee (a new institution to be established according to the proposal), and Party discipline inspection committee (DIC).[30] The three committees, each with its own different personnel, would be responsible to the Party Congress. When the Party Congress is adjourned, the Party committee would lead the executive committee and the DIC. The Party committee would make decisions based on the principle of collective leadership. The executive committee would implement policies, giving responsibility to the leading cadre (*shouzhang fuzezhi*), for the sake of efficiency. To increase the authority of the DIC, its members could attend and speak at the executive committee's meetings, review documents issued by the executive committee, and watch policy implementation; the DICs personnel should be appointed vertically, free of control of the Party committee and executive committee within the same domain.

Despite these innovative ideas, one can still find the institutional linkage between this proposal and the old norm favoring power concentration. First, the plan proposes that Party committees lead executive committees and DICs when party congresses are adjourned. In other words, the proposal still assumes that Party committees are superior to executive committees and DICs. Second, the main function of DICs is supposed to be watching executive committees, rather than Party committee. In other words, the proposed relations between Party committees on the one hand and executive committees and DICs on the other would be an institutional combination of vertical control and parallel checks and balances.

It is unclear whether China's new Party leadership will put this kind of proposal in its reform agenda. In view of the Party's tradition of democratic centralism and its current experiment with reform of the Party committee system, a more likely scenario is that plenary sessions of Party committees will become major venues for collective decision-making, while standing members of Party committees will be responsible for policy implementation. In other words, a division of power might occur within a local Party committee following the norm of "fusion of power," but not between two parallel Party organizations.

Introducing Electoral Mechanisms into the Party

Electoral competition was absent during the Mao era. It was not until the early 1980s that the reform elite under Deng began to allow limited electoral competition within the Party. At the 12th Congress in 1982, delegates were allowed to add names to, and delete names from, the list of nominees for the Central Committee provided by the leadership.[31] At the 13th Congress in 1987, the election rules for the Central Committee were further reformed to require more nominees than the number of seats (*cha e xuanju*). With the reform, the number of candidates for membership in the Central Committee must exceed the number of slots by 5 percent.[32] The marginal difference in number between candidates and seats, plus the Party's control of the nomination process, has significantly limited the voters' free choice and veto power, but it nevertheless prevents the most disliked nominees from being elected to the Central Committee. For instance, the Party mobilized delegates to make sure that some candidates would be elected at the 15th Congress, but delegates intentionally voted for others, forcing the Party to discard this practice at the next Congress. In selecting preliminary candidates for the new sixteenth Central Committee, the Party took several rounds of consultations to shorten the name list from 514 to 375, but only 32,200 Party heads at the county level and above were involved in recommending possible candidates and it was the Politburo Standing Committee that finally decided the list. During the 16th Congress, delegates, who were grouped into 38 delegations, preliminarily elected 198 full members out of 208 candidates and 158 alternate members out of 167 candidates. When delegates as a whole formally elected the Central Committee on November 14, 2002, all candidates preliminarily elected by the 38 delegations were elected to the Central Committee.[33] As can be seen from the procedures for (s)electing Central Committee members at the 16th Congress, Party leaders obviously prefer coordination and consensus building to electoral competition and majority votes. The "margin of elimination"(*cha e*) remains the same (5 percent) as 15 years ago, when the rule of "more nominees than the number of seats" was first introduced into the Party. Also, this rule has not been applied to the (s)elections of Politburo members and higher Party and state leaders, although some scholars in China argue that even the Party general secretary should be subject to real elections.

Electoral competition for Party positions is more significant at the grassroots level, where village Party branches in some regions have experimented with the two-ballot system since 1992. At the first stage, candidates are recommended by ordinary villagers through secret votes and then nominated by township Party committees. At the second stage, village Party members elect the secretary and other Party branch members.[34] The significance of the two-ballot system is to prevent those most disliked from being elected, but the system cannot guarantee that those elected are the most liked by Party members or ordinary villagers, since official candidates are determined by township Party committees. In other words, villagers have a certain veto power, but not comprehensive voting power. In 2002, the Party mandated that all who want to be village Party secretaries must first stand for election to the village committee, subjecting Party cadres to the electoral process.[35] After the 16th Congress, Party leaders in Yaan City, Sichuan province, conducted an experiment of convening annual meetings in a township Party Congress. More than 82 percent of candidates for delegates to the Congress were self-nominated or recommended by ordinary Party members, rather than being appointed by upper-level Party cadres. Through secret vote, one village Party secretary failed to be elected, while another ordinary Party member at the same village won a majority of votes.[36] The institutional roots of these intra-Party elections can be traced to the relatively competitive village elections for village committees initiated in the 1980s.

Institutional Constraints

In developing intra-Party democracy, Chinese leaders have adopted a cost-efficient and risk-averse strategy to improve existing institutions within the Party's traditional system of democratic centralism. Democratic centralism is defined as a system that practices centralism on the basis of democracy while carrying out democracy under centralized guidance. It emphases theoretically both free input from Party members before decisions are made by the leaders and strict discipline to implement Party decisions, once made. Such a dialectical principle can provide either opportunities or constraints for the reform elite in the ongoing undertaking of Party building, depending on which variable, centralism or democracy, is emphasized by the Party.

In the past, the principle of democratic centralism was elaborated by Mao, who noted that "individual Party members are subordinate to the organization, that the minority is subordinate to the majority, that lower Party organizations are subordinate to the higher ones, and that all the constituent organizations and members of the Party are subordinate to its central leadership" (*geren fucong zuzhi, shaoshu fucong duoshu, xiaji fucong shangji, quandang fucong zhongyang*). The phrase "central leadership" is ambiguous; it can refer to the National Party Congress, the Central Committee, the Politburo and its Standing Committee, or, historically, Mao himself. While the 8th Party Congress in 1956 used "the National Party Congress and the Central Committee" to replace "central leadership" in the revised Party Constitution, "central leadership" was adopted again by the Party's 9th Congress (1969), 10th Congress (1973), and 11th Congress (1977). Since the 12th Congress in 1982, the phrase "the National Party Congress and Central Committee" has been reinstated in the Party Constitution.[37] Furthermore, at the 15th Congress, the Party called for improving the systems of Party congresses and committees, suggesting a trend toward expanding power sharing among the Party elite via strengthening the two existing institutions. If the National Party Congress, an "electoral college" for selecting the Central Committee and a rubber stamp for endorsing Party Constitution revision, is to actually transform itself into the "highest decision-making organ" in the future, the empowered organ may provide an ongoing institutional forum where delegates meet once a year, and from which they periodically supervise the Central Committee. Likewise, if collective decision-making is seriously practiced at plenary sessions of the Central Committee, the process may provide a new channel for *all* committee members to participate actively in nationwide Party affairs. If these institutional innovations are implemented successfully, they will add more "democratic elements" into the dialectical principle of democratic centralism.

On the other hand, the sacred idea of centralism has set a parameter for developing intra-Party democracy. Obsessed with the idea of centralism, the Party tends to accept a *single* power center as an unshakable norm, making it very difficult to establish horizontal check-and-balance mechanisms within the Party. For the same reason, intra-Party electoral competition is marginal because top Party leaders usually nominate candidates for the lower-level positions. While the Party Constitution stipulates that local party congresses elect Party committees at the same level (Article 25), it also authorizes Party organizations at the higher level to appoint or transfer the principal leaders of Party organizations at the lower level when local party congresses are adjourned and the appointment and transfer are considered necessary (Article 13). In fact, provincial Party secretaries usually are appointed by the center leadership, rather than elected by provincial party congresses. In the case that the provincial Party Congress elects the Party secretary, the only candidate is either incumbent or predetermined by the center leadership. The Party Constitution requires local Party committees make policies according to resolutions made by party congresses at the same level, and upon instructions given by Party committees at a higher level (Article 26). It is unclear how China's new leaders will redefine such an ambiguous relationship and establish political accountability on the part of local Party committees within the framework of democratic centralism. This demonstrates the inexorable impact of past choice of rules on current Party building.

CONCLUSION

Recent leadership transition in China has been a mixture of institutional formalization and political personalization. The succession of the top leadership is contingent upon the previously selected path of ending the tenure system. While the age and term limits for Party leaders are yet to be formalized, the gradual development of these informal rules clearly follows the institutional trajectory started in the past—starting with setting term limits for state leaders and age limits for provincial and ministerial officials, followed by attaching Party leadership to state leadership, and finally by abolishing the life-tenure system for national Party leaders. However, Jiang's retention of the CMC chairmanship, following the precedent created by Deng in the 1980s, has left an exception for the retiring paramount leader. This incomplete leadership transition hints at China's progress and difficulties in formalizing its informal politics.

China's new leaders have attempted to develop intra-Party democracy through theoretical and institutional innovations. The advancement of the "Three-Represents" idea reflects the Party's effort to reconcile its traditional doctrine with a growing pluralistic society. Although the Party is eager to redefine itself as the vanguard of the Chinese people, it cannot easily divest itself of the old coat—the vanguard of the working class. Using "two vanguards" to identify the Party vividly demonstrates the impact of past choice of doctrines on current ideological innovation. Institutionally, China's new leaders hope to develop intra-Party democracy through sharing power with more Party elites and allowing limited electoral competition within the Party. These measures are aimed at enhancing the Party's art of leadership and raising its capacity to resist corruption, prevent degeneration, and withstand risks. No signs indicate that the new leadership is going to change the one-Party ruling system or discard the principle of democratic centralism for the foreseeable future. The preexisting rules have provided both constraints and opportunities for political actors in a new round of the game.

It may be worthwhile to recall that prior to Taiwan's democratic breakthrough in 1986, the ruling Nationalists (Kuomintang, or KMT) led by Chiang Ching-kuo had planned to reform the KMT *before* comprehensive reforms of the whole society, but the Nationalist Party's authoritarian internal structure did not change until many years after Taiwan's political democratization. Can China's new leaders reach the goal of developing intra-Party democracy without *concomitantly* democratizing the whole society? Even if institutional innovations within the Party make the leadership more responsible to its members, such changes do not render it accountable to society as a whole. In the absence of meaningful restraints on the Party's monopoly of power and the consequent blurring of lines between Party and state authority, China's institution building is likely to be incomplete and fraught with theoretical inconsistency and strategic ambiguity. In other words, path dependency, rather than path breaking, is instructive as a means to observe China's leadership transition and institution building.

NOTES

* The author wishes to thank Lowell Dittmer, Xiaobo Hu, and the anonymous reviewers for their constructive comments and suggestions. Views expressed in this article are the author's alone. @ 2004 by the Regents of the University of California. Reprinted from *Asian Survey*, vol. 44, no. 2, pp. 255–275 by permission of the Regents.

1. Elisabeth Rosenthal, "China's Communists Try to Decide What They Stand for," *New York Times*, May 1, 2002.
2. Jiang Zemin, speech at the Central Party School, May 31, 2002, *New Chinese News Agency*, <http://www.xinhuanet.com>.
3. Jiang Zemin, *Report to the 16th National Party Congress* (November 8, 2002) [in Chinese] (Beijing: Remin Chubanshe, 2002), p. 52.
4. Douglass C. North, *Institutions, Institutional Change and Economic Performance* (Cambridge: Cambridge University Press, 1990).
5. Robin Cowan and Philip Gunby, "Sprayed to Death: Path Dependency, Lock-in and Pest Control Strategies," *Economic Journal*, vol. 106, no. 435 (May 1996), pp. 521–42.
6. Hua Guofeng gave his chairmanship to Hu Yaobang one year earlier than the 12th Congress (1982), Hu Yaobang left his office prior to the 13th Party Congress (1987), and Zhao Ziyang was replaced by Jiang Zemin in 1989, three years before the 14th Party Congress (1992).
7. The fourth plenary of the fourteenth Central Committee convened in September 1994 announced that leadership transition from the second generation (Deng) to the third (Jiang) had been completed. For a discussion of formal and informal power being brought back into close alignment by Jiang, see Lowell Dittmer, "Chinese Leadership Succession to the Fourth Generation," in Gang Lin and Xiaobo Hu (eds.), *China after Jiang*, (Woodrow Wilson Center Press and Stanford University Press, 2003), p. 33.
8. Hu Wei, *Zhengfu Guocheng* [Process of Government] (Zhejiang: Zhejiang Renmin Chubanshe, 1998), p. 94.
9. One can speculate that Jiang's name might have been added to the predetermined seven-member list of the CMC at the last moment. This speculation is

supported by some reliable stories that during the 16th Party Congress high-ranking military officials strongly demanded that Jiang stay in the CMC. This does not mean that Jiang was really prepared to retire before the 16th Congress. However, by not listing his name in the original list, it could justify the retirement of six senior CMC members who were over 70, such as Chi Haotian, Zhang Wannian, Yu Yongbo, Fu Quanyou, Wang Ke, and Wang Ruilin.

10. See *People's Daily*, November 16, 2002; New Chinese News Agency [accessed on November 16, 2002], <http://www.xinhuanet.com> and <http://www.chinaview.cn>.
11. The essence of "Three Represents" is to redefine the Party as an ever-innovating organization corresponding to China's ongoing socioeconomic and cultural changes, with its ruling constituency (*zhizheng jichu*) being expanded from the working class to the public.
12. Erik Eckholm, "China's New Leader Promises Not to Sever Tether to Jiang," *The New York Times*, November 21, 2002.
13. This group, besides Deng himself, includes PRC President Yang Shangkun, Vice President Wang Zhen, former PRC President Li Xiannian, former NPC chairman Peng Zhen, Central Advisor Commission (CAC) Director Chen Yu, and CAC Vice Directors Bo Yibo and Song Renqiong.
14. Cheng Li, "Jiang's Game and Hu's Advantages," *Foreign Policy in Focus*, November 21, 2002, <http://www.fpif.org>.
15. Zhu Guanglei, *Dangdai Zhongguo Zhengfu Guocheng* [Process of Government in Contemporary China] (Tianjin: Tianjin Renmin Chubanshe, 1997), p. 77.
16. Prior to 1993, Politburo Member Yang Shangkun served as PRC president, Politburo Standing Committee Member Li Peng served as premier, Politburo Member Wan Li served as NPC chairman, and former PRC president Li Xiaonian served as CPPCC chairman.
17. Seven provinces, municipalities, and autonomous regions where the Party secretary does not serve as provincial people's congress chairman are Beijing, Shanghai, Tianji, Hubei, Guangdong, Xinjiang, and Tibet. Interesting, Party secretaries in these localities except for Tibet are all Politburo members, too busy to have an additional job in their domain. See New Chinese News Agency, *Local Government* [accessed on April 15, 2003], <http://news.xinhuanet.com/ziliao/2002-02/20/content_476046.htm>.
18. Xiaobo Hu, *Political Economy of Decentralization and Resource Allocation in Contemporary China* (Dissertation, Duke University, December 1994).
19. Joseph Fewsmith, "The Sixteenth Party Congress: A Preview," *China Leadership Monitor* (Hoover Institution, 2002), <http://www.chinaleadershipmonitor.org>.
20. "Political civilization" refers to advanced political ideas, political institutions and civilized political behavior. For a more detailed discussion of "Three Represents," "two vanguards," and "political civilization," see Gang Lin, "Ideology and Political Institutions for a New Era," *China after Jiang* (Stanford University Press, 2003), pp. 40–46
21. Jeremy Page, "China Opens Up Political Debate to Strengthen Party," *Reuters News*, July 20, 2002.
22. The following seven paragraphs except for one are a summary of this author's earlier discussion of intra-Party democracy, but with significant revisions and

supplements. See Gang Lin, "Ideology and Political Institutions for a New Era," in *China after Jiang*, pp. 46–60.

23. Mao Zedong, *Selected Works of Mao Zedong*, vol. 2 (Beijing: Remin Chubanshe, 1986), pp. 820–21; Deng Xiaoping, *Selected Works of Deng Xiaoping*, vol. 2 (Beijing: Remin Chubanshe, 1993), pp. 331, 341.
24. Hu, *Zhengfu Guocheng*, pp. 87–88.
25. New Chinese News Agency, *Minzhu Zhengzhi Xin Pianzhang* [A New Chapter in Democracy], October 20, 2002, <http://www.xinhuanet.com>; Duoweinews, December 19, 2002, <http://www.duoweinews.com>.
26. Gao Fang, *Zhengzhixue yu Zhengzhi Tizhi Gaige* [Political Science and Reform of Political Institutions] (Beijing: Zhongguo Guji Chubanshe, 2002), pp. 411–13, 416–18, 952–53.
27. Fang, *Zhengzhixue yu Zhengzhi Tizhi Gaige*, p. 919.
28. Jin Taijun, "Xinshiji Zhongguo Zhengzhi Gaige Ruogan Zhongda Wenti de Sikao" [Thought on Several Important Issues regarding China's Political Reform in the New Century], *Zhongguo Zhengzhi* [Chinese Politics], vol. 4, no. 11 (2001), p. 30; Wang Changjiang, et al., *Xinshiji Dang de Jianshe de Weida Gangling—Xuexi Jiang Zemin Zongshuji Qiyi Jianghua Fudao* [Great Platform for Party Construction in the New Century—Instruction to Studying General Secretary Jiang Zemin's "July 1" Speech] (Beijing: Zhongyang Dangxiao Chubanshe, 2001), pp. 126–30.
29. Jiang, *Report to the 16th National Party Congress*.
30. Li Yongzhong, "Guanyu Gaige Dangwei 'Yixing Heyi' Lingdao Tizhi de Sikao" [On Reforming the Leading System of "Combining Executive and Legislative Functions into One Organ" within Party Committees], *Tizhi Gaige* [System Reform], no. 4 (2002), pp. 29–30.
31. James Wang, *Contemporary Chinese Politics: An Introduction* (NJ: Prentice Hall, 1989), p. 81.
32. Minxin Pei, *From Reform to Revolution: The Demise of Communism in China and the Soviet Union* (Cambridge, MA: Harvard University Press, 1994), p. 73.
33. He Ping and Liu Siyang, "Dang de Xinyijie Zhongyang Weiyuanhui Danshengji" [The Birth of the New Central Committee of the CCP], November 14, 2002, <http://www.xinhuanet.com>.
34. Lianjiang Li, "The Two-Ballot System in Shanxi Province: Subjecting Village Party Secretaries to a Public Vote," *China Quarterly*, no. 42 (1999), p. 107.
35. Jean C. Oi, "State Responses to Rural Discontent in China: Tax-for-Fee Reform and Increased Party Control," *Asia Program Special Report 107: Crisis in the Hinterland: Rural Discontent in China* (Washington, DC: Woodrow Wilson International Center for Scholars, January 2003), p. 7.
36. "Dangdaibiao Changrenzhi Gaige Xin Changshi" [A New Experiment of Reforming Local Party Congress System], *Zhongguo Guangbowang* [Chinese Broadcasting Net], December 24, 2002, <http://www.cnradio.com>.
37. Gao, *Zhengzhixue yu Zhengzhi Tizhi Gaige*, p. 476.

CHAPTER 4

BUILDING A NEW POLITICAL ORDER IN CHINA: INTERPRETING THE NEW DIRECTIONS IN CHINESE POLITICS

Weixing Chen and Guoli Liu

Building a new political order has become the central theme of Chinese politics in post-Deng China not a clearly defined goal of the Chinese leadership, but the direction that Chinese politics are pointing to and it will be the ultimate challenge for the fourth generation of Chinese leadership produced at the 16th National Congress of the Chinese Communist Party (CCP).

Chinese politics in the reform era has been portrayed as an ephemeral transitional phase either of liberalization or fatal undermining of the old regime by civil society. Chinese politics in the reform era, however, has rarely approached either extreme. The CCP has not been as bold politically as it has been economically to democratize, despite the magnitude of the material and societal since the economic reform; in the meantime, the CCP has not actively mounted a rearguard action against civil society's growing demands and power. In fact, China's leadership and institutions have shown the capacity to cope with the rapid pace of socioeconomic change and to address new issues and challenges raised by the success of reform and openness. China's leadership and institutions, however, are experiencing increasing difficulties in addressing the issues and challenges raised by their reform and openness today as this proceeds. The *People's Daily's* New Year's editorial for 2002 stated "it is necessary to handle the new situations and issues in a proper way, in order to create a stable economic and social environment for promoting all-round reform and development." It is clear that a stable economic and social environment cannot be created, given the nature of the challenges the CCP faces, unless a new political order can be built in post-Communist China. The CCP legitimacy and China's social solidarity have severely eroded due to the demise of Communist ideology, decay of the CCP itself, government corruption, the widening gap between the rich and the poor, high unemployment rate, rising popular pressure and resentment (especially from the peasantry), and problems derived from inevitable conflict between free market and one-Party rule. It goes far beyond just policy response for the CCP to rise to these challenges: it requires the transformation of the CCP, the establishment of the citizens' petition access to power, and the establishment of the rule of law within Chinese political context, the three dimensions needed to build a new political order in post-Communist China. In interpreting the new directions in Chinese politics, this chapter examines the transformation of the CCP, the establishment of petition access, and the rule of law within the Chinese political context.

PARTY TRANSFORMATION

Building a new political order in China must start with the transformation of the CCP itself. Party transformation has always been the CCPs way in reacting to the dynamics of reform and openness. The reality in post-Deng China is that the Party is indispensable to the preservation of the order of reform and openness. But to preserve it, the CCP must be attuned to the new reform conditions by transforming itself. If Deng's legacy lies in his success in depoliticizing the Chinese polity, economy, and culture, Jiang Zemin's legacy will be largely determined by how he will respond to immediate social and political crises brought about by the demise of Communist ideology and Deng Xiaoping's depoliticization and to the long-term demand for a new economic and social order in post-Deng China. The historic task of building "socialism with Chinese characteristics" for Jiang and the fourth generation Chinese leadership is building a new reformed political order in China, which Jiang's politics point to.

Jiang's politics are encapsulated in the "three stresses" (stressing politics, political study, and political moral spirit), the combination of "rule by law" with "rule by virtue," and the "three representatives" (the CCP represents the most advanced culture, the most advanced forces of production, and the interest of the overwhelming majority of the Chinese population). The "three stresses" was first advocated by Jiang Zemin before the CCPs 15th National Congress in 1997. Following the CCPs 15th National Congress, a political campaign of "three stresses" was carried out within the Party and government, which did not end until 2001. The short-term political consideration for Jiang to put forward the "three stresses" was to consolidate his own power within the Party and strengthen his unified leadership. Deng was able to use the power shaped by Mao's politics and the power abd finesse launching China's reform and openness. But this power had been complicated by Deng's depoliticization, which made it more difficult for Jiang Zemin, who did not have the charisma or image of paramount leaders like Mao Zedong and Deng Xiaoping. Stressing politics was thus stressing Jiang's politics and unified political leadership within the CCP and the political cohesiveness of the CCP that had severely deteriorated. Jiang's means to define his leadership was the "three stresses"; his endeavor to adapt the CCP to new conditions in post-Deng China.

The "rule by virtue" idea was advanced by Jiang Zemin on January 11, 2001 at a national conference, which was participated in by the heads of the propaganda departments. Jiang stressed at the conference that the CCP must govern the country by combining "rule by law" with "rule by virtue." "Rule by virtue" resembles the Chinese aphorism: *xiushen qijia zhiguo pingtianxia*. That is, cultivate oneself and make oneself useful to the society (*xiushen*), look after the family and have strong sense of family responsibilities (*qijia*), look after the country (*zhiguo*), and peace and harmony under heaven (*pingtianxia*). China's economic reform started in an environment of moral and ideological decay following the Cultural Revolution, while traditional Chinese culture, which had been severely devastated by years of revolution and political campaigns, was further devastated by money worship in economic reform. Culture power is important for the Jiang leadership primarily because (1) the means of political control has almost been exhausted, (2) Party and government officials have not been constrained by the CCPs own rules, and (3) a code of conduct for Party members and for the population is badly needed in absence of official ideology.

The "Three Represents," formally put forward by Jiang Zemin in February 2000, is the capstone of Jiang's politics. "The most advanced culture" means that the CCP should serve as an integrative force representing positive things in China's reform and development. On the defensive side, it means an advanced culture is not a response to moral decay and influence of Western culture since China's economic reform. The most advanced forces of production emphasize both the importance of economic development and the Chinese economic development. The post-Deng leadership must try to maintain a sustained economic growth in China, while at the same time it must stress the importance of the CCP leadership for economic development in China. Representing the interests of the overwhelming majority of the Chinese population, for the first time, raises the question of development for whom and for what in China as well as the question of the CCPs political base in China in a post-Communist era. First of all, it is a response to the widening gaps between the rich and the poor and between the privileged and the unprivileged. Representing the interest of a majority of the population is not just a matter of letting the wealth of the rich trickle down to the poor, which may or may not happen, but to make sure that the overwhelming majority are the beneficiaries of China's economic growth. Second, it redefines the CCPs political base and tries to accommodate the demands of the intellectuals, entrepreneurs, and other emerging social-economic classes that are the engines of China's economic development and incorporate them into China's political order. Jiang Zemin made his intention clear in his speech on CCPs eightieth anniversary that emerging capitalists in China should be allowed to join the CCP. To allow capitalists to join the CCP would require change in the CCP Constitution and a redefinition of the CCP, having significant ramifications. Third, it emphasizes the importance of the CCPs traditional political base—workers and peasants and the importance of reincorporating them into China's changed social and political order. Representing the advanced forces of production indicates that the CCP will stick to reform and openness as advanced forces of production must be reflected in economic growth and the interest of the people must be measured economically. "Representing the interest of the overwhelming majority of the people" is the core of the "Three Represents," and the direction it points to is to build a new political order in China on the basis of sustained economic growth.

The problems resulting from Mao Zedong's "politics in command" were economic, while the problems resulting from Deng's politics of depoliticization were political and social. Jiang's politics places emphasis on economic growth as this directly concerned people's standard of living and well-being, but places equal emphasis on politics, ideology, and culture. It is politics that will guarantee China's economic growth will benefit the majority of the population. It is economics, politics, ideology, and culture that will determine the outcome of the endeavor to build a new political order in China. In putting forward the theme of "Three Represents," Jiang tries, for the first time since economic reform, to make the goal of the CCPs reform program consistent with the CCPs goal.

"Prosperity for the majority of the population" is the natural next step to Deng Xiaoping's "letting few individuals get rich first." Workers and peasants, especially unemployed workers and peasants, have been left without any sense of social purpose since the 1990s. To a large extent they have become the victims of the current "socialism with competitive capitalism." The CCP must try to incorporate workers and peasants into China's social and political order, because they are the majority. If "Socialism with Chinese Characteristics" emphasizes the CCP leadership and the role of the state in China's market economy, it is a test for the CCP at this stage of China's economic reform to improve their standard of living and social status through policies of redistribution and resource allocation and in the process make them the new middle classes in China. The basis for "prosperity for the majority of the people" is sustained economic growth, while the expansion of the private arena is a necessary condition for sustained economic growth as state-owned enterprises are in deep trouble and the prospect of reforming state-owned enterprise looks bleak. The CCP cannot try to protect and expand the private arena on the one hand and keep private property owners or capitalists out of the political order on the other. To allow capitalists to join the CCP, as Jiang indicated in his speech on the CCPs eightieth anniversary, seems to be the first step toward incorporating them into China's political order, which directly concerns the nature of the CCP as a Communist Party.

China's corruption is structured corruption, a result of the bad combination of market greed and the lack of checks and balances in the government. If market economy can be taken for granted, the elimination of structured corruption in China must start with the concurrent restructuring of institutions and the establishment of rule of law. China and the Chinese have suffered much by relying on "*qingguan*" (clean officials). It is the system that can be trusted, not individuals. Structured corruption in China is inherent in the system and can only be resolved by building institutional mechanisms of checks and balances and through the rule of law—not by anticorruption campaigns. While the rule by law has been repeatedly emphasized since the economic reform, it is time for the transition from "rule by law" to "rule of law" as rule by law in the absence of institutional mechanisms of checks and balances is to blame for many of the problems the CCP is facing. Realizing the limitations of rule by law in the context of one-Party rule, Jiang Zemin stresses that rule by law must be combined with rule by virtue in China. Even though laws and virtues belong to different domains and can hardly be combined, it may be the first step for the transition from rule by law to rule of law, because rule of law will be the inevitable alternative if rule by law, whether or not combined with rule by virtues, results in more problems than solutions. Institutional restructuring and the establishment of rule of law will represent significant departures from the CCPs normal politics.

To Jiang's credit, order was not disrupted and economic growth was sustained from 1992 to 2002; at the same time problems mentioned above worsened. If economic growth was a way out of the difficult situation for Deng in post-Mao China and the CCPs legitimacy could be based on their ability to deliver economic goods during the Deng era, the CCPs legitimacy can only partly depend on China's economic growth as the social and political problems resulting from Deng's depoliticization are piling up and discontent against the Party is widespread. Building a new political order through first transforming the CCP is the way to get out of the difficult situation for Jiang and the ultimate challenge for fourth-generation Chinese leadership after Jiang. Great space and differentiation have been created in China, and individualism has developed over the last two decades. Chinese society today is more diverse economically and pluralized politically. Under these circumstances, Party transformation is part of the search for new bases of social solidarity and the CCPs political legitimacy. To be successful in this endeavor, the CCP may have to meet the CCP members and unorganized and transformed citizen-masses halfway, either through institutions or on the street.

ESTABLISHING CITIZENS' POLITICAL PETITION ACCESS

To respond to rising popular pressure and resentment, the CCP has tried, for stability and survival, to establish a citizens' political petition access on three fronts: The People's Congress system, Offices of Correspondence, and village elections. Democratization was not the CCPs objective in establishing these institutional outlets, but these outlets do provide a petition access for citizens. The People's Congress has become a voice since the economic reform, which will be discussed later, and any Chinese citizen can write to the Offices of Correspondence to complain about government officials, but the village elections electoral process of seems far more significant. Letting over 700 million Chinese peasants elect their own representatives for the Village Committee (VC) is an important aspect in the process of building a new political order.[1]

The dilemma faced by the CCP since the economic reform was how to decentralize economic initiative to peasants and increase their functional efficiency while maintaining macroeconomic and political control over them. China's economic reform in the late 1970s and early 1980s was a process of empowering the peasantry through relaxation of control by the state. Chinese peasants were empowered by two institutional changes: The implementation of various forms of the Household Responsibility System (HRS) in the countryside in 1979 and dismantling the people's commune system in 1984. The downward transfer of authority to cultivate land from the collective to the household returned to the peasants with control over their own labor and economic activity, while dismantling the commune system enabled peasants to move freely. On the positive side, China became the fastest growing economy in the 1980s, and Chinese peasants contributed enormously to economic growth. About 30 percent of China's general social output value increase, 35 percent of its national industrial output value increase, and 45 percent of its total export was contributed by rural enterprises alone.[2] On the negative side, village governments were paralyzed by implementation of the HRS and by dismantling the people's commune system. VCs that were supposed to manage village affairs after dismantling the people's commune system fell short of their expectations. According to a 1994 Renmin Ribao report, more than 800,000 village-level organizations in the countryside throughout China were not functioning and had to be rebuilt soon.[3] The breakdown of village government had three interrelated consequences.

First, it made it difficult for the state to enforce their policies and laws (such as compulsory grain procurement, birth control, tax collection, environmental protection, etc.) in the villages. The collective economy and the framework of the people's commune system used to be the economic and organizational basis for the state to enforce village policies. With implementation of the HRS and dismantling the people's commune system, the state's ability to enforce laws and policies in the countryside had been greatly handicapped. Village leaders had no incentives to offer villagers for compliance, and they did not have necessary means to enforce state policies themselves. Second, it resulted in a surge of rural lawlessness. Murder, beatings, robbery, abduction and the selling of women and children, illicit gambling, drugs, secret societies, and extravagant expenses on ceremonies, etc. were all flourishing in rural China since economic reform.[4] Jiang Liu, minister of agriculture, describing one situation in the countryside in 1995, as "the vicious power of local bullies, village tyrants, and other hoodlums is running amok in the countryside."[5] It finally led to the worsening of relations between village cadres and villagers, as many former village leaders, free of supervision from above by Party and government authorities and from below by villagers after dismantling of commune system, became village tyrants and turned village assets and properties into their personal wealth. Peasants make up over 70 percent of China's total population. It was fear of chaos and the sense of urgency to solve the political crisis in the countryside where most of China's population still lived that drove the case for village elections.[6]

The importance of village elections to the CCP was three twofold. First, the CCP could not afford lawlessness in China's countryside where over 70 percent of China's population still lived; nor enslaving peasants either, as rural development was the key to success in China's modernization program. Organizing peasants through elections would enable the CCP to control the peasantry without enslaving them and without having negative economic consequences. Second, only when peasants were organized could state policy be carried out and state laws enforced and villagers conduct their own affairs and better develop their economy. Third, it was hoped village elections would create opportunities for capable villagers who could develop and promote the village economy and, at the same time, increase accountability of village leaders and improve relations between village cadres and villagers. Village elections thus represented a middle course between the people's commune system and the absence of organization after dismantling the commune system.

The National People's Congress (NPC) passed the "Organic Law of Villagers' Committee" in 1987, and since then many rounds of elections have been held in China's countryside. Village elections provide an electoral participation process for Chinese peasants, even though these elections are not designed to run against the CCP, the source of all political power in China. According to the Organic Law, VC members are chosen in popular elections, where all adult registered villagers have the right to vote and stand for office. The VC, the standing working institution at the center of village elections, is defined in Article 2 of the Organic Law as a mass organization through which villagers manage their own affairs, educate themselves, and meet their own needs. Villagers are empowered by the Organic Law to elect VC members to manage affairs on their behalf, even though the VC has not been empowered in the relationship with Party authorities.

Technically the village Party organization exercises its leadership over this electoral process in three ways. First, the village Party secretary serves as head of the village election committee, stipulated in village election laws in most provinces. As head of the village election committee, the village Party secretary has enormous influence over the process, but the village Party secretary is not elected by villagers. It screens candidates before each village election for the VC, and in many cases, decides on final candidates. Village groups (VG) submit the names of their candidates to the village Party organization for screening and approval before each election.[7] Candidates unendorsed by the village Party secretary will have a hard time becoming candidates, and they will have an even harder time winning the election. Villagers typically do not vote for candidates who run "against the state."[8] The village Party secretary is also responsible for mobilizing and organizing village voters and administering the actual election. He/she decides the method of voting and oversees the actual voting.

Next, Party control over village government remains strong, judging not only by overlapping Party branch membership and VC membership and the number of Party members in VCs, but also that the Party branch appoints VG leaders who recommend candidates for the VC and are responsible for implementing VC decisions within their groups. Finally, the village Party organization is still the source of political power in village policy. The supreme decision-making body in the village is the Villagers Assembly (VA). The Organic Law stipulates that the VC is accountable and reports to the VA. In reality, the VA is nonexistent in most villages. In some places, it is the Villagers' Representatives' Assembly (VRA) that has come to perform the function of the VA. The major problem with the VA or VRA, however, is that it is either a leaderless body or a party-controlled body. There is not an institutional framework through which the VA/VRA can function properly. The VA/VRA can only be as effective as the VC wants it to be. In terms of working relationships between the VC and the VA, the VA is the supreme decision-making body in theory only. It is the other way around in practice. There is a disproportionately high percentage of Party members who are representatives. Again, most, if not all, members of the VC and the village Party organization are among the representatives.[9]

Village elections arise from the imperative of economic development and the necessity of state control in an environment of decentralizing policy in post-Mao China. The imperative of economic growth is not likely to disappear as the CCP legitimacy in the reform is, to a large extent, dependent upon China's economic growth. State control cannot be sacrificed either as it concerns the CCP authority and the state's capacity to address issues of reform. As such, this electoral process should be viewed as an integrative part of building a new political order during the reform era. Village elections illustrate that building a new political process is a major aspect in redefining the CCPs relationship with the village. We could generalize five relationship types between village Party organization and VC since the introduction of village elections: coordinating (between the VC and the village Party branch), all-encompassing (the village Party branch making all decisions), drifting (the village Party branch having a hard time exercising leadership over the VC, as the VC chair is "drifting" most of the time), conflictual (between the VC and the village Party branch), and integrating (the village Party secretary also serving as the VC chair). It seems that the trend has been from the all-encompassing type to the coordinating type.[10]

Direct elections would not be limited to the village level as the process proceeds. Joseph Cheng recently examined direct town and township head elections in China.[11] It is interesting and significant to examine whether the success in local elections will encourage Chinese leaders to expand direct elections to the county, then province, and eventually national levels. Democratic elections will provide a new legitimate foundation to the new political order in China in the long run.

RULE OF LAW IN THE CHINESE POLITICAL CONTEXT

China is a country with more than 2,000 years of the "rule of men." In a certain sense, to establish the authority of law and replace the rule of men with the rule of law is one of the most important social and political reforms in China today. The long tradition of the rule of men hindered China's move toward legal rational authority. Revolutionary movements in twentieth century China destroyed traditional regimes. However, traditional authority patterns as embodied in old culture continue to affect people's thinking and behavior. The Cultural Revolution of 1966–76 represented a period of lawlessness and chaos. The Chinese debate over the rule of law in the late 1970s and early 1980s originated in the far-reaching political reaction against the Cultural Revolution. The policy to create a rule-of-law state started taking shape as early as 1978, at the Third Session of the 11th National Party Congress. The CCP determined that the way to avoid any future cultural revolutionary politics was through the entwining of democratization and legalization. The Congress Communique stated:

> In order to safeguard people's democracy, it is imperative to strengthen the socialist legal system so that democracy is systematized and written into law in such a way as to ensure the stability, continuity and full authority of this democratic system and laws; there must be laws for people to follow, these laws must be observed, their enforcement must be strict and lawbreakers must be dealt with.[12]

The communique called upon judicial and procuratorial personnel to maintain their independence and guarantee equality of all people before the people's law and deny any one the privilege of being above the law.

China's legal reform can be interpreted as "a movement to enhance procedural legality at the expense of arbitrary power."[13] After witnessing and personally suffered during the chaotic and violent era of the Cultural Revolution, Deng Xiaoping said in 1978:

> Democracy has to be institutionalized and written into law, so as to make sure that institutions and laws do not change whenever the leadership changes or whenever the leaders change their views. . . . The trouble now is that our legal system is incomplete . . . Very often what leaders say is taken as law and anyone who disagree is called a lawbreaker. That kind of law changes whenever a leader's views change. So we must concentrate on enacting criminal and civil codes, procedural laws and other necessary laws. . . . These laws should be discussed and adopted through democratic procedures.[14]

Deng's determination to open China to the outside world—and transform its domestic economy—also led to the rapid development of Chinese laws. A Sino-Foreign Joint Venture Law was enacted in July 1979. The 1982 Constitution promises to protect the lawful rights and interests of foreign investors. James V. Feinerman points out that China's opening to the outside world has been a driving force for legal reforms.[15] Legal reforms certainly have promoted both foreign trade, investment, and domestic economic growth as China is becoming increasingly integrated into the global economy.[16]

The demand for establishing the rule of law initially came from three sources. First, Chinese leaders like Deng Xiaoping who experienced the lawlessness of the Cultural Revolution fully realized the significance of building a system of law and order. Second, the rule of law is perceived to be indispensable to addressing the issues and challenges raised by China's reform and openness and an essential part of China's drive for modernization. Third, China's increasing contact with the outside world and growing foreign investment in China requires a legal system that provides stability, transparency and predictability.

The NPC has the power to promulgate basic laws under the Constitution adopted in 1982. Its Standing Committee has the authority to promulgate and amend laws with the exception of those enacted by the NPC. The staffs of the NPC and the State Council, engaged in drafting legislation, have developed into sizable bodies of specialists. Debate on proposed legislation in the NPC is also becoming more and more active and outspoken and now sometimes influences legislation under discussion. Major pieces of legislation must still receive prior Party approval, and much of their content is decided before the NPC becomes involved. The NPC has had a strong leadership in the recent past when CCP Politburo Standing Committee members Qiao Shi and then Li Peng (1998 to the present) have been Chairmen of its Standing Committee. Li is the number two figure in the Chinese political hierarchy. NPCs legislative and supervisory roles have been strengthened under him whether his active involvement was aimed at enhancing his power and political influence or not.

The people's congresses—bodies of deputies elected (under CCP supervision) from the local to the national levels—are the closest China comes to representative bodies. In 1990, Peng Chong of the NPC already defined supervision by the people's congresses as follows: "In major cases, the people's congress may request a report from the people's procuracy and the courts, and also conduct its own investigation. If [the people's congress] finds error, it may ask the procuracy or the courts to correct the case according to law."[17]

In a pioneer study of the NPC, Kevin O'Brien found that reform-minded officials from lower-level parliaments in China believe that cooperative cooption of the CCP is much more effective in promoting parliamentary independence, and through it China's constitutional and democratic development, than is institutional quarantine. This belief is corroborated by findings that in the West, parliaments have historically developed their institutional independence and capacities much more effectively during periods in which they sought to act in cooperation with a dominant executive, rather than periods where they sought to act independently from such an executive.[18]

In a more recent study, Murray Scot Tanner found that since Chinese reformers called for more rapid development of socialist democracy and rule by law, lawmaking has become an increasingly large, important, and contentious part of policymaking.[19] A sort of professional legislator mentality is developing among many of the NPCs delegates. This mentality attaches growing value to constitutional and legal procedure, relatively free debate, the legislature's organizational autonomy and increased NPC oversight of government ministries. A far more positive view of the rights enshrined in China's Constitution has also emerged among some delegates.[20] Legal reform and its heavily propagandized popularization have heightened individual consciousness in China about legal concepts, legal rights, and substantive justice. This heightening of consciousness is due partly by the influx of Western ideas into China and partly to the legal reforms themselves.[21]

The role of law in China differs from the role of law in the West. A democratically elected legislature is the basis of legitimacy in the West, and the rule of law is superior to governmental and nongovernmental organizations. In China the Party's legitimacy derives from its successful leadership and its commitment to economic development. The rule of law is secondary to the rule of the Party, and the legislature, the NPC, is definitely secondary to the Party. A citizen must obey Party decrees and officials as well as laws and state officials. This basic fact has not been changed by recent increases in legal codification, though it is important to note that the Party is also bound by legislation.[22] However, establishing the rule of law in China is becoming increasingly important since the 1990s in order for Chinese leadership to rise to the challenges raised by China's reform and openness in the 1990s.

The rule of law is a Western tradition. The legal order is a vital part of any Western social order. The place of law in the Western tradition of thought and action is unique. "The West has exalted law as a fundamental basis of unity in society. Belief in the existence of a 'fundamental law,' to which governments must adhere or risk being overthrown as despotisms, has been characteristic of European thought at least since the eleventh century. This belief finds expression in the English concept of the Rule of Law as well as in the German idea of the Rechtsstaat, not to mention the American Constitutional requirement of the due process of law."[23]

According to Stanley B. Lubman, basic principles of the rule of law include the following: legal rules, standards or principles must be capable of guiding people in their conduct; the law should, and for most part, actually guide people; the law should be stable; the law should be the supreme legal authority; the courts should be able to do their work impartially and without direct interference from the political system.[24] In the last decade, Chinese discussions of legal institutions and legal theory are consistent with the rule of law as that concept is understood in the West today.[25] The rule of law has been called for in China.

Law is not a tool of class dictatorship, and legal institutions such as the legislature, the Procuracy and the courts must be independent; the state and the

Party must be subject to law; the Party may not supplant the state and policy may not supplant the law; the NPC must not be a "rubber stamp" and its members should be elected in public campaigns; political power must be divided by a system of checks and balances and laws should be enacted to establish a system of constitutional government that will define procedures for amending the constitution; administrative agencies must be permitted to act only within the legal competence, and an administrative court and administrative procedure should be established to exercises control over official arbitrariness; legislation and implementation of law must be aimed at maximizing citizens' rights and freedoms and restricting government powers; citizens' rights and freedoms may not be restricted except through the exercise of due process. These views are not just the product of a transitory moment in Chinese history.[26]

Transition to the rule of law has involved three institution-building efforts. The first is the attempt to employ legislation and administrative rules as essential tools to govern China. The Chinese leadership, departing from previous reliance on policy declarations and disregard of formal legal rules, have moved to elevate such rules into primary sources of authority. The second area of institution-building includes efforts to revive legal education and to recreate the Chinese bar. The third effort is to construct a substantive criminal law and criminal procedure.[27]

Rule of law has both a private and a public dimension—private in guaranteeing predictability for economic transactions and resolving private dispute, public in restraining the powers of officialdom and regulating transfer of political power.[28] In Ronald C. Keith's analysis, "The struggle for the 'rule of law' originated in the politically inspired correlations domestic stability and economic reform."[29] Establishing the rule of law will provide a viable social and political framework for stability and sustainable economic development. Constitutionalism is the key for the rule of law.

Since 1978, the Chinese government has strongly embraced the perspective that economic markets require strong laws. A huge number of national statutes relating to commercial regulation have, as a result, been adopted in the last few decades. For example, the legislature adopted contract laws governing domestic and foreign transactions in the early 1980s. Patent and Trademark Laws were also adopted. A Copyright Law, introduced in 1979, was finally passed in 1990. A Company Law to govern private, collective, and state enterprises was passed in the 1990s. The first national Securities Law was adopted in 1998, as well as a law to allow for establishment of a bond market. A unified Contract Law came into effect in 1999. Other national laws passed during this flurry of legislative activity included an Advertising Law, Arbitration Law, a Law against Improper Competition, Insurance Law, Audit Law, and a Chartered Accounting Law. Collectively this mass of statutes represents a concerted effort by the government to adopt a modern legal framework to support a market economy.[30]

At an international symposium in August 2000 on "twenty-first Century China and Globalization" in Beijing, the participants were asked to list the most important issues facing China. Interestingly, most respondents named "maintaining fair justice and judicial independence" as China's top priority. An exhibition of antieconomic crime campaign by the Beijing municipal government revealed that, between 1996 and 1999, thousands of economic criminal cases were persecuted involving 8.7 billion yuan.[31] It is clear that without strict enforcement of the rule of law, the fruits of Chinese economic developments will be eaten away by corrupt officials. Thus establishing the rule of law is a central measure for the success of Chinese political reform and a necessary step for ensuring sustainable economic development.

According to Max Weber, there are three types of authority patterns: traditional, charismatic, and legal-rational legitimation.[32] Weber's analysis is based on European experience. It is interesting to examine whether the Weberian ideal types can be used to study China's authority patterns. The current leadership wishes to strengthen legal rational authority. The perception that many Chinese have been ruled for decades by arbitrary and frequently hypocritical cadres has led many Chinese to believe that government should be based on universally applicable rules, and that under such a government certain rights ought to be recognized and protected by the uniform role application. Without charisma, Jiang Zemin, the third generation of Chinese leadership, in contrast to Deng's informality regarding official titles, simultaneously holds the positions of General Secretary of the CCP, President of the PRC, and Chairman of the Central Military Committee. Obviously Jiang's authority is more institutional than personal. The current leadership strongly wishes to strengthen legal-rational authority. Because China has moved into a new era of modernization, the new leaders including Hu Jingtao's (the fourth generation of Chinese leadership) authority has to be based on legal-rational legitimacy. At the official level, a public commitment has been made on rules according to law despite the fact that, in practice, China still has a mixed pattern of traditional, charismatic, and legal-rational authority. Such a mixed pattern is likely to persist for a while. Modernization of China, however, depends on a successful transition to legal-rational authority, while legal-rational authority will further promote China's effort in building a modern, democratic, and civilized country.

The 15th Party Congress held in 1997 adopted rule according to law. The NPC amended the 1982 Constitution in 1999. One key Constitutional amendment states: "The PRC should implement rule according to law, and build a socialist state based on rule of law."[33] The rule of law, if successfully established and implemented, will provide a solid foundation for China's market economy, and it is indispensable to the building of a new political order in China.

Xin Chunying, a leading scholar at China's Academy of Social Sciences, summarizes China's struggle for the rule of law in the last two decades as follows.[34] First, there is nothing more important than the Party commitment in power to the highest authorities of the constitution and the law. The fact that the authority of the Party's policies are above the constitution and laws, the authority of Party's institutions and organizations are above the State legislative and judicial organs has generated severe consequences in social life. In order to establish the rule of law, the ruling Party must act within the framework of the Constitution and laws.

Second, an administrative system according to law must be established. For a long period of time, China has neglected the legal restraining of administrative power. There were no unified regulations or standards for administrative acts, no specific demarcation lines between different administrative powers, no unified procedures for administrative actions, no legal ways to restrain and affix the responsibility when public officials violated the law and disciplines when they neglected or were derelict in their duties. The 1982 Constitution stresses the principle of administration according to law. The Administrative Litigation Law of the PRC was adopted and went into effect in 1991. It is the first law to protect the citizen's rights to bring public officials to court through formal legal procedure in Chinese history. The State Compensation Law, the Law of Administrative Review, the Law for Administrative Punishment, and other related laws were adopted and implemented thereafter, they have promoted the standardization of the exercise of the administrative power.

Third, China has speeded up the process of legislation on economic laws during the transition to the market economy. The General Principles of Civil Law, the Cooperate Law, the Law on Chinese–Foreign Equity Joint Ventures, the Law on Foreign Capital Enterprises, the Economic Contract Law, the Banking Law, etc., have led economic activities onto the legal track. China has also taken part in the economic globalization process, and has participated in and ratified a number of international economic agreements.

Fourth, the Chinese legislature has made serious efforts to build a legal system that provides guidance for all aspects of social life. Through more than two decades of efforts, a system with the Constitution as its base, including administrative, civil law, economic law, marriage, labor, social welfare, natural resources and environment protection, criminal, procedure, and military laws, has been formulated. The number of laws since 1978 in China have rapidly increased. The NPC and its Standing Committee passed 251 laws from 1979 to 1999, and local people's congresses passed over 6,000 laws.[35] The social and economic conflicts that used to be dealt with by administrative methods are addressed more and more through law and judicial process. Building and consolidating legality are primarily political tasks. Regardless of how much legislation is promulgated and how many judges are trained and installed in the courts, legality will not grow unless the Party-state fosters and maintains a commitment to it and alters the allocation of power between the courts and the rest of the Party-state.[36]

It seems that Chinese reformers have adopted a combination of functional and instrumental approaches to law. The first is restoring equilibrium to the social order when that equilibrium has been seriously disrupted. The second is enabling members of society to calculate the consequences of their conduct, thereby securing and facilitating voluntary transactions and arrangements. The third is teaching people the right beliefs, feelings, and the right actions—that is, to mold the moral and legal conceptions and attitudes of a society.[37] Law was almost totally identified as an instrument for social control throughout the history of the PRC until the economic reform began to promote other functions that now jostle for attention. There has been frequent expression of the need for more laws and a strong legal system to maintain "political stability and good social order." The instrumental use of the courts as part of the state control apparatus is demonstrated by nationwide campaigns to punish crime, and join in the general struggle to maintain social order.[38] The rule of law is a critical link of political and economic reforms. Establishing the rule of law will provide a viable framework of social and political stability and sustainable economic development.

When China joined the World Trade Organization (WTO) in 2001, the Chinese government agreed to abide by all of the WTO rules—from protection of foreign intellectual property to elimination of local content requirements that China had imposed on many wholly foreign-owned joint venture manufacturing companies.[39] Entry into the WTO is a seminal event in China's economic history and the history of the world trading system. It shows the commitment of China's leadership to accelerate domestic economic reform, pushing China more rapidly toward a market economy. China's rising trade reflects its emergence as perhaps the world's preeminent manufacturer of labor-intensive goods. China's total goods' imports and exports in 2001 reached US$509.8 billion, with exports US$266.2 billion and imports US$243.6 billion. China has become the world's sixth-largest foreign trader behind the United States, Germany, Japan, France, and Britain. China's foreign trade volume ranked eleventh in 1998, and tenth in 1999.[40] China's entry into the WTO will usher in a period of radical change in the Chinese legal system. Many laws will be revised to meet international standards. As China commits itself to open its legal service market internationally, much pressure will be put on China's fledging legal profession. China is still in the early stage of developing the rule of law. The legal system established on the basis of a planned economy is now changing to one based on market economic concepts. As China entered the WTO, the new legal system must adhere to international standards, especially in civil and commercial law areas.

The establishment of the rule of law in China is one of the largest social infrastructural projects in the history of mankind. This project is organically linked to China's transition to the market economy. The ruling dictum is "market economy is a legal economy," meaning that a healthy market economy is necessarily regulated by law. It was considered that a healthy market was possible only if there was a level competition ground, which required a high degree of regularity, predictability, and transparency. The traditional reliance on policies and individuals could ill-suit the needs of a market economy, which flourished in places that generally practice the rule of law. This perceived logical relationship between requirements of a market economy and the rule of law is to a large extent underlined by the advocacy on the rule of law by central leadership since late 1992, when construction of a socialist market economy was made the target of future reform and development.[41]

China's move toward the rule of law will facilitate its participation in world affairs. At the same time, China's growing participation in global organizations will certainly further promote the development of a system based on the rule of law. China's successful transition from the rule of men to the rule of law requires a fundamental transition of authority patterns from traditional and charismatic authority to legal-rational authority, a strong commitment by the leadership to follow the laws even if such practice comes into conflict with the interests of the elites, the growth of the popular awareness of rights and duties defined by law, and the growth of a legal profession including judges, prosecutors, and lawyers who take the supremacy of law and professionalism very seriously. The doctrine that the current leadership espouses, which urges replacement of the rule of man by the rule of law, implies that relations between state and Party must change and that the CCP must surrender at least some of its authority to law.[42] Equality of all before the law is a principle expressed in China's Constitution and Criminal Procedure Law and much discussed in the Chinese media. Under this principle, Party cadres are not above the law and offenders who violate the law must be punished according to the law. The rule of law, essential to a modern industrial society, is the means by which human activities can be regulated, and one purpose of the legal system is to regulate and restrain the behavior of government officials. The rule of law necessarily assumes the existence of rights. When government abuses its power, citizens should have the right to seek legal remedies against their government. While the law also regulates the behavior of citizens, the scrutiny to which the law subjects the government should be more stringent than that upon the individual. As no one should be above the law, judicial independence is crucial to the rule of law.[43]

Chinese lawyers are growing rapidly in number, and have been playing an increasingly important role in safeguarding legal rights and interests of the citizen. In the 1996 Law of Lawyers, lawyers are defined as "legal practitioners who have obtained business licenses according to the law and provide legal service for the society." Corresponding requirements for lawyers' practices, businesses, rights, and duties are also set forth in the Law. Before the adoption of the Law, private lawyers simply did not exit. All lawyers were legal workers serving the country and the government. The Law of Lawyers represents remarkable progress.[44] However, there remains a paucity of legally trained professionals to act as lawyers, judges, and bureaucratic officials. In 1992 there were only 50,000 lawyers in China. By 2000, there were only 150,000 lawyers in China, though there are over 50,000 new law students and plans to increase the number of lawyers to 300,000 in the next decade. According to a report by the Central People's Broadcasting Station on July 13, 2002, only 70 percent of China's 200,000 lawyers have law degrees, and only 30 percent of China's current judges have law degrees. Obviously China must strengthen its legal education process to establish the rule of law.

China's legal reform has made enormous progress but still confronts daunting challenges. Pitman B. Potter notes that the legal system plays an

increasingly significant role in social, economic, and even political relationships. Legal norms drawn largely from foreign experiences have been
selected and applied through a plethora of newly established institutions.
The role of law as a basis for governmental authority has become a legitimate
and significant issue in the broader political discourse. Despite these achievements, law in China remains dependent on the regime's policy goals.
Particularly where political prerogatives are at stake, legal requirements
appear to pose little restraint on state power. From the perspective of pragmatic development as suggested by Michael Dowdle, China has made very
impressive progress in its transition to the rule of law. Pragmatic development refers to a strategy in which developmental process begins without
knowing what the end-state of the development process might or should
look like. Legal development is more properly conceived of as pragmatic
rather than reductive.[45]

China's economic, legal, and political reforms have had an impact on the
country's political institutions. There are clear signs that the political system
has adapted to the new circumstances and that China's political system is
increasingly institutionalized. Institutionalization here means increased
structural differentiation, more regularized decision-making processes and
more state autonomy from society.[46] As the former Vice President of the
Chinese Academic of Social Sciences Li Shenzhi points out, implementing
the rule of law would bring about fundamental political changes, improve
human rights in China, and let China join the world and earn the respect of
other countries. Thus, the only way to meet the challenge of globalization
was to establish institutions that were compatible with it—democracy and
the rule of law—and not try to rely on market forces alone.[47]

SARS AND ITS POLITICAL IMPLICATIONS: AN AFTERTHOUGHT

A mysterious flu-like disease first called "atypical pneumonia" appeared in
China's Guangdong province in November 2002. In February 2003 the
Chinese government reported the disease to the World Health Organization
(WHO). On March 15, 2003, the WHO issued a travel alert, identifying the
illness as severe acute respiratory syndrome (SARS) and calling it a "worldwide health threat." The initial response by Chinese officials to the disease
was sluggish, and mass media kept a low profile in SARS reporting. The initial sluggish response to the SARS, to a certain degree, was affected by political factors. China went through a generational shift of top party and state
leaderships at the 16th CCP National Congress in November 2002 and the
First Session of 10th NPC in March 2003 respectively. A desire to maintain
stability during the leadership transition plus the deeply ingrained bureaucratic impulse to maintain secrecy undoubtedly contributed to China's
failure in reporting SARS in a timely and accurate fashion.

On April 9, the Vice Minister of Health reported only 22 confirmed SARS
cases in Beijing and four deaths. On the same day, however, Dr. Jiang

Yanyong (a retired military doctor) publicly declared that he knew that there were at least 120 cases at three military hospitals in Beijing. Western media's coverage of Jiang's story quickly caused alarm among Chinese elites and people who had access to news from abroad. As of April 18, a total of 1,512 SARS cases had been reported on the Chinese mainland, with 37 cases and four deaths confirmed in Beijing. Claiming that SARS was under effective control, the health officials promised that it was safe for people to travel or work in China. However, Western media had mounting suspicions that the Chinese government might be covering up the severity of the disease, triggering uncertainty and panic among the general public.

A dramatic turning point came on April 20, 2003 when a press conference on SARS sponsored by the Information Office of the State Council was held in Beijing. The conference, originally to be given by the health minister and the mayor of Beijing, was held by the new executive Vice Minister of Health, Gao Qiang, who admitted that there were 339 confirmed SARS cases in Beijing, as compared to the 37 cases previously stated. On the same day, the State Council declared the dismissal of two senior officials—the health minister, Zhang Wenkang, and the mayor of Beijing, Meng Xuenong, for their "negligence." A directive was issued to both officials and medical institutions at all levels nationwide, stipulating that intentional cover-ups of SARS cases or refusing to admit suspected and identified patients would be punished severely. The dismissal of senior officials, along with the increased openness in SARS reporting, represent a level of public accountability not seen before, opening a new chapter in reforming China's political structure toward a more responsive and service-based administration. In a speech made on April 22, Premier Wen Jiabao reiterated that all localities and workplaces must report SARS in a timely and accurate manner. In cases of failure to comply, local and departmental leaders will be held strictly responsible.[48] By May 8, more than 120 central and local government officials had been dismissed, demoted, or suspended from their duties due to their slow response to SARS. A national task force was established on April 23. Vice Premier Wu Yi was designated as the head of the SARS Control and Prevention Headquarters of the State Council.

SARS inflicted patients in more than twenty countries with a total of 8,098 confirmed cases in which 5,327 were from Chinese mainland, 1,755 from Hong Kong, and 346 from Taiwan. Among the total number of deaths of 774, 349 occurred in Chinese mainland, 299 in Hong Kong, and 37 in Taiwan.[49] Clearly China is the epicenter of SARS outbreak. To curtail the further spread of SARS, the Chinese government took strict preventive measures. For instance, the State Council trimmed what was to be the "Golden Week" (May 1 holidays) to only three days in 2003. Citizens were advised to stay at home instead of taking mass travel. The municipal government of Beijing ordered the closing of all movie theaters, Internet cafes, and other places of entertainment on April 28. On July 24, 2003, WHO lifted travel advisory it had issued for Beijing. The medical crisis appeared to be over. The political repercussions, however, are still being felt. In the aftermath of the health crisis, the political question raised by SARS is whether the government's belated demands for more open reporting, transparency and accountability, and for putting the people's interests first can translate into a more open political system.[50] Media coverage of the SARS crisis served to popularize the term "right to know." SARS linked the "right to know" with people's health. If the term sticks, it may enlarge China's political discourse.

According to Joseph Fewsmith, China's SARS crisis offers a dramatic example of how ostensibly nonpolitical issues drive demands for better governance. The SARS crisis, occasioning as it did the sacking of high- and mid-level cadres for negligence of duty, highlighted issues of accountability. These issues in China extend well beyond SARS to broad concerns about government performance and the prevention of corruption. By challenging the Chinese to consider not only the accountability of their government, but also issues of openness, trust, responsiveness, and the "right to know," the SARS crisis seems likely to provide a major impetus to new thinking about relations between society and state.[51]

In politics, credibility is associated with the government's legitimacy and efficacy. The initial cover-up of SARS crisis damaged Chinese government's credibility. The mishandling of the outbreak demonstrated to both the leaders and ordinary citizens the long accumulated malady of the bureaucratic machine. This made it imperative to reform it to become a more efficient and responsive administration.

When the newly elected President Hu Jintao and Premier Wen Jiabao finally decided to take bold measures to deal with the SARS crisis, they gained widespread support among the Chinese people. The SARS crisis demonstrated that the Chinese government was not well prepared for handling this type of sudden crisis. On the other hand, the remarkably coordinated efforts after April 20, 2003 in the fight against SARS also demonstrated that the Chinese government still controls significant amount of political and social capital in dealing with a health crisis. When the top leaders are determined and the political machines are mobilized, decisive measures can be taken in a short period of time. The fact that Beijing was able to build a special hospital for SARS patients from the ground up in one week indicates that the system could perform efficiently under extraordinary pressure. Over the long run, successful governance cannot rely on extreme crisis management measures. It seems that Chinese leaders have learned some valuable lessons from the SARS crisis. Since the bird-flu cases emerged in the winter of 2003–04, Chinese officials at all levels have taken the situation very seriously. New cases of bird-flu have been reported timely and dealt with quite effectively so far. In February 2004, Vice Premier and Health Minister Wu Yi emphasized the Chinese government must take decisive measures against the growing AIDS crisis. More openness in mass media in reporting health crisis and social problems will put great pressure on the government to respond to such problems in a more timely and more transparent way. How well the Chinese government will be able to handle crises like these and address other related issues will certainly affect the success or failure of building a new political order in China.

CONCLUSION

The direction that the transformation of the CCP and the establishment of citizens' political petition access and rule of law point to is building a new political order in post-Communist China. China's economic reform and openness have created conditions for development of personal difference, opening up spheres of action not subject to collective control. In the meantime, problems such as high unemployment rates, corruption, fallouts of the welfare system, widening gaps between the rich and the poor, unequal and unfair treatment, intolerable burdens on peasants, etc. have contributed to widespread grievances and resentments in Chinese society. Under such circumstances, leadership in the reform era requires flexibility and sensitivity to stability and popular pressures. Party transformation and the establishment of the citizens' petition access and rule of law could be viewed as the CCPs responses to issues and challenges raised by China's reform and openness but they delineate the dimensions of a new political order that is being built in China.

NOTES

1. For an empirical analysis of local election in the early 1990s, see M. Kent Jennings, "Political Participation in the Chinese Countryside," *American Political Science Review*, vol. 91, no. 2 (June 1997), pp. 361–72.
2. *Renmin Ribao* (People's Daily), overseas edition (December 27, 1994), p. 1.
3. Ibid. (October 31, 1994), p. 1.
4. The first national Astrike hard campaign since the economic reform was conducted during 1983–84 to crack down on crimes, which showed the seriousness of the situation. Statistics for those 2 years, however, is not available.
5. Daniel Kelliher, "The Chinese Debate over Village Self-Government," *The China Journal*, no. 37 (January 1997), p. 66.
6. See Kevin J. O'Brien, "Implementing Political Reform in China's villages," *The Australian Journal of Chinese Affairs*, no. 32 (July 1994), pp. 33–60; Daniel Kelliher, "The Chinese Debate over Village Self-Government," *The China Journal*, no. 37 (January 1997), pp. 63–86; Jean C. Oi, "Economic Development, Stability and Democratic Village Self-Governance," in Maurice Brosseau, Suzanne Pepper, and Tsang Shu-ki, eds., *China Review 1996* (Hong Kong: The Chinese University Press, 1996), pp. 125–44; M. Kent Jennings, "Political Participation in the Chinese Countryside," *American Political Science Review*, vol. 91, no. 2 (June 1997), pp. 361–72; Melanie Manion, "The Electoral Connection in the Chinese Countryside," *American Political Science Review*, vol. 90, no. 4 (December 1996), pp. 736–48; and John Dearlove, "Village Politics," in Robert Benewick and Paul Wingrove, eds., *China in the 1990s* (Vancouver: UBC Press, 1995), pp. 120–31. Chinese scholarship includes Zhang Houan, *zhongguo nongcun jiceng zhengquan* (Local Government in China's Countryside) (Chengdu: sichuan renmin chubanshe,

1992) and Xu Yong, *zhongguo nongcun cunmin zizhi* (Villagers' Self-Government in China's Countryside) (Wuhan: huazhong shifan daxue chubanshe, 1997).

7. Weixing Chen's field research in 1999 revealed that the same procedure was followed in Shandong's Qufu, Laixi, and Pingyi.

8. Lianjiang Li and Kevin J. O'Brien, "The Struggle over Village Elections," in Roderick MacFarquhar and Merle Goldman, eds., *The Paradox of China's Reforms* (Cambridge, MA: Harvard University Press, 2000).

9. Sylvia Chan, "Village Self-Government and Civil Society," in Joseph Cheng, ed., *China Review 1998* (Hong Kong: The Chinese University Press, 1998), p. 245.

10. Mao Junjie and Chen Yuanzhang, *Anoncun liangwei guanxi xianzhuangjiduice* (The Current Relationship between the VC and Village Party Branch and Solutions), *zhongguo dangzhenganbu luntan* (The Chinese Cadres' Forum) (January 2001), pp. 21–2.

11. Joseph Cheng, "Direct Elections of Town and Township Heads in China: Significance and Limitations of a New Direction in Chinese Politics," in Guoli Liu and Weixing Chen eds., *New Directions in Chinese Politics in the New Millennium* (Lewiston: Edwin Mellen Press, 2002), pp. 37–78.

12. *Peking Review* (December 29, 1978), p. 14.

13. Anthony Dicks, "The Chinese Legal System: Reforms in the Balance," *China Quarterly*, no. 119 (September 1989), p. 570.

14. Deng Xiaoping, *Selected Works of Deng Xiaoping* (Beijing: Foreign Languages Press, 1984), p. 158.

15. James V. Feinerman, "The Rule of Law Imposed from Outside: China's Foreign-Oriented Legal Regime since 1978," in Karen G. Turner, James V. Feinerman, and R. Kent Guy, eds., *The Limits of the Rule of Law in China* (Seattle: University of Washington Press, 2000), pp. 304–24.

16. See Thomas G. Moore, "China and Globalization," in Samuel S. Kim, ed., *East Asia and Globalization* (Lanham: Rowman & Littlefield, 2000), pp. 105–31; and Elizabeth Economy and Michel Oksenberg, eds., *China Joins the World* (New York: Council on Foreign Relations Press, 1999).

17. "A Discussion of the Various Kinds of Supervision by the People's Congress and the Sanding Committee," *Fazhi Ribao*, November 1, 1990, p. 3.

18. Kevin O'Brien, "Chinese People's Congresses and Legislative Embeddedness: Understanding Early Organizational Development, *Comparative Political Studies*, vol. 27 (1994), pp. 80–107.

19. Murray Scot Tanner, *The Politics of Lawmaking in Post-Mao China: Institutions, Processes and Democratic Prospects* (New York: Clarendon Press, 1999).

20. Chapter 2 of the 1982 Constitution defines the Fundamental Rights and Duties of Citizens. Among the rights guaranteed by the Constitutions are: All citizens are "equal before the law." All citizens who have reached the age of 18 have the right to vote and stand for election. Citizens enjoy freedom of speech, of the press, of assembly, of association, of procession, and of demonstration. Citizens enjoy freedom of religious belief. The freedom of person or citizens, the personal dignity of citizens, and the home of citizens are all inviolable. Citizens have the right to criticize and make suggestions to any state organ or functionary. Citizens have the right and the duty to work, and the right to rest. Citizens have the right to material assistance from the state and

society when they are old, ill, or disabled. Citizens have the duty as well as the right to receive education. Women enjoy equal rights with men in all spheres of life, political, economic, cultural, and social, including family life. It is obvious that the Constitution covers extensive rights. The key is how to realize all the rights provided by the Constitution and how to deal with violations of citizens' rights by powerful organs. "The Constitution of the People's Republic of China" (1982), in James C.F. Wang, ed., *Contemporary Chinese Politics: A Introduction*, seventh edition (Upper Saddle River: Prentice Hall, 2002), pp. 379–81.

21. Lubman, *Bird in a Cage*, p. 307.
22. See Gabriel A. Almond and G. Bingham Powell, Jr. eds., *Comparative Politics Today: A World View* (New York: HarperCollins, 1992), p. 510.
23. Harold J. Berman, William R. Greiner, and Samir N. Saliba, *The Nature and Functions of Law*, fifth edition (Westbury: Foundation Press, 1996), p. 6.
24. Stanley B. Lubman, *Bird in a Cage: Legal Reform in China After Mao* (Stanford: Stanford University Press, 1999), p. 34. Richard H. Fallon, Jr. provides an interesting analysis of the concept of the rule of law and its four ideal types: Historicist, formalist, legal process, and substantive. See Fallon, "The Rule of Law as a Concept in Constitutional Discourse," *Columbia Law Review*, vol. 97, no. 1 (January 1997), pp. 1–56.
25. For representative literature in Chinese language, see Guo Daohui, *Lishi Xin Kuayue: Zouxiang Minzhu Fazhi Xin Shiji* (A Historic Leap Over: Towards a New Century of Democracy and the Rule of Law) (Wuhan: Hubai Renmin Chubanshe, 1999); Gong Peixiang et al., eds., *Dandai Zhongguo de Falu Geming* (Chinese Law Revolution in the Contemporary Era) (Beijing: Falu Chubanshe, 1999); and Wang Renbo, Chen Liaoyuan, *Fazhi Lun* (On the Rule of Law) (Jinan: Shangdong Renmin Chubanshe, 1998).
26. Lubman, *Bird in a Cage*, pp. 124–25. For a critical and systematic analysis of China's legal theories and debates on key legal issues, see Ronald Keith, *China's Struggle for the Rule of Law* (London: St. Martin's Press, 1994).
27. Ibid., p. 138.
28. Kathryn Hendley, *Trying to Make Law Matter* (Ann Arbor: University of Michigan Press, 1996), p. 12.
29. Ronald C. Keith, *China's Struggle for the Rule of Law* (London: St. Martin's Press, 1994), p. 21.
30. Eric W. Orts, The Rule of Law in China, *Vanderbilt Journal of Transnational Law*, vol. 34 (January 2001), (<http://web3.infotrac.galegroup.com>, accessed on March 19, 2002).
31. Based on Guoli Liu's notes from the conference and the Beijing exhibit.
32. Max Weber, "Politics as a Vocation," in David Held et al., eds., *States and Societies* (New York: New York University Press, 1983), pp. 111–12. First published in 1919.
33. See *Falu Fagui Shiyong Shouce* (Handbook of Laws and Legal Rugulations) (Beijing: Jincheng Chubanshe, 2000), p. 25.
34. Xin Chunying, *Chinese Legal System and Current Legal Reform* (Beijing: Legal Press), pp. 344–51.
35. Liu Xiaolin, "China Moves toward the Rule of Law: 50 Years of Legal Development in the New China," *People's Daily*, October 7, 1999, p. 1.
36. Lubman, *Bird in a Cage*, p. 299.
37. Berman et al., *The Nature and Functions of Law*, pp. 29–31.

38. Stanley Lubman, "An Introduction: The Future of Chinese Law," *China Quarterly*, no. 141 (March 1995), p. 10.
39. Nicholas R. Lardy, *Integrating China into the Global Economy* (Washington, DC: Brookings Institution Press, 2002), p. 2.
40. *China Daily*, May 9, 2002.
41. Linda Chelan Li, "The Rule of Law Policy in Guangdong: Continuity or Departure? Meaning, Significance and Progresses," *China Quarterly*, no. 161 (March 2000), p. 213.
42. Lubman, *Bird in a Cage*, pp. 4 and 5.
43. Zhenmin Wang, Vice Dean at the Tsinghua University School of Law, recalled when he was a law student. Most students associated law with concepts such as jail, execution, death penalty, police, army, and criminal tribunal. For a long time, it was difficult to see law in terms of rights and justice in China. Today, Chinese students are beginning to associate the law with ideas such as protection of civil rights, dispute resolution, equity, and justice. The reflects the progress that has been made in the attitude of the Chinese toward the rule of law. See Zhenmin Wang, "The Developing Rule of Law in China," *Harvard Asia Quarterly*, Autumn 2000, <www.fas.harvard.edu/~asiactr/hag/200004/0004a007.htm>.
44. Zhenmin Wang, "The Developing Rule of Law in China," <www.fas.harvard.edu/~asiactr/hag/200004/0004a007.htm>.
45. Michael W. Dowdle, "Rule of Law and Civil Society: Implications of a Pragmatic Development," in Pitman B. Potter and Michael W. Dowdle, eds., *Developing Civil Society in China: From the Rule by Law toward the Rule of Law* (Washington, DC: The Woodrow Wilson Center, Asia Program, 2000), pp. 13–22.
46. John P. Burns, "The People's Republic of China at 50: National Political Reform," *China Quarterly*, no. 159 (September 1999), p. 586.
47. See Joseph Fewsmith, *China Since Tiananmen: The Politics of Transition* (New York: Cambridge University Press, 2001), p. 128.
48. Susan V. Lawrence, "The Plague Reaches Much Deeper," *Far Eastern Economic Review*, May 1, 2003.
49. World Health Organization, <http://www.who.int/csr/sars/country/table2003_09_23/en/>. Accessed on February 25, 2004.
50. Joseph Fewsmith, "China and the Politics of SARS," *Current History*, vol. 102, no. 665 (September 2003), pp. 250–55.
51. Ibid., p. 255.

CHAPTER 5

NEW INSTITUTION BUILDING OR MUDDLING THROUGH IN THE CHINESE COUNTRYSIDE

Yang Zhong

INTRODUCTION

The rural situation in China has been a trouble spot for the Chinese government since the late 1980s. Rural problems are often summarized as *san nong wenti* (three rural issues), that is, *nongmin* (peasants), nongye (agriculture), and *nongcun* (rural areas). The three rural issues entail both economic and political dimensions. The peasant problem refers to the peasants' declining income, poor living conditions, low education level, and the difficulty in controlling peasant population. The agricultural problem involves the low profitability of Chinese agricultural products, scarce agricultural land use, low agricultural technology levels, and the vulnerability of Chinese agricultural economy in world competition after China's accession to the WTO. These two problems lead to the overall rural problems (*nongcun wenti*) of instability and potential chaos in the Chinese countryside.

The *san nong* problems can be understood along two dimensions: economic and political. Problems on the economic level are easy to understand but difficult to solve. World economic history tells us that industrialization always occurs at the expense of agricultural economy in the process of modernization. It is inevitable that Chinese farmers' interests will be sacrificed in China's modernization drive. Chinese leaders do realize the severity of China's rural problems. However, they find themselves in a dilemma: namely that they have limited viable economic options to solve the rural economic problems even if they want to. Chinese leaders neither have the desire nor the resources for using heavy-handed administrative methods (such as price fixing and massive subsidies) to solve the *san nong* problems. Instead, it seems that the Chinese government has basically adopted passive, reactive, and delaying tactics vis á vis its rural population. In other words, Chinese leaders are betting on time: they hope that, over time, China rural economic problems will eventually be solved or at least ameliorated through urbanization, rural migration into the cities, and endurance by the Chinese peasantry.

The risk of taking such a strategy is the possible political fallout and instability resulting from the deteriorating economic condition in transition in China's vast rural areas. China's rural economic problems have been complicated and exacerbated by the rigid and decaying political structure and institutional norms at the Chinese local government level. It does not seem that Chinese leaders are prepared to prevent and contain potential political fallout. As a matter of fact, rural instabilities such as peasant riots and sit-ins already occur frequently. Fortunately for the Chinese government these rural disturbances have not happened in a large-scale and organized fashion.

This paper takes an institutionalist approach to study village politics in China by focusing on the institutional arrangements of Chinese village authorities. It is argued in the paper that despite of the official push for autonomous and democratic governance at the village level, village authorities in China still primarily function and are treated as a convenient policy-implementation arm for the higher governmental authorities. Township/town government depends heavily upon the village administrative establishment and village officials to implement the central, provincial, and local governments' policies. Higher governmental authorities depend primarily on two authoritative powers available to them to control village officials and their behavior: power over the village cadre personnel and power over the village officials' financial compensation. Such institutional constraints have prevented the villagers' committee in rural China to be a genuine democratic and autonomous village government even though in most places it is procedurally elected now.

It is also argued in the paper that the authority of village officials during the reform era in China has been gradually declining. On the one hand, village officials find it increasingly difficult to implement state policies in the villages. A common complaint by Chinese village officials these days is that the villagers have become increasingly unruly and difficult to govern. On the other hand, village officials are becoming more irrelevant than ever in villagers' life due to the return of private farming (i.e. the "household responsibility system"), the declining dependency of peasants upon village officials in their daily life, the massive migration of villagers to the urban areas, and the rise of traditional political and social forces such as kinships and clans in the Chinese countryside.

Chinese leaders are faced with two different approaches to the mounting problems in China's rural areas: muddling through and institutional changes. The choice may well determine the success of China's modernization drive and its future. Thus far the Chinese government seems to have taken a cautious and reactive muddling approach. The Chinese countryside may not necessarily spark a major system collapse in the PRC, but it is extremely unlikely that the CCP could count on the peasants' support as it did during the Nationalist era if the Party faces another serious crisis like the 1989 Tiananmen events. What is more likely to happen is that the Chinese peasantry may be a contributing factor to the crisis if no serious institutional changes will take place at Chinese local levels soon. The author argues that the ultimate solution may lie in the reorientation of state policies and democratization of the political structure at higher levels.

ORGANIZATIONAL STRUCTURE OF CHINESE VILLAGE ADMINISTRATION

Prior to 1949 the Chinese governmental authorities had historically relied upon unofficial or semiofficial networks (e.g. the *bao jia* system) and local forces such as the local gentry class (*xiangshen*) to rule Chinese villages. This dramatically changed in 1949 after the communist victory. Land was redistributed to Chinese peasants who were by and large left alone in the initial two to three years after 1949. However, a new central government policy was adopted in 1955 to encourage the formation of agricultural cooperatives to prevent income polarization among peasants.[1] Afterwards, direct governmental control was gradually but surely extended into the countryside. The rural collectivization drive was finally completed in 1958 with the establishment of the people's communes.

The people's communes, which replaced townships and the township governments, were both economic and political organizations (*zhengjing heyi zuzhi*). They could even be compared to a military regiment with little autonomy for members. Villages were organized and turned into "production brigades," which were one level below the communes and were also both an economic and political organization. Chinese peasants were controlled in an organized fashion under the commune system as they had never been before in Chinese history. The commune system was formally abolished in the early 1980s and replaced by townships that existed prior to 1958. With the abolishment of communes, production brigades (*shengchan dadui*) were also abolished and replaced by "villagers' committees" (*cunmin weiyuanhui*). By the end of 1995, close to 750,000 villagers' committees, with more than 4 million village officials, were formed.[2] About half the village committees exist in geographically integral villages (*zirancun*) and the other half are found in administrative villages (*xingzhengcun*).[3]

There is no formal government at the village level in China since, according to the PRCs constitution, the township/town government is the most basic level of government. Yet there does exist an informal and quasi-governmental administration in Chinese villages, including the village CCP branch, the villagers' committee, a village economic organization often called the General Company of Agriculture, Industry and Commerce" (*nonggongshang zong gongsi*) and several auxiliary "mass" organizations. These village organizations form the "village Inc." in rural China. Even though it is not easy to define the exact legal status and role of the above village authorities, the village governmental administration is treated and viewed as a policy implementing arm of the Chinese central government, as well as Chinese local governments at various levels. Officials or cadres of the village administration, though not formal state employees, are treated and perceived as foot soldiers of the Chinese central and local governments in actually implementing polices from above in the vast Chinese countryside.

The Village Party Branch

According to the Constitution of the Chinese Communist Party, a Communist Party branch (*dangzhibu*) should be established in any work unit or place where there are three or more full Party members. A Party branch, a smaller unit than a Party committee, is the grassroots or primary Party organization in China. Therefore, a Communist Party branch exists in every Chinese village. A Party committee is set up in villages where there are significantly large numbers of Party members. The structure of the village Party branch is fairly simple. The Party branch is headed by a Party secretary and one to two deputy secretaries, officially elected by a general membership meeting and serving a 3-year term. In reality, though, an overwhelming majority of village Party secretaries and deputy secretaries are decided upon by township/town Party authorities and all Party secretaries and deputy sec-retaries have to be approved by higher Party organizations. Other members or cadres of the village Party branch also include a person in charge of Party organizational affairs (*zuzhi weiyuan*), a person in charge of propaganda (*xuanchuan weiyuan*), and a person in charge of Party discipline (*jilu weiyuan*). Three auxiliary "mass" organizations (i.e. the Communist Youth League, the Women's Association, and the People's Militia) are also under the leadership of the village Party branch.

The Chinese Communist Party Constitution defines the primary Party organizations as the "militant bastions of the Party in the basic units of soci-ety" and attaches eight functions to these organizations, including the most important function of "propagating and carrying out the Party's line, prin-ciples and policies, the decisions of the Central Committee of the Party and other higher Party organizations, and their own decision."[4] The village Party branch serves an especially crucial function as the institutional control mech-anism in the PRC since there is no formal governmental authority at the village level. The village Party branch, not the villagers' committee (to be explained later), is the decision-making body in the village and the villagers' committee primarily implements the decisions made by the village Party branch. All major decisions concerning village affairs have to be approved by the Party branch before formal adoption by the villagers' committee. This is how higher Party and governmental authorities make sure that decisions made by village administration conform to the Party line and policies.

The village Party branch secretary is no doubt the most important and powerful village official (the "first-hand") in the village. The village Party branch secretary serves as the personification and chief representative of the Party at the village level. A consensus among Chinese township/town officials is that the economic development and good governance of a village depends most importantly on having a capable village Party secretary. That is why in the Chinese system the village Party secretary is given so much power. All major decisions concerning village public affairs have to be approved first by the village Party secretary. The villagers' committee chairman usually serves literally as a lieutenant (deputy Party secretary) to the Party secretary. One of the crucial powers held by the Party secretary is his control over personnel decisions and recruitment of new Party members in the village. The village Party branch secretary is obviously influential in the selection of key personnel in the Party branch. In addition, the village Party secretary also plays an important role in the nomination and election of key officials on the villagers' committee due to the fact that the village Party secretary heads the organizing committee of the villagers' committee election and this committee plays a crucial role in the selection in the final slate of the villagers' committee candidates in consultation with township/town governmental authorities.

The Party secretary also has the final authority over village public financial and budgetary matters. Usually all major village expenditures have to be approved by the village Party secretary. The power of the Party secretary over financial matters is especially significant in well-to-do villages where there are a significant number of village-owned enterprises. After the dissolution of communes, many villages formed an economic entity called Economic Cooperatives (*jingji hezuo she*) or Agricultural, Industrial, and Commercial Corporation (*nonggongshang gongsi*) to continue running the village-owned enterprises that were already in existence during the commune era. These economic organizations, which represented the collective rural economy, were greatly expanded during the 1980s and 1990s in many rural areas (such as southern Jiangsu province) and provided many of the funds for the village's expenses for public projects and welfare.[5] The village Party secretary usually serves as chairperson of these economic organizations. As a result the village Party secretary controls major economic activities in the village. The village Party secretary is one of few fully compensated officials in Chinese villages.

In recent years, the influence of the village Party branch in many rural areas has declined. A 1994 Chinese Communist Party Central Committee document admitted that about 75 percent of rural Party primary organizations were in a state of paralysis (not functioning).[6] It is becoming increasingly difficult even to gather enough Party members for a general meeting in many villages. In some well-to-do villages Party members have to be paid to attend Party meetings and functions and Party members also receive an annual cash bonus at year's end.[7] Decline of the primary Party organizations in rural China is reflected in the dwindling Party membership since it is becoming increasingly difficult for the Party to recruit new Party members from the peasantry. In fact, many village Party branches have not recruited new members in a decade due to declining Party ideological attraction of the Party to young peasants and the village Party branch's declining influence and power.[8] A related problem is the *laozhishu* or "old (or aging) Party secretary" phenomenon in the Chinese countryside. According to a study of village Party branches in one Chinese county in the mid-1990s, the average age of village Party secretaries was 47 and more than a third of the village Party secretaries in the county had served in their position for over two decades.[9] Dwindling Party membership and functional decline of village Party branches have seriously undermined the CCPs institutional control in China's rural areas.

The Villagers' Committee

The other important body of the village administration is the villagers' committee, which has actually evolved for over 20 years in China. The establishment of the villagers' committee can be traced back to the late 1970s when the "household responsibility" system (*jiating lianchan chengbao zhi*) was introduced to the Chinese countryside. With the introduction of the "household responsibility" system, the old political structure of communes and production brigades became obsolete due to poor fit between the new economic system and the old political structure. Like the "household responsibility" system that first emerged independent of governmental forces and support, the villagers' committee, the new form of village self-government that replaced the production brigade, was also initially a spontaneous creation at the grass-roots level in two counties in Guangxi province without government sanction.[10] The early villagers' committees were only responsible for managing neighborhood affairs.[11] Later on, they became a comprehensive administrative organization and a policy-implementation tool for the Chinese government. Under the villagers' committee, peasants are further organized into small villagers' groups (*cunmin xiaozu*). Each small villagers' group is composed, on average, of 30 to 35 households with a elected leader. Small villagers' groups evolved from small production teams (*shengchan xiaodui*) during the commune era. The organizational structure of the villagers' committee and small villagers' groups resembles very much the *bao jia* system that existed in precommunist rural China.

Villagers' committees in China are usually made up of three to six members, including a committee chairman (often referred to as the "village head" or *cunzhang*), an accountant, a woman leader (*funu zhuren*) in charge of women's affairs (primarily in the area of family planning) and a member in charge of village public security (*zhian baohu*). Each serves a 3-year term. The villagers' committee chairman is usually the first deputy Party secretary of the village Party branch and it is common that some other villagers' committee members also serve concurrently as key officials in the village Party branch. Usually the chairman and the accountant are the only fully paid officials of the villagers' committee.

The current Chinese Constitution stipulates that the chair, the deputy chair, and other members of the villagers' committee be elected by villagers. Even though elections of production brigade leaders and villagers' committee members were held in many provinces prior to the late 1980s, these elections were often conducted in an ad hoc fashion and most village leaders were still directly appointed from above. Endorsed by Peng Zhen, then Chairman of National People's Congress (NPC), the NPCs Standing Committee in 1987 passed the *Organic Law of the Villagers' Committee* on a trial basis, which legally provided for election as the means to choose villagers' committee officials.[12] (The *Organic Law* was adopted on a permanent basis in 1998.)[13] Initially, adoption of the village committee system met resistance from some local government officials and the Organizational Department of the Chinese Communist Party Central Committee, especially in 1989 during the aftermath of the Tiananmen democracy movement. If it were not for Peng Zhen's strong support, villagers' committee elections would not have survived after 1989.[14] The fact that it took the Chinese government almost a decade to revise the 1987 provisional *Organic Law* and to adopt it on a permanent basis indicates the cautiousness and hesitance of the Chinese government over this practice.

Yet, by the late 1990s (more than a decade after the adoption of the *Organic Law*), there was little consensus on the exact percentage of Chinese villages that had had villagers' committee elections, let alone competitive and democratic elections. The reported figures of Chinese villages that have experienced varying degrees of open elections range from one-third to 50 percent.[15] The assessment of the nature and significance of the villagers' committee elections is just as controversial. It is almost impossible to make any sweeping and generalized statements about the democratic nature and significance of villagers' committee elections in China due to the fact that there is so much variation in villagers' committee election practice from village to village, from region to region, and from province to province in the vast Chinese countryside.

Many analysts of villagers' committee elections seemingly have a cautiously optimistic evaluation of these elections. Some argue, for example, that the village election exercise has made Chinese peasants more aware of their political rights and serves as, in Peng Zhen's words, "a democratic training course" for Chinese peasants.[16] Some others contend that villagers' committee elections have made it possible to replace corrupt and unpopular leaders.[17] More importantly, it is hoped that such elections have the potential to lead to wider democratization in China, such as elections of town/township and county government officials in the near future.[18]

Other studies have questioned the meaningfulness of the villagers' committee elections in many parts of the country. Yang Zhong's study of village elections in southern Jiangsu province finds that these elections are highly orchestrated and mobilized.[19] He Qinglian argues that villagers' committee elections have revived traditional Chinese evil forces in the countryside such as clans and hooligans and these elections have been made a convenient vehicle for these forces to come to power and dominate Chinese rural politics.[20] In their empirical study of villagers' committee elections in Jiangsu, Yang Zhong and Jie Chen found that only around half of the eligible voters in southern Jiangsu villages actually showed up to vote in these elections in the late 1990s, even though the Chinese press routinely reports voter turnout in these elections at above 90 percent.[21] This low voter turnout raises the question: what are the subjective factors motivating Chinese peasants to participate in villagers' committee elections? This question was partially addressed by the study of Yang Zhong and Jie Chen based on data collected from a representative survey in southern Jiangsu province. Their main findings in the study include that those who tended to vote in village elections were people with low levels of internal efficacy and democratic values, high levels of life satisfaction and interest in state and local public affairs, and that anticorruption sentiment did not seem to play any role in these village elections. Peasants with higher levels of internal efficacy and democratic orientation stayed away from the elections.[22] (These findings are very similar to those found in a voting behavioral study of Beijing residents in local Peoples' Congress elections in Beijing in 1995.)[23]

These findings call into question the competitiveness and democratic nature of villagers' committee elections in the Chinese countryside. It seems that the peasants' voting behavior in the case of Jiangsu fits the *disengagement model* that was used to conceptualize constrained and limited political participation among formal Soviet citizens.[24] Implied in this model is that individual political values and orientations do play a role in what political activities citizens choose to participate in and how actively they become involved. Indeed, in the constrained and limited elections nonvoting is often used by many as a protest vote. Even though the case study was conducted in Jiangsu, it is highly possible that this behavior exits in many other parts of the Chinese countryside due to the similar institutional constraints and limitations placed on village elections in many other parts of China.

There are at least three common institutional constraints on villagers' committee elections in China (with slight regional variations). The first concerns the nominating process. Forming alternative political parties is de facto banned in China. Therefore, the nominating process of candidates to villagers' committee elections is operated totally under the one-party system. Even though *hai xuan* or total open nomination has been practiced in many Chinese village elections, in most places the nomination of villagers' committee officials is still significantly controlled by the township/town government and the village Party apparatus. The final slate of candidates is usually decided by the village election organizing committee headed by the village Party secretary and approved by the township/town government. If there is some "gap" between the authority favored candidates and the popular candidates, the village organizing committee is expected to "persuade" the villagers to accept the authority-approved candidates. One of the criteria used to judge whether a nominating process is successful or not is to see whether the authority-preferred candidates also happen to be the candidates favored by the villagers.[25]

A second constraint in the villagers' committee electoral process is the constraint on electoral campaigns by the candidates. In any democratic election, candidates are allowed and expected to publicize their positions on issues and their platforms to their constituency in an open and free fashion. In other words, they need to "sell" themselves to their electorate to gain support and votes. In the villagers' committee elections in China, however, the final list of candidates is often officially announced only days prior the actual vote and election regulations often forbid or discourage open campaigning and soliciting votes. The only legitimate and open campaigning that a candidate can do in most village elections is to make a short speech in front of the village voters minutes before voting on election day, even though private lobbying and behind-the-scene campaigning are fairly common in many village elections. The absence of free and open electioneering on the part of the candidates significantly reduces the competitiveness of villagers' committee elections in China.

A third and fundamental institutional limitation on villagers' committee elections in China is the dominating role that the village Party apparatus plays in village governance after the election is over. As mentioned earlier, even though the villagers' committee is officially designated as an "autonomous" and "self-governing" body by the Chinese constitution, it is generally treated as a subordinate to the village Party apparatus. A circular issued by CCPs Central Committee in 1990 made it clear that the villagers' committee should be "under the leadership of the Party."[26] *The Organic Law of the Villagers' Committee*, which governs villagers' committee elections, activities, and functions, emphasizes the central role of the village Party branch in village "self-governance."[27] While the village Party secretary is the most powerful official in the village, the villagers' committee chairman is usually the "second hand," or even the "third hand" in some cases, in the village administration. In other words, even if the chairman of the villagers' committee is elected in a perfectly democratic fashion, the election only elects a deputy to the village Party secretary who is not subject to popular and democratic election and confirmation. A survey of more than a hundred villagers' committee chairs conducted in several townships and towns in Zhejiang province in 1998 shows that close to 80 percent of them felt that the village Party secretary had more power in their village due to the institutionalised leadership role of the Party.[28]

An institutional block for popular election of Party secretaries in Chinese villages is that, according to CCPs constitution, only Party members can elect Party officials. There have been trial efforts in recent years in some parts of China to bypass that limitation to inject popular input in the election (or selection) of the village Party secretary. One experiment that has been tried in Anhui province and Shanxi province since 1999 is to allow villagers to vote informally for the nominees for the village Party secretary position and then village Party members will choose a candidate to be the village Party secretary from the list of candidates already approved by the villagers in the first round of voting.[29] This practice will certainly make the Party secretary more accountable and responsive to the villagers. It, however, will not change the subordinate position of the villagers' committee chair.

Village Assemblies and Village Representative Assemblies

In addition to the village Party apparatus and the villagers' committee, there are two other official village organizations, that is, village assemblies (*cunmin huiyi* or *cunmin dahui*) and village representative assemblies (*cunmin daibiao huiyi* or *cunmin daibiao dahui*). According to the Organic Law of Villagers' Committees governing village self-governance in China, village assemblies are the ultimate decision-making body in deciding (by majority vote) on the most important issues concerning the villagers, such as the allocation of village public finance and expenditures and plans for raising money for village public projects such as schools and roads.[30] Any villager over the age of 18 is a member of the village assembly in his/her village and has the right to vote in the assembly meetings. It is suggested in the Organic Law that village assemblies should be convened at least once a year to discuss villagers' committee's work report and to evaluate villagers' committee members' performance.[31] Obviously, the village assembly is supposed to be a form of direct democracy. Yet, in reality, village assembly meetings are rarely convened due to the organizational and practical difficulties in gathering enough villagers for assembly meetings and in running the meetings smoothly.[32] The only time that a village assembly meeting is held is the villagers' committee election.

Because of the impracticality of holding regular village assembly meeting, a new organization, the village representative assembly, has been created and utilized as a form of a representative body in many Chinese villages. The village representative assembly is supposed to have the same functions and power of the village assembly and is often referred to as the "village People's Congress." Interestingly enough, however, the *Organic Law* does not specify how village representatives are chosen except that one villager representative should be elected by every 5–15 households, even though many local authorities have set up rules and regulations on the election of village representative assembly members.[33] The composition of village representative assemblies varies from village to village. In some places the village representative assembly consists of elected village representatives (one representative per 10–15 households), small village group leaders and villagers' committee members; in some other places the assembly also includes deputies to county and township people's congresses from the village; and still in some others the village Party secretary and other village Party branch cadres are automatic members of the village representative assembly.[34]

The practice and effectiveness of village representative assemblies vary significantly from region to region and from province to province. In villages where there is strong pressure from the higher authorities to make the village representative assembly work and sufficient support and cooperation from the village Party branch, the village representative assembly is able to perform its functions as a representative organ of the villagers, a crucial decision-making body and an effective monitoring instrument over the village government.[35] Yet in most villages, either the village representative assembly is rarely convened and utilized or the assembly meetings are held as a formality (*zouxingshi*) in a meaningless fashion or used as merely a legitimizing body to approve the decisions already made by the village Party branch and/or the villagers' committee.

VILLAGE OFFICIALS: SERVING THE VILLAGERS OR THE CHINESE STATE AUTHORITIES?

As indicated earlier, Chinese village officials (such as the village Party secretary, villagers' committee chair, and other villagers' committee members) are not officially state employees, civil servants, or Party functionaries on the state payroll or *bianzhi*. They are officially referred to as "village cadres" or "grassroots cadres." The overwhelming majority of village cadres are terminal officials without prospect of promotion to township/town official positions due to age and educational requirements for these positions. Only a few young and educated village cadres are expected to become township/town officials and they are considered the extremely lucky ones since, with the promotion to township/town positions, their residential status (*hukou*) is changed from rural to nonrural and they become state employees with a steady salary and benefits, or "people eating emperor's grain" (*chi huangliang de ren*). In some economically developed regions, however, village cadres are reluctant or unwilling to be promoted to formal state employees at township and town levels since compensation and benefits as village cadres are much better than the fixed low salary of township/town officials.

An overwhelming majority of the village officials in China are natives of the particular village they serve. Some village Party secretaries are appointed to serve in another village where no appropriate local person can be found to serve or no local villagers are willing to serve. A substantial number of village cadres are demobilized People's Liberation Army (PLA) soldiers (*tuiwu junren*). Demobilized PLA soldiers have some advantages in serving as village cadres. First of all, many demobilized soldiers had already become Party members at a relatively young age (at the end of their military service) since joining the Party while in military service is easier than joining the Party in civilian life. Second, demobilized PLA soldiers are perceived to be better educated technically and are more politically progressive or loyal to the Party since the PLA is often described as "a big communist school" (*gongchan zhuyi da xuexiao*). Third, demobilized PLA soldiers are often perceived as more open-minded and visionary since they have traveled and lived in far away places and therefore they are considered good candidates as capable leaders for rural China. Finally, demobilized PLA soldiers are said to have the *guanxi* (or personal network) advantage due to their close connections and relations with their former buddies in the military living in various parts of the country.[36]

In the 1990s an increasing number of "rural talents" (*nongcun nengren*), such as successful rural collective enterprise managers, peasant businessmen, and peasants who are successful in growing special crops, fruits, or vegetables, have been recruited or elected into the village nomenclature to form a new breed of village elite (*nongcun jingying*).[37] In the first villagers' committee elections in Guangdong province in the late 1990s, for example, close to 40 percent of the newly elected village officials were economically talented villagers (*jingji nengren*).[38] An obvious advantage to these people, not necessarily having sufficient education or Communist Party members, was their successful business or economic backgrounds and skills that local authorities and villagers felt could be applied to management of village affairs. These new rural elites also tend to have extensive personal networks through their business dealings that can be crucial assets for developing the village economy. In addition, they tend to be more original and creative in their thinking to solve village problems.

Regardless of backgrounds or origins, village officials in many respects are more often perceived and treated as Party and state officials instead of nonstate "autonomous" community leaders by both local Chinese governmental authorities and Chinese villagers. Chinese village officials serve primarily as implementers, facilitators, and enforcers of policies made by various levels of government, representatives of higher governmental authorities in Chinese villages, and links or agents between Chinese peasantry and Chinese state authorities. One of the villagers' committee's responsibilities (as defined in the *Organic Law*) is to "publicize [the PRCs] Constitution, laws, regulations, and state policies."[39] Even though the relationship between the township/town government and the villagers' committee is supposed to be "guidance" and the latter should "provide cooperation, support, and assistance to the township/town government's work,"[40] in reality the township/town government acts as the immediate superior "boss" to the village officials, who are then obligated to carry out policies from the higher governmental authorities.

Indeed, the township/town government depends heavily upon the village administrative establishment and village officials to implement the central, provincial, and local governments' policies. Supervision of village officials' policy-implementation efforts is often difficult due to the distant geographical location of many villages from the site of township/town government and the lack of modern communication means between villages and the township/town government. Generally there are three ways that the township/town government uses to monitor policy implementation by Chinese village officials: signing a performance contract, site visits, and calling village officials to the township/town government to report their work.

Like the policy implementation relationship between the county government and the township/town government, a similar pressurized performance contract system also exists between key village officials (i.e. village Party secretaries and villagers' committee heads) and the township/town government. The contract with numerical policy targets usually covers the crucial policy issue areas such as family planning (specific birth rates and number of abortions and sterilizations performed), social order and stability in the village, village economic development (such as village economic growth, increase in villagers' income and construction of public facilities in the village), and the collection of fees and taxes. In addition to these usual standing policy issues, village officials have to carry out ad hoc policies such as achieving particular sanitation and living standards, mandatory subscription of newspapers by the village authorities, coercion of peasants into buying particular life insurance, and pressuring peasants to grow a particular type of agricultural product.[41]

The township/town government periodically (on a semiannual or annual basis) conducts evaluations of village officials' performance to achieve the goals specified in the contract. Personal conduct and the moral character of village officials, such as engaging in illegal and immoral activities (such as gambling, prostitution, and corruption) are also components of this periodical evaluation. Failure to achieve the numerical targets in the performance contract and ad hoc policies may result in monetary punishment and/or demotion. Village officials often adopt extreme measures under pressure in order to fulfill both the contracted and ad hoc policy goals, especially in the areas of family planning (such as forced abortion and sterilization) and fee/tax collection.

Township/town officials often pay visits to villages to evaluate job performances by village officials and to listen to the voices of the villagers. These visits are usually conducted at year's end and for specific reasons or occasions. Chinese villagers frequently complain that township/town officials do not visit their village often enough and when they do visit they are often hosted by village officials with lavish meals and are less interested in talking to the ordinary villagers about what is really going on in the village.[42] Therefore these visits are becoming less meaningful these days. Apart from township/town officials' visits to the villages, village officials are often summoned to the township/town government to report on their work and to attend meetings and seminars to study governmental documents, policies, and directives.

Chinese township/town governments depend primarily on two authoritative powers available to them to control village officials and their behavior: power over the village cadre personnel power and power over the village officials' financial compensation. The township/town government is directly responsible for the village cadre management. Key village officials (especially the Party secretary and deputy Party secretaries), as mentioned previously, are basically selected and appointed by township/town government even though they are procedurally and formally elected by Party members in the village. Also, as mentioned earlier, the township/town government also plays an important role in the election of villagers' committee members, including the chairperson. Township/town government also often dismiss elected villagers' committee chairs even though it does not have the official authority to do so. According to a Chinese newspaper report, 57 percent of villagers' committee chairs in Qianjiang city, Hubei province were dismissed by local township/town governments between 1999 and 2002. A main reason was the alleged disobedience of these village officials to the township/town government and officials.[43] The personnel files of village officials are kept at the township/town government. Village officials in many places are sent to township/town Party schools on a regular basis for leadership training and ideological indoctrination, even though some villagers' committee members are not Communist Party members.

In many villages there exists a miniature nomenclature system and cadre reserve list. Promising and educated young people, such as the secretary of the Communist Youth League (CYL), are targeted for promotion to become future key village cadres. Even though there is no tenure system for village cadres, the village Party secretary and other key village cadres usually serve long terms. The mentality of a typical village Party secretary is that he is to serve in his position as long as he is willing to serve, does not make any major mistake, and has the trust of the key township/town Party and government officials. In some places, retirement age for the village Party secretary is set at 55 for women and 60 for men, the same practice as with regular state employees and cadres.[44] Sometimes township/town government and village officials feel obligated and compelled to "make job arrangements" (*anpai gongzuo*) for villagers' committee chairs who fail to win reelection.

One example is Jiangxia village in Jiangsu province.[45] Jiangxia village held its fifth villagers' committee election in February 1999 with a new nomination method: "sea election" (*haixuan*) or free nomination for the final slate of candidates. As usual, the village Party secretary led the election organizing committee. What was interesting was that the sitting villagers' committee chair was serving as deputy chair of the organizing committee and he was also a member of the village Party branch. The sitting chair was also running for reelection and he was the favored internal candidate (*neiding renxuan*) of the village Party branch. After the "sea election" of the initial nominees, the villagers' committee sitting chair, a village deputy Party secretary, and the village accountant came in first, second, and third. The election organizing committee decided that there should be only two final candidates for the chairman position of the villagers' committee in the general election. Therefore, the sitting villagers' committee chair and deputy village Party secretary became the final candidates. The village Party branch and the town government (which governs the village) felt relieved since both candidates were acceptable to the Party establishment. However, the village Party branch was still promoting the sitting chair in his reelection bid and was expecting him to win in the general election.

To most people's surprise, the sitting chair lost the election to the deputy village Party secretary in the general election. It was a humiliating defeat for the sitting villagers' committee chair. The town government felt it was obligated to find a suitable job for the villagers' committee chair since he had served in the village leadership group for a long time. What the town government decided to do was to appoint the outgoing villagers' committee chair to be the deputy village Party secretary and asked the newly elected villagers' committee chair to resign from his position. In other words, the old and new villagers' committee chairs simply switched positions and in the meantime they both continued to serve as members of the village Party branch. What was even more ironic was that before this election only three village officials (i.e. the village Party secretary, the villagers' committee chair, and the village accountant) received full salary compensation. After the election, the outgoing villager who was also appointed as deputy village Party secretary was also added to the village official payroll, thus increasing the financial burden to the village.

Indeed, the Chinese township/town government has the final authority over financial compensation for village officials. As indicated earlier, village cadres as nonstate employees are not on the state payroll. Yet key village cadres, including the village Party secretary and villagers' committee chair, are usually treated as full-time village officials (*quantuochan ganbu*) and do receive a quasi-salary in the form of a "stipend" or "compensation" for their village work. The money comes from fees collected from the villagers, income from village-owned enterprises, payments from renting village land, etc. Ironically, the amount of monetary compensation for village cadres is not decided by the villagers who contribute the money, but rather by the township/town government depending on the level of the economic development in the village and the performance of the village cadres. Such a compensation system is said to prevent the possible abuse of public funds by village officials. In addition to the salary compensation, the township/town government also authorizes the use of village public fund as a monetary bonus reward for the village cadres at year's end.

In fact, the monetary compensation is a major factor that attracts many peasants to pursue village cadre positions, especially that of village Party secretary and chairmanship of the villagers' committee. Village cadres in economically developed regions are compensated much more generously than those in the poorer areas. In Jiangxia village in southern Jiangsu province, for example, the village Party secretary in 1999 was compensated about 43,000 *yuan* plus 25,000 *yuan* bonus; while the villagers' committee chairman in the same village made about 44,000 *yuan* from both salary and bonus that year.[46] This kind of income is even better than that of many formal state cadres and urban residents. Obviously the southern Jiangsu province, one of the most developed rural areas in China, is an exception rather than the rule. Village Party secretaries and villagers' committee chairs in central Sichuan province only received about 100 to 200 *yuan* a month for their work.[47] Even this seemingly small amount of income means a lot for most villagers in poorer regions of China.

In addition to official monetary compensation, Chinese village cadres also enjoy "hidden" benefits and gray income. Dining on village public funds by village cadres is a widespread phenomenon and a serious corruption issue in Chinese rural areas. Gifts (such as cigarettes and wine) and favors are almost expected of villagers in return for services provided by village cadres. Village cadres are also exempted from mandatory labor service to the state each year.[48]

The relationship between village cadres and township/town government officials is one of mutual dependency. Chinese township/town government officials depend heavily on village cadres for policy implementation in the rural areas. Because of this dependence, township/town officials often turn a blind eye to the wrong-doings and abuses by village cadres. On the other hand, village cadres owe their position and power to township/town officials. As mentioned earlier, the township/town government controls the selection of village cadres. In addition, the township/town government decides the legal income or monetary compensation of village cadres. Under the current village cadre compensation system, village officials are more responsive and accountable to the township/town government and officials than to the villagers since the former controls their purses. In recent years, properly held VC elections have presented a challenge for township/town officials in many places since some of these newly elected village cadres are no longer willing pawns of township/town government and reluctant to carry out government policies not compatible with local interests.

THE WEAKENING ROLE AND AUTHORITY OF VILLAGE OFFICIALS

The authority of village officials during the reform era in China has been gradually declining. On the one hand, village officials find it increasingly difficult to implement state policies in the villages. A common complaint by Chinese village officials these days is that the villagers have become increasingly unruly and difficult to govern. On the other hand, village officials are becoming more irrelevant than ever in villagers' life. Village cadres, in the eyes of many Chinese villagers, have become merely tax and fee collectors and enforcers of unpopular governmental policies (e.g. family planning). In a survey of 1,000 peasants in Ningxia province, when asked whom they rely upon in time of need and trouble, 55 percent of the peasants chose family members, 19 percent said they would go to the township/town government, 10 percent chose relatives and friends, and only 5 percent would go to village cadres for help.[49] The same survey also shows that the majority of peasants preferred to voice their opinions and complaints to township/town or even higher authorities rather than to village officials.[50]

What is even worse is that many Chinese villages have become "paralyzed villages" (*tanhuancun*).[51] A "paralyzed village" is a village that exhibits one or more of the following symptoms: the village Party branch and the villagers' committee exist in name only and do not perform normal functions anymore; traditional clans and village forces have become, in effect, informal village authorities; Party and governmental policies (such as family planning and tax/fee collection) cannot be implemented; and there is a general breakdown of village order.[52] A major cause for the paralysis in many Chinese villages is extreme poverty. In these poor villages the township/town government has difficulty in finding villagers willing to serve in village Party and villagers' committee leadership positions due to the fact that village cadres cannot be properly compensated: the village is too poor to collect enough fees to pay the village cadres.

A number of factors have contributed to the general decline of the power and authority of village officials. One factor is that villagers depend much less upon the village authorities and officials for their livelihood. In the previous collective commune system prior to the 1980s, village officials had many resources under their control and the villagers were heavily dependent upon the mercy and goodwill of village officials for their work assignments and incomes. In addition, village officials also had the recommending power and influence in the military draft, job placement, and joining the Communist Party. For young villagers in those years, joining the army or the Communist Party was considered an extremely desirable step for them in climbing the official ladder to become a member of privileged officialdom or changing their residential status (*hukou*) from rural to urban. Under the current "household responsibility" (or private farming) system, however, peasants are by and large economically independent and self-sufficient. Since there are also economic opportunities outside officialdom and freedom of movement and employment in urban areas, joining the army and the Party are no longer the only attractive options as they used to be for peasant youth's career development.

Another contributing factor, indeed, is the fact that, unlike the prereform period when villagers were tied and confined to the rural areas, tens of millions of Chinese peasants, especially young and able-bodied male peasants, have left the rural areas to the cities to work and to live (the "floating population" in China). According to one study, 20 percent of China's rural labor force worked outside their villages in 2000, and, among them, 69 percent were male and 74 percent were between 18 and 40 in age.[53] In many villages in Sichuan province, for example, close to two-thirds of rural labor force had left the countryside by the late 1990s.[54] More and more farmers have given up farming altogether to avoid paying land taxes due to the low profitability of farming.[55] The absence of a large number of able-bodied male peasants from villages has complicated the work of village officials in effectively implementing higher authorities' policies.

A third factor has been the moral decline of village officials and the lack of fairness in village governance since the 1980s. Villagers' committee elections have not eradicated corrupt officials and made village official more accountable to the villagers. In fact, Chinese village officials are often perceived to be crooks who are mainly interested in enriching themselves. In another survey of approximately 1,000 peasants conducted in 1996 by a research center of Chinese Ministry of Agriculture, about 80 percent of the respondents believed that village officials were corrupt and used their power and position to benefit themselves instead of working for the villagers.[56] In the same survey, close to 60 percent of the peasants said that bribery and *guanxi* (or connections) were the most effective means to get things done, and, not surprisingly, corruption among village officials was a top concern for Chinese peasants.[57]

A fourth factor contributing to the decline of power on the part of village authorities is the privatization drive in the late 1990s of the village collective enterprises. Village collective enterprises led rural industrialization in China in the 1980s and have been hailed as one of the most successful achievements in Chinese economic reform.[58] Yet beginning in the late 1980s village collective enterprises started to show problems common to state-owned enterprises (SOEs): wasteful expenses, debt, profit/loss, overstaffing, and job security. These problems stemmed from collective ownership of the enterprises that resulted in lack of clear responsibility on the part of management.[59] After Deng Xiaoping's 1993 publicized southern tour, and especially after 1996, local governments were encouraged to reform the village enterprises' ownership system to solve the village collective enterprises' inefficiency problems. By the late 1990s most collective village enterprises, including those in southern Jiangsu province that prided themselves with their collectivist rural economic structure, were either totally privatized or changed into shareholding companies (commonly known as "changing ownership system" or *zhuanzhi*) based largely on the ownership share model.[60] A direct consequence of the privatization of village collective enterprises is that the village authorities have lost a major revenue source and the power of job placement in these enterprises since the enterprises were previously under the control of village government and officials.

Finally, the revival of traditional kinships and clans in Chinese villages poses as a competing force to village authorities in China. Kinships and clans, which were strong rural political forces in traditional China, were suppressed but were never eradicated during the Mao era and resurfaced in the reform era.[61] Apart from traditional kinships and clans, secret societies, which were common scenes in rural China prior to the Communist era, have also sprung up since the 1990s in the Chinese countryside.[62] The main reason for the resurgence of kinships, clans, and secret societies is the peasants' need to depend on some kind of organization or association for better protection of their interests because they feel they can no longer trust the official village authorities to do so. As a matter of fact, traditional cleavages such as kinships and clans have played a prominent role in villagers' committee elections in rural regions, especially poor and remote rural regions.[63] In some places many "undesirable elements" or even "evil forces" (based largely upon kinship and clan support) have come to power in Chinese villages via village election anud have become a resistant force to carrying out township government policies.[64]

CONCLUSION

The implementation of governmental policies in Chinese villages has faced increasing difficulties and resistance. As the Chinese government is becoming increasingly dependent on village officials for state policy implementation, the authority of these village officials has weakened and become more irrelevant due to the return of private farming (i.e. the "household responsibility system"), the declining dependency of peasants upon village officials in their daily life, the massive migration of villagers to the urban areas, and the rise of traditional political and social forces such as kinships and clans in the Chinese countryside. The village administration has, in large part, a tax and fee collection agency for itself and the Chinese state that does not provide much service to the villagers. In addition, Chinese village governments, under pressure from higher governmental authorities, are increasingly relying upon negative punishments and fines to enforce state policies, which further alienates the Chinese peasantry.

There is little doubt that the old village political structure has decayed in many rural areas in China and more villages are becoming "paralyzed." To salvage its control over the peasantry and to reduce the level of tension between the village government and the villagers, the Chinese government introduced the concept of "village self-government" and election of villagers' committee in the late 1980s. This rural political reform has yet to become a magical solution to China's rural problems. On the one hand, genuine democratic elections and autonomous governance have not occurred in many villages due to the dominant role of village Party branch and interference from the township/town government in the election process of the villagers' committees and in village governance. This results in the loss of credibility and legitimacy on the part of the village government. On the other hand, in villages where more successful democratic village elections are held, the township/town government is finding that the village government is less willing to cooperate with the state authorities to implement unpopular state policies.[65] In neither case is the state policy-implementation capacity in rural China improved. The ultimate solution may lie in the reorientation of state policies and democratization of the political structure at higher levels.

NOTES

1. On the origins and formation of agricultural cooperatives and communes in the 1950s, see Center for Agricultural Economic Research, (Chinese) Ministry of Agriculture, ed., *Dangdai zhongguo nongyie biange yu fazhan yanjiu* [A Study of Contemporary Chinese Agricultural Reforms and Development] (Beijing, China: China Agricultural Press, 1998), pp. 26–116.

2. See *Zhongguo xinshiqi nongcun de biange* [Changes in the Chinese Countryside in the New Era], Party I (Beijing, China: Chinese Communist Party History Press, 1998), p. 1745.

3. Geographical villages or zirancun refer to individual villages that are physically separate from other villages. Two or more small geographical village often are joined together to form an "administrative" village. See Liu Zhenwei, *Nongmin yu nongcun zuzhi jiangshe* [Peasants and the Development of Rural Organizations] (Guiyang, China: Guizhou People's Press, 1994), p. 54.

4. Add a footnote from CCPs Constitution (Article 32).

5. On the Agricultural, Industrial, and Commercial Corporation in southern Jiangsu, see Zhang Ming, *Sunan cunji zuzhi yanjiu* [A Survey of Village-Level Organizations in Southern Jiangsu] (Suzhou, China: Suzhou University Press, 1997), pp. 33–39.

6. Minxin Pei, "Creeping Democratization in China," *Journal of Democracy*, vol. 5, no. 4 (1995), p. 73.

7. Such phenomenon exists in southern Jiangsu province. Author's Interview File 02070301.

8. See Deng Sanlong, *Diceng wenti: "qipinguan" mianlin de nandian yu duice* [Problems at the Bottom: Local Officials' Dilemma and Responses] (Beijing, China: China Personnel Press, 1998), p. 112.

9. Ibid.

10. Villagers' Committees first appeared in two counties: Yi Shan and Luo Cheng in Guangxi province. Later on, similar organizations were also found in a number of other provinces such as Sichuan and Hebei, see Bai Gang, *Guanyu gaishan cunmin zizhi lifa de baogao* [Report on improving the legislation of village self-governance], Working Paper, No. 971103 (Beijing, China: Center for Public Policy Research, Chinese Academy of Social Sciences, 1997), p. 2.

11. See Kevin O'Brien and Lianjiang Li, "Accommodating 'Democracy' in a One-Party State: Introducing Village Elections in China," *The China Quarterly*, no. 162 (2000), p. 466.

12. Initially, the adoption of this village election system met resistance from some local government officials and the Organizational Department of the Chinese Communist Party Central Committee, especially during the aftermath of the Tiananmen democracy movement in the summer of 1989. If it were not for Peng Zhen's strong support, the village election system would not have survived. See Chun Gao, *Cunmin zizhi: zhongguo nongcun de zhidu chuangxin* [The autonomy of peasants: An institutional innovation in rural China], *Dangdai zhongguo yanjiu* [Modern China Studies], no. 1 (1997), p. 121.

13. This revised *Organic Law* is more comprehensive, providing specific clauses on the implementation of village self-government in China.

14. On the adoption of villagers' committee election system in China, see Tianjian Shi, "Village Committee Elections in China: Institutionalist Tactics for Democracy," *World Politics*, vol. 51, no. 3 (April 1999), pp. 385–412.

15. Kevin O'Brien and Lianjiang Li, "Accommodating 'Democracy' in a One-Party State: Introducing Village Elections in China," pp. 485–86.

16. Sylvia Chan, "Research Notes on Villagers' Committee Election: Chinese-Style Democracy," *Journal of Contemporary China*, vol. 7, no. 19 (1998), p. 519; and Chun Gao, *Cunmin zizhi: zhongguo nongcun de zhidu chuangxin*, p. 121.

17. See, for example, Kevin O'Brien and Lianjiang Li, "Accommodating 'Democracy' in a One-Party State: Introducing Village Elections in China," p. 488; and Tianjian Shi, "Voting and Nonvoting in China: Voting Behavior in Plebiscitary and Limited-Choice Elections," *The Journal of Politics*, vol. 61, no. 4 (1999), p. 1135.

18. See Tyrene White, "Reforming the Countryside," *Current History*, vol. 91, no. 566 (1998), p. 267; Robert Pastor and Qingshan Tan, "The Meaning of Chinese Village Elections," *The China Quarterly*, no. 162 (2000), p. 512; and Daniel Kelliher, "The Chinese Debate Over Village Self-government," *The China Journal*, vol. 37 (1997), p. 86.

19. Yang Zhong, "Village Democracy in China: The Case of Southern Jiangsu Province," in Thomas J. Bellows, ed., *Taiwan and Mainland China: Democratization, Political Participation and Economic Development in the 1990s* (New York, NY: Center of Asian Stueies, St. John's University, 2000), pp. 269–300.

20. He Qinglian, *Difan eshili de jiuqi* [The rise of local evil forces], *Er shi I shiji yuekan* [21st Century Monthly], vol. 41 (1997), pp. 129–34.

21. See Yang Zhong and Jie Chen, "To Vote or Not To Vote: An Analysis of Peasants' Participation in Chinese Village Elections," *Comparative Political Studies*, vol. 35, no. 6 (August 2002), pp. 686–712.

22. Ibid.

23. See Jie Chen and Yang Zhong, "Why Do People Vote in Semicompetitive Elections in China?" *The Journal of Politics*, vol. 64, no. 1 (February 2002), pp. 178–97.

24. For more discussion on the disengagement model, see Wayne DeFranceisco and Zvi Gitelman, "Soviet political culture and 'covert participation' in policy implementation," *American Political Science Review*, vol. 78, no. 3 (1984), pp. 603–21; Theordore H. Friedgut, *Political Participation in the USSR* (Princeton, NJ: Princeton University Press 1979) and "On the effectiveness of participatory institutions in Soviet communities," *Research Paper* no. 42 (1981), Hebrew University of Jerusalem. The competing theoretical framework in the study of Soviet citizens' voting behavior is the mobilization model that emphasizes the mobilization nature of Soviet psudeo elections. See Robert Sharlet, "Concept Formation in Political Science and Communist Studies: Conceptualizing Political Participation," *Canadian Slavic Studies*, vol. 1 (1967), pp. 640–49; Alexander Shtromas, "Dissent and Political Change in the Soviet Union." In Erik P. Hoffmann and Robbin F. Laird, eds., *The Soviet Polity in the Modern Era* (New York: Aldine, 1984); and Philip Roeder, "Modernization and Participation in the Leninist Developmental Strategy," *American Political Science Review*, vol. 83, no. 3 (1989), pp. 859–84.

25. Author's Interview File 98060101.

26. See Wang Zhenyao and Bai Yihua, eds., *Xiangzhen zhengquan ji cunweihui jianshe* [Strengthening the Township/Town Government and the Villagers' Committee] (Beijing, China: China Social Press, 1996), p. 168.

27. See *Zhonghua renmin gongheguo cunmin weiyuanhui zuzhifa* [People's Republic of China's Organic Law on Villagers' Committee] (Beijing, China: Law Press, 1998), p. 4.

28. See He Baogang and Lang Youxing, *Cunmin xuanju du xiangcun quanli de yingxiang: du zhejiang gean de fenxi* [The Impact of Village Elections on Village Power Structure and Its Operation: A Case Study in Zhejiang], *Xianggang shihui kexue xuebao* [Hong Kong Journal of Social Sciences], no. 16 (Spring 2000), p. 103.

29. See Lianjiang Li, "The Two-Ballot System in Shanxi Province: Subjective Village Party Secretaries to a Popular Vote," *The China Journal*, no. 42 (July 1999), pp. 103–18; and Huang Weiping, Zhang Dinghuai, and Yang Longfang, eds., *Zhongguo jiceng minzhu fazhan de zuixin tupe* [A New Breakthrough in China's Grassroots Democracy] (Beijing, China: Social Sciences Documentation Press, 2000), p. 180.

30. *Zhonghua renmin gongheguo cunmin weiyuanhui zuzhifa* [People's Republic of China's Organic Law on Villagers' Committee], pp. 7–8.

31. Ibid., p. 7.

32. See Wang Zhenyao and Bai Yihua, eds., *Xiangzhen zhengquan ji cunweihui jianshe* [Strengthening the Township/Town Government and the Villagers' Committee], pp. 130–31.

33. *Zhonghua renmin gongheguo cunmin weiyuanhui zuzhifa* [People's Republic of China's Organic Law on Villagers' Committee], p. 8.

34. Wang Zhenyao and Bai Yihua, eds., *Xiangzhen zhengquan ji cunweihui jianshe* [Strengthening the Township/Town Government and the Villagers' Committee], pp. 136–37.

35. For example, Lan Youxing and He Baogang reported some successful stories of village representative assemblies in their study of some villages in Zhejiang province. See Lan Youxin and He Baogang, *Cunmin huiyi he cunmin daibiao huiyi—cunji minzhu wanshan ji chanshi* [Village Assemblies and Village Representative Assemblies: Efforts to Perfect Village Democracy], *Zhengzhixue yanjiu* [Political Science Studies], no. 84 (2000), pp. 57–58.

36. See Chen Guangjin, *Xiancun jingying jiuqi he chengzhang de aomi* [The Secret of the Rise and Development of Rural Elites], in Liu Yingjie et al., eds., *Zhongguo shihui xianxiang fenxi* [An Analysis of Chinese Societal Kaleidoscope] (Beijing, China: China City Press, 1998), p. 376.

37. See ibid. for more on the new rural elites in China, pp. 337–94.

38. See Guo Zhenglin, *Cong nongcun guanliqu dao cunweihui: guangdong shishi cunmin zizhi de beijing, guocheng yu wenti* [From Rural Administrative District to Villagers' Committee: Background, Process and Problems in the Adoption of Village Self-governance in Guangdong Province], *Yazhou yanjiu* [Asian Studies], no. 31 (June 1996), p. 34.

39. *Zhonghua renmin gongheguo cunmin weiyuanhui zuzhifa* [People's Republic of China's Organic Law on Villagers' Committee], p. 4.

40. Ibid.

41. See Ma Rong, Liu Shiding, and Qiu Zeqi, eds., *Zhongguo xiangzhen zuzhi diaocha* [Survey of Township Organizations in China] (Beijing, China: Hua Xia Press, 2000), pp. 192–96.

42. This is a common complaint that I hear during my field trips to the Chinese countryside.

43. See <http://www.duoweinews.com>, September 12, 2002.

44. Such practices exist in Jiangsu province, for example. Author's Interview File 99061201.

45. This case study was based on one of my field research trips to rural Jiangsu province in 1999. The name of the village is a fake to maintain anonymity.

46. Author's Interview File 99061201.

47. Author's Interview File 97062301.

48. Chinese peasants are required to perform mandatory manual labor for the state for 7 to 14 days each year. Their most frequently performed labor service is to clear up river beds and planting trees. Now peasants are allowed to pay money to substitute for their manual labor. The state authorities use the money to hire other people to do the labor.

49. See Li Kang, "*Zhengtong renhe zhiyu jiceng shiqu: ningxia nongcun qianren chouyang diaocha fengxi*" [Smooth Governance at Grassroots Level: A Survey of One Thousand Chinese Peasants in Ningxia], in Li Xueju, Wang Zhenyao, and Tang Jinsu, eds., *Xiang zhen zhengquan de xiangshi yu gaige (The Reality and Reform of Township and Town Government)* (Beijing, China: China Social Sciences Press, 1994), p. 286.

50. Ibid., p. 296.

51. On paralyzed villages, see Kevin O'Brien, "Implementing Political Reform in China's Villages," *The Australian Journal of Chinese Affairs*, no. 32 (July 1994), pp. 51–53.

52. See Tian Huisheng, *Xiangzhen zhengquan jianshe* [Building Up Governmental Authorities at the Township/Town Level] (Beijing, China: Economic Science Press, 1990), pp. 173–74.

53. Chen Jinsong and Yu Xian, *Er ling ling ling nian zhongguo nongcun jingji xingshi fenxi yu er ling ling yi nian zhanwan* [An Analysis of China's Rural Economic Situation in 2000 and its Prospect in 2001], *Zhongguo Nongcun Jingji* [Chinese Rural Economy], no. 194 (2001), p. 5.

54. See Yuan Yayu, *Zhongguo nongye xiandaihua de lishi huigu yu zhanwang* [A Historical Review and Prospect of China Rural Modernization] (Chengdu, China: Sichuan University Press, 1999), pp. 228–29.

55. Ibid., pp. 264–65.

56. See Agricultural Research Center (of Chinese Agriculture Ministry), *Dangdai zhongguo nongye biange yu fazhan yanjiu* [Evolution and Development of Contemporary Chinese Agricultre] (Beijing, China: China Agriculture Press, 1998), p. 221.

57. Ibid., pp. 222–23.

58. More on village collective enterprises, see William A. Byrd and Lin Qinsong, eds., *China's Rural Industry: Structure, Development, and Reform* (Oxford, England: Oxford University Press, 1990).

59. See Xu Yuanming, Shi Xunru, and Zhou Faqi, *Jiangsu xiangzhen qiyie xinlun* [New Theories of Township and Village Enterprises in Jiangsu] (Nanjing, China: Jiangsu People's Press, 1997), pp. 105–14.

60. For more on ownership reform of village collective enterprises in Jiangsu and Zhejiang, see Qin Hui, *Jiangzhe xiangzhen qiyie zhuanzhi anli yanjiu* [Case Studies of Ownership Reforms of Township and Village Enterprises in Jiangsu and Zhejiang Provinces], USC Seminar Series No. 13 (The Chinese Hong Kong: Hong Kong Institute of Asia-Pacific Studies, The Chinese University of Hong Kong).

61. See Bai Shazhou, *Zhongguo erdeng gongmin: dangdai nongmin kaocha baogao* [China's Second-Class Citizens: A Report on Contemporary Peasants] (New York, NY: Mirror Books, 2001), pp. 283–90. Also see Anita Chan, Richard Madsen, and Jonathan Unger, *Chen Village under Mao and Deng*, second edition (Berkeley, CA: University of California Press, 1992), pp. 324–26.

62. Bai Shazhou, *Zhongguo erdeng gongmin: dangdai nongmin kaocha baogao*, pp. 314–15.

63. See He Baogang, *Kinship, Village Elections and Structural Conditions in Zhejiang*, EAI Working Paper No. 47 (Singapore: East Asian Institute, National University of Singapore, 21 July 2000), p. 17.

64. Ibid., pp. 6–7.

65. See He Baogang, *Xiangcun xuanju diaocha shuibi* [Investigative Notes on Village Elections], *Ershiyi shiji* [Twenty-First Century], no. 58 (April 2000), pp. 131–32; and Author's Interview File 97070201.

CHAPTER 6

CRAFTING VILLAGE DEMOCRACY IN CHINA: ROLES AND STRATEGIES OF NATIONAL POLITICAL ELITES

Youxing Lang

This study argues that village elections and self-governance in rural China represent a deliberation of the reformers to solve crises in rural areas after the collapse of the People's Commune system. This chapter aims to examine the roles and functions of national political elites in the process of village elections. In the first section, it tries to trace how the villagers' self-government emerged, and why national political elites were willing to implement village election and replace the People's Commune with this democratic vehicle. In the second section, this study attempts to explore how reform-oriented political elites won, through all their difficulties, to allow the Organic Law of villagers' committee pass; this law is one of the important aspects of the elites' crafting. In the following two sections, the roles of senior political elites are discussed respectively, particularly Peng Zhen, the officials at the Ministry of Civil Affairs (MCA) and in particular Wang Zhenyao and his elite network. I then show how officials at the MCA have promoted village elections through building a sound macroenvironment, designing laws, rules and regulations, making institutional arrangements, and three cooperative projects, and the the conclusion.

BACKGROUND OF POLITICAL ELITES' CRAFTING VILLAGE ELECTIONS

When studying the transition to democracy, some scholars have presented explanations to this question: why and when do political elites or actors choose democracy?[1] As regards the village elections in rural China, the question is: Why were Chinese political elites willing to choose rural, not urban, communities as a starting point for China's democratization? Thereby, two questions should be first offered: Why did the Chinese government initiate village elections at the beginning of the 1980s? Why did the Chinese Government choose village election and self-governance but not other forms as a substitute for the People's Commune?

The emergence of village elections and self-governance has a profound historical background. Most importantly, it is the rural economic reforms that thoroughly changed the rural economic, political, and social relationships. The fundamental changes in the rural economic and political relationships were a basic background. First, the household production responsibility system had led to profound changes, with new patterns emerging in economic relationships in the rural economic system that would provide a fitting economic basis for village self-government and village elections. Second, since the reform and opening to the world, the rural social structure and rural politics had greatly changed. For example, the household production responsibility system had enabled the peasants to win a small status of freedom. Third, many social problems such as social security and order, conflicts between village cadres and villagers, gambling, fighting, stealing, and killing, had emerged as somes of the Central government's major concerns. Central government's concern was fully displayed in a summary of the (Chinese Communist Party's) CCPs 1982 national countryside work conference: "Recently some rural organizations are lax, some ever at a standstill or semistandstill, that result in there are many affairs no one changed."[2] Furthermore, few villagers cared and managed the public affairs. Therefore, dealing with the breeding and spreading of unhealthy tendencies became the common central issue of the villagers and Central government, and the latter were thinking how to rebuild the rural organizational system after the dissolution of the People's Commune and the establishment of the new economic system. Naturally, the village committee that had emerged at the beginning of the 1980s in the Guangxi Autonomous Region quickly came into the Central government's view.

The problems, such as social unrest occurring in many rural areas, did not naturally form a sufficient reason to implement village elections and self-governance. The questions are: why did the central government choose this form of village election and village self-government but not other forms? Did it have no other choice?

Confronting the dissolution of the People's Commune, the CCP had several alternatives. Their first choice was to maintain authoritarian control, although the names of local administrative system would be changed. Their second choice was to let nature take its course without any active actions or measures. Their third choice was establishing a new political system that would be different from the People's Commune and Production Brigade. First and second choices seemed not to be feasible. The first choice would obviously directly conflict with the household responsibility system and would not be well coordinated within the new economic system, resulting definitely in terminating rural economic reform, while "to let nature take its course" was not a wise choice. At that time, the peasants' demands and the top leaders' concerns about rural control exerted pressure upon the government, which would bring about a possibility to supply a new alternative.

There are other possible reasons as to why the CCP chose village self-governance, but not other forms as a substitute for the People's Commune. One is the lesson of the People's Commune regime. Peasants had no freedom and few democratic rights, which resulted from the planned economics, and needed the support of an authoritarian polity. The new rural economic system would offer one possibility in changing local power structure that would be different from the old one.

Another is the restoration of the People's Congress System, an incentive to give peasants more freedom and rights to deal with their own affairs. After the end of the Cultural Revolution (CR), the CCP decided to restore the People's Congress System. The resolution by the third Plenary Session of the eleventh Central Committee of the CCP was instructed to strengthen the People's Congress system and gradually allow the people to exercise direct democracy at basic-level government and grassroots social lives. In his report to the sixth Plenary Session of the eleventh Central Committee of the CCP, Deng Xiaoping pointed out, "At this moment, we specially need to emphasize democracy. Because, in long post, democratic centralism had not really been implemented, if we stress centralism to the neglect of democracy, there will be few democratic factors." He further suggested guaranteeing democratic rights conscientiously for workers and peasants.[3] China held the first deputies election to the People's Congress in 1979 at a local level after the CR.[4]

Furthermore, the new village organization, which first emerged in Guangxi at the beginning of the 1980s, offered one model for Central Government leaders who was eager to design one organization as a substitute for the dissolution of the People's Commune and brigade system. Yan Minfu, a former vice minister of MCA (who was directly responsible for the department of Basic-Level Governance and Community Development among the ministers and vice ministers of MCA), revealed that the Central government chose village committees as a substitute for the People's Commune based on MCAs summary report of local experiences such as the village committee, the agency for motion (*yi shi hui*), or management committee (*gui wei hui*), public security group (*zhi an xiao zu*).[5] At that time village committees and village elections accorded with actual situations and demands: the rural new economic system after other economics abandoned freedom and democratic rights.

However, village elections and self-governance would not necessarily automatically make rural China emerge based on the reasons mentioned above, because the crucial matter was the incumbent elites' choice. As Amy B. Epstein pointed out, the democratic seeds being planted in China's villages were not by dissidents or even by the masses, but by reformers in the Chinese government.[6] The benefits of implementing village elections, such as the improvement of the relationship between the cadres and masses gave political elites (and in particular the central leaders) sufficient confidence to see that the CCPs legitimacy in rural China would be built more effectively through village elections.

In short, implementating village elections was one result in a series of policies made by the national leaders who were on a quest as to how to better organize rural government and maintain village social stability after agricultural reform.

POLITICAL ELITES' GAME AND THE PROCESS OF THE PASSAGE OF THE ORGANIC LAW

According to game theory, a game is composed of five elements: the actors that play the game; the sequence of choices actors face; the information actors have about the game; all the logically possible outcomes of the game; and preference over all outcomes of all actors.[7] Actually the types of resources actors can employ are very important in the process of a game besides the five elements mentioned above.

The process of Organic Law on the Village Committee of the People's Republic of China enacted is an interesting case. Regarding the game players, there are two characteristics in China's Organic Law. First, the masses' influence on Organic Law formulation and enactment was very weak. At the beginning of the reform, the pressure from peasants could scarcely influence the choices of political elites: "when elections were first introduced into rural China, peasants hardly had any say in the process."[8] Second, the defender was not opposite the challenger. Both are situated inside the system (*ti zhi nei*). In a sense, they share the same motive, namely, both wanted to enhance party control over rural China.

Information about the game is also important, mainly covering two dimensions: whether there is adequate information available and if there is accurate or appropriate information available on the game to the players. The players rely on this information to make judgments as to which alternative should be taken. Regarding village elections and self-governance, more important is what information the reformers and the opponents had. Actually most of the disputes about village self-governance involved the truth of the information the disputers had. For example, whether or not village elections are helpful to rural social stability is, to an extent, dependent on the information. Because rural China is so huge and complicated, people easily find one case to support their own stand.

There were some groups and specific political elites at the central government who supported and wanted to embark on village elections. Peng Zhen was one of a few CCP senior veterans who strongly supported implementation of village self-governance. The numbers of this group mainly came from the MCA. The Organization Department of the CCP Central Committee was the major representative at the centers who opposed village election. First, remove the masses and then simply presume there were two players: the reformer and the opponent. Here the letters ND, OD, RG, OG, RC,

OC will be used as the main symbols for the principal alternatives in preference ordering. Village election and self-government should replace the appointment system after the commune's end; the higher authorities and village party branches do not control or manipulate village elections. This alternative is a new model, denoted as ND. OD represents the unchanged, namely maintenance of an appointment model usually existed in the Maoist era, an old model. RG represents this situation: facing strong opposition, the reformer gives in, giving up his endeavor to conduct political reform in rural China. OG, on the contrary, represents the opponent's giving in. RC and OC represent the compromises made by the reformer and the opponent respectively.

Theoretically 12 possible outcomes can be derived from the combinations of alternatives, but four possible outcomes are significant: NDOD, NDOG, RGOD, and RCOC.

1. NDOD: The choice of the New Model by the reformers and Maintenance of the Maoist Era Model by the opponents. The NDOD means the outcome is in a stalemate and no action.
2. NDOG: The choice of the New Model by the reformers and giving in by the opponents. The outcome NDOG means that the opposition find themselves in a marginal position and has to agree with the reform without any conditions attached, while the reformer can implement the village election according to desires.
3. RGOD: Giving in by the reformers and Maintenance of Maoist Era Model by the opponents. The outcome RGOD means rural China remains the status quo of the appointment way; namely, the village head is appointed by higher authorities but not elected by villagers.
4. RCOC: The choice of compromise by both reformers and opponents. RCOC means the reformer has encountered opposition and has to make concessions; equally the opponent cannot absolutely oppose village self-governance. The result is just a compromise. However, this can be divided into two types: one is RDC, meaning although the reformer encountered opposition and had to make a concession to the opponent, they can embark upon village self-governance under their dominance; another is ODC, meaning that there would be limited reform under the opponent's control.

Obviously, NDOG is the most preferred by the reformer and the least by the opponent. If this outcome could not be pursued completely, the reformer would by all means try to avoid the outcome of RGOD. Thus, second best for the reform player would be opting for RDC. NDOD is the worst outcome for both reformer and opponent, both sides being anxious that chaos would not result from the local level leadership crisis. Theoretically, RGOD and RDOG are the worst for the reformer and the opponent respectively. Thus, the reform player prefers alternatives from greater to lesser: NDOG>RDC>ODC>NDOD>RGOD. Equally, the opposition player orders his preference in this way: RGOD>ODC>RDC> NDOD>RDOG.

It is crucial to the reformer and the opponent to avoid the worst outcome and win the most preferred one. The dilemma being the worst of the reformers is probably the most preferred of the opposition and conversely the worst for the opponent is the most preferred of the reformers. The possible outcomes of bargaining are to a great extent dependent on these four aspects: players' position and relation to the issue under bargaining, players' capabilities, the players' strategies and tactics, and the context of the issue being bargained upon. Shi Tianjian argues that the intelligence, skill, and sophistication of political actors are key factors in their understanding of institutional constraints, their formulations of preference, and their design of strategies to pursue their goals.[9] The position is defined not only in terms of the player's position in governmental hierarchy, but also in terms of specific organizations; for example, the MCA or the Organizational Department of CCP Central Committee or National People's Congress (NPC). The capabilities are defined not only in the players' formal authority to make decisions, but also on informal resources such as seniority. The alternative in the course of action is called "tactics."

NDOD is one of the possible outcomes. This outcome means that the reformer hoped to conduct political reform to adapt the changing countryside with the economic reform, but the conservatives opposed any changes in the rural political system. Both sides were in a stalemate, resulting in rural chaos and instability and a power vacuum. But this situation could not last for a long time because peasants needed social order and stability, whereas the government could not endure social chaos either. Rural China needed a political agency, new or old, to fill the vacuum. Actually this is a game of moves, a sequential bargaining. Both sides considered alternatives within the changing context.

Then, the question is that which alternative is the most probable. RGOD seems impossible, namely, impossible to return to the Maoist model. Since economic reform policies had been implemented in rural China at the end of 1970, whereas the commune system had actually collapsed since the beginning of 1980s, it seemed impossible to completely remain under the appointment way without any changes.[10] The symbolic event is that the 1982 Chinese Constitution affirms the legal position of the villagers' committee and village elections. Furthermore, the Commune system collapsed in 1983, never to return. However, it was difficult to approach the outcome of NDOG, because China was just at the initial stages of reform and opening to the world, the orthodox power still spread all over the Chinese society. It would be not possible to carry out village elections according to the reformers' desires without opposition.

Therefore, RCOC is the most possible outcome, in which both sides compromise. The question thus became which one, RDC or ODC, would be the final outcome? It seems the situation turned the scales in favor of the reformer. First of all, some top national leaders supported establishing villagers' committees and conducting village elections. After all, as in China's institutional context, the key actors are decisive, "the final decision outcome may be derived from their final positions."[11] Peng Zhen, a supreme leader, gave a strong support to the reformer (the next section will focus on his role in detail).

Second, the information the reformer collected was helpful to the implementation of village self-governance. The opponent's major reasons or superiority against village elections was "the leadership of the Party," concern with social stability, governmental tasks' accomplishments, and the peasants' capacity of conducting democratic elections. The opponent feared that village election would lead to the erosion of party organs in the countryside and thereby the party would lose its leading role in rural communities, and also social chaos would emerge in rural China; therefore clan powers would be resurrected. Foremost, they feared that if villages became autonomous, village cadres would disregard local governments' instructions. Additionally, some people doubted that peasants were really capable of thinking, making decisions, and solving their problems.

Cui Naifu, a former minister of Civil Affairs, denied all these concerns and charges above. He said, "Through years of my investigation and research I feel this law is conducive to stability and unity of our nations as a whole. It improves the awareness and the ability of the villagers to mater and manages their own affairs."[12] The information collected by the MCA strongly supported Cui's statement. All in all, the reformer used these messages and evidence to exert influence on other actors, including some senior national leaders, proving the necessity and possibility of village elections and self-governance.

Third, the reformers chose a relatively suitable strategy. Shi Tianjian stresses the importance of the strategic choice: "the key to their success lies in their strategic choice to handle Chinese reform incrementally."[13] It seems that these reformers acknowledged the path-dependent theory. They chose an incrementalist and pragmatist strategy: If only peasants were allowed to conduct village elections, no matter how local cadres strictly manipulate the village elections, whether or not these elections were conducted was only as a matter of form. This strategy indeed obtained a space and opportunity for the survival and development of democracy in rural China.

These factors well illustrate that the situation turned the scales in favor of the reformer. One matter marked it well: in 1984, the Central government empowered the reformers at the MCA to draft the *Villagers' Committee Organic Rules*, and in April 1997, in the view of the importance of this law, the fifth session of the 6th Peoples' National Congress suggested to change the title of <Villagers' Committee Organic Rules> into <The Organic Law of Villagers' Committees of People's Republic Of China>.[14] The first round of the debate/struggle ended with the reformers' winning. The mark of winning is the Organic Law of Villagers Committees passed in November 1987, but this was the result of compromise made on both sides. The mark of this compromise is that the Organic Law was provisional. In fact many representatives of 6th NPC did not approve the draft of the "Organic Law," which pushed NPC to revise it again, but the revised bill could not be passed yet. Consequently, Peng Zhen had to compromise with the opposition on this law. He had to trade concessions for passing it, suggesting that the Standing Committee of NPC pass the law under the provisional. At last this law was enacted through many disputes and compromises. Unlike some laws, which were little but advance discussions, there were many discussions and disputes on the Organic Law and it attracted much notice particularly by the local cadres.[15]

Yet, there was still tremendous resistance during the process of exercising the law. Both game players came to grips with the implementation. Especially after the 1989 crackdown, antivillage election and self-government forces gathered, and blamed Zhao Ziyang for being responsible for the introduction of the Organic Law, which was said to set China on the road of "peaceful evolution." The opposition was still concerned about policy implementation and potential instability. As a result, efforts to implement the law were suspect in many places. As the representative of the reformer and a strong supporter of village elections, the political elites at MCA had to convince high Party leaders that village elections would strengthen state control in rural China and guarantee smooth implementation of Party policies. At last Senior Party leaders (such as Bo Yibo and Song Ping) came to the rescue. Due to their strong support, the law could continue to be implemented, and the provincial governments were asked to set up "village self-governance demonstration units."

However, resistance did not completely disappear; the opposition was not entirely defeated, whereas the game therefore was not over. At present, the debate was focusing on the Party leadership. Many of the opponents began to argue that village elections would threaten and weaken the legitimacy of the party's grassroots organizations. The whole context would be yet beneficial to the MCAs proposals. The senior Party's leaders still supported village elections. Jiang Zemin and Li Peng were also the backers of village elections. More importantly, village elections caused international society attention (particularly the United States). NGOs highly praised village elections, which spurred the top national leaders on to further support village elections. And, since the mid-1990s, due to their heavier burden, the farmers' appeals mushroomed and rural instability once again raised its head, which resulted in the worsening of the relationship between cadres and villagers. Furthermore, more and more local leaders had begun to feel the positive side of village elections. It is within these contexts that the State Council decided to revise the Provisional Organic Law after a 10-year trial. The new Organic Law was adopted on November 1998, with some of the reformers' proposals absorbed into the law.

Yet, this outcome does not mean that the opposition had finally surrendered. Naturally, one had come out blatantly repudiating village elections or self-governance after several rounds of elections, namely around 10 years of practice. Therefore, debates, arguments, and disputes shifted the focus to the word "guiding" and the role of the party in village elections or villager's self-governance. The fact is that their appeal for Party leadership won the attention of the highest leaders. For example, Jiang Zemin and Li Peng argued that "China would not follow the western approach with a separation of powers, a multiparty system, and privatization."[16] As the representative of the antivillage elections after 1995, the Party' organizational departments successfully inserted Article 3 into the Organic Law (revised in 1998): "The rural grassroots unit of the CCP should work under the Charter of CCP and play a core role in leadership. Under the guidance of the Constitution and other laws, the unit should also support and ensure villagers in developing self-governance activities and performing democratic duties," which clearly did not exist in the 1987 Provisional Organic Law.

We have seen a distinguished characteristic in rural political change: bargaining or negotiating on the Organic Law between the reformer/advocator forces and conservative/opposition forces, whereas this characteristic shaped the manner and extent of implementing village self-governance in rural China.

SENIOR POLITICAL ELITES AND VILLAGE ELECTIONS

Adam Przeworski makes an in-depth analysis of the important choices made by actors in moving their countries toward democracy.[17] Ambrose Y.C. King pointed out, "Ironically, it was the leader of an authoritarian party who used nothing less than his authoritarian power to engineer and legitimate a democratic breakthrough."[18] G. Pasquino first used the notion and term of "swing man" which was originally conceived with respect to military figures.[19]

Peng Zhen was a "swing man" in village elections, the most critical decision-maker of village elections among national leaders.[20] He enjoyed supreme authority in China's political system. There are many stories showing how Peng Zhen persuaded senior party conservatives and provincial and local leaders to pass the Organic Law. He addressed seven speeches for the law. Larry Diamond's argument is particularly true for China's case that "the most favorable development for democratization is a firm and forceful commitment to the process on the part of a country's leadership."[21] Shi Tianjian argues that at that time national leaders except for Peng Zhen "had little influence over the implementation of the Organic Law," ever after the June 4th 1989 incident, "Most national leaders were indifferent to electoral reform."[22]

In 1981, some peasants from Shancha People's Commune in Yishan of Guangxi Autonomous Region established its village committee, while the traditional production brigade's management system was broken through. Peng Zhen paid special attention to that case, ordering the NPC and MCA to make an investigation and summarize Yishan's experience, then promote it. In April 1982, in the speech for the draft of the new Chinese constitution, Peng Zhen suggested the villagers' committee to become a mass autonomous organization, whereas the NPC should list it as an article of the new constitution. He urged the NPC to work out the regulations for village committees after the practice of villagers' committee mature. He declared on November 11th of 1982 at the report of the draft of People's Republic Constitution of China that the villagers' committee had been listed into the constitution.

Wang Zhenyao, a chief architect of village elections (the next section will focus on his role in detail), reveals that when Premier Zhao Ziyang proposed to establish government offices in villages (*cui gong suo*) as a substitute for the production brigade's management system, Peng Zhen strongly opposed this proposal. At that time many local leaders strongly supported Zhao's proposal.[23] Peng Zhen thought Zhao's proposal was unconstitutional. "What is the nature of the urban resident committee or the village committee? This is a local autonomous organization that has been stipulated by Article 111th of the constitution," he said, "the rule from the constitution is foundation for RC or VC." Thus, "all leaders at every level should take some measures to bring resident committee or the village committee into full play according to the rules laid down in the constitution." He believed that a training seminar for 800 million Chinese peasants to learn how to participate in politics is a process that has no precedent in China but one through which the remnants of China's feudalistic past will be erased along with "backward practices."[24]

Peng Zhen's most important contribution to village elections is the passing of "the Organic Law" and implementing it as his best. Cui Naifu admitted the Organic Law was drafted under the direct leadership of Peng Zhen. According to Cui, Peng Zhen was the kind of man who never shot an arrow without having good aim.[25] He said, "When the law was adopted in 1987, it was termed as 'provisional,' which is very rare in China's legislation history. This says much about the uneasiness felt by many people." Cui admitted MCAs pressure was very heavy. Peng Zhen's three observations drove forced MCA to draw up the law. The first observation was that self-governance in rural China was mandated by the 1982 Constitution. The second observation is that, corresponding to village self-governance, the role of township government should be one of "guiding" (*zhi dao*) rather than "leading" (*ling dao*). The third observation is that the power of the officials must be restricted and they could never be allowed to do whatever they desired to do.[26]

As a result of his great efforts, on November 24, 1987, just before Peng Zhen's resignation from chairman of the 6th NPC Standing Committee, the NPC officially issued the Organic Law on Village Committees of the People's Republic of China (for trial implementation).

After the Tiananmen demonstration, the opposition criticized the village elections, regarding it as an example of "bourgeois liberalization." Consequently, it seemed that "efforts to implement the law nationwide were suspended."[27] On February 1990, after having understood Cui Naifu's strong support to village self-governance, Peng Zhen expressed that he would not worry about the fate of village elections or village autonomy, and suggested the minister write some articles to advocate democratic management.

Bo Yibo, another CCP senior veteran, also gave in his time—strong support to village elections. He came to the rescue. "Bo's backing for village self-governance was decisive," then Song Ping, a number of CCPs politburo, "puts the controversy over the Organic Law to an end." In August 1990, Song Ping instructed that the law should be implemented rather than debated at a national Conference on the Construction of Village-level Organizations.[28] In late 1990, the Central Committee of CCP endorsed the trial law. It began to be enacted in 1991 in many areas of China.

WANG ZHENYAO AND HIS COLLEAGUES AT MCA

When looking at the initial stage of village elections and self-governance, two questions arise first: who were the key operators at national level and how did they operate? Since there are many political elites, the notion of elite differentiation needs to be taken further. Accordingly, we draw our attention to locating the main craftsmen of village democracy and consider what position and "resources" they possess in terms of political system.

Wang Zhenyao: A Chief Actor

In one report, the International Republican Institute (IRI) argued that the leadership on the village elections from 1990 to 1997 within the MCA was "unquestionably strong due to Wang Zhenyao." That report listed his roles: with his colleagues' assistance, he promoted direct election practices and procedures; developed training handbooks and civic education posters; inspired provincial election officials to take an interest in and support village elections.[29] Anne F. Thurston regards Wang Zhenyao as being "representative of many of the younger, educated reformists now occupying key positions in the middle ranks of the Chinese government."[30] Paul Grove also points out that Wang Zhenyao was "the chief architect of the implementation strategy," while the MCA is a key partner who has done its endeavors to seek the international cooperation and assistance technically and financially for implementing village elections.[31]

Wang Zhenyao was born in 1954 in a very normal village in Henan province. As a son of a peasant, he knows the peasants' hardships and eager desires very well. In 1977, he became a university student at the first university entrance examination after the downfall of "four persons-gang." During his university study, he majored in world history, writing one thesis on Yugoslavian autonomy for his bachelor's degree. At that time, he believed that Yugoslavian autonomy was a way to solve socialist countries' totalitarianism. We can link Wang's throwing himself into village elections with his university studies. In 1986, he was granted his master's degree of law from Central China's normal university, where now has a leading academic research center on village elections and rural politics. After graduation, he was appointed to one position at the Central Institute of Policy for the Countryside, being engaged in a study on policies for the countryside.

He was then appointed to the position of the head of the Division of Rural Work in 1988 when MCA established the Department of Basic-Level Governance and Community Development, and then appointed vice director of this department from 1994 to 1997. Since 1988, he had been in charge of village elections until he left this post in 1997.

Wang Zhenyao has visited more than 1,000 villages over the years to oversee village elections. By and large, his ideas on village elections are a kind of procedurism, incrementalism, and tactics. His main points on village democracy are the following.

First, after his assessing senior party leaders such as Peng Zhen and criticizing Chinese intellectual elites, Wang Zhenyao confirms the importance of procedures and presents the path of democratization in China: Chinese democratization should advance step by step. The democratic procedures are particularly important to China's democratization. In his view, the procedural path is the best or most reliable one for Chinese democratization. He pointed out that the main question is senior party leaders such as Peng Zhen were not skilled in procedural operations; namely they had no ability in operation procedures, although they had firm faith and were thirsty for democracy. Regretfully, many Chinese people do not like to discuss this issue. Wang also criticized Chinese intellectuals. It seems to him that Chinese intellectuals have two main shortcomings. One is that they do not care about discussing procedures and are not actually good at operating democracy, but just focusing on democratic principles; another is that they lack the equality idea, while citizen's equality is the most important precondition of democratic politics.

Second, Wang Zhenyao gives an explanation of the relationship between peasants and the possibility of democracy: there is no direct relationship between democracy and education levels; rather crucial to democracy is the kind of interest relationships. What villagers are concerned about is whether candidates can truly act on their behalf. On the other hand, as soon as farmers are granted the vote in village elections, their behaviors demonstrate differently. They create and invent many measures and institutions to participate in politics, restrict and supervise power. "Sea election" is a typical case. However, he admitted that at the beginning of village elections, people were not used to them, thus it was necessary to train the common people with government guidance.

Third, he expounds the relationship between clans and village elections. It is very natural for Chinese peasants to live within different kinds of clans. People do not necessarily worry about it and it is understandable for some candidates to use clans as a resource for village elections' competition, since there are no other political parties but the CCP existing in rural China.

Fourth, and finally, he argues that the suitable strategies are very important for political elites to conduct democratic reform and implementing village elections. Chinese democratisation must be a gradual, accumulative process; any rash act might block the rural democratic progress. Wang guards against the radical thoughts that expect a democratic system to be perfect. A gradual policy to promote village elections adopted by the MCA has been proved to be correct.

The Core Members of the Elites' Network: Wang, Zhan and Their Colleagues at MCA

Why could Wang Zhenyao succeed in the process of implementing village elections? There is no single variable to explain this. However, this question turns our attention to the question of elites and elitist groups. This study contends that formal or personal networks provide a social structure, which may seem to facilitate smooth and successful rural democracy construction. Networks can provide elites with access to the decision-making processes. In contrast, some officials are likely to contact or be dependent on individuals; Wang Zhenyao obviously prefers and feels the need to operate with officials within his elite chain. Actually, the officials in China's political systems have certainly been long aware of the networking, informal or formal. The officials at MCA also employ network to perform their task in promoting village self-governance.

This network is more vertical and based on Wang's position and personal relations. The elites clustered around Wang include his colleagues, the officials from the Civil Affairs, local officials, and even village heads. Wang's cluster is the main carrier of rural democratization of China: he was a leading player in this cluster.[32] Given the "soft" task of village self-governance as well as MCAs weak position in power structure and hierarchy broaden their base of support for implementing village self-governance, however, they had to construct contacts depending on informal institutions and particularly personal relationships. In doing this, they may invest their feeling on a personal relationship and provide benefits such as an opportunity to visit abroad. This is a reward, which, in return, reinforces network ties. However, with the institutionalization of their role, Zhan Chenfu, Wang's successor, and Zhan's colleagues more and more adopted the institutional network for promoting village democracy.

The networks originated as a strategy for implementation of village self-governance, providing the executors a base to perform their task. These network ties provide an informal or formal mechanism along which information can be exchanged, resources can be obtained, and activities can be conducted. For example, because the Fujian Department of Civil Affairs has been actively embedded in the network, Fujian has obtained some special support from MCA time and again. For instance, MCA has introduced foreign NGOs several times to observe village elections in Fujian, but never to Zhejiang. Zhejiang has never been actively embedded in MCAs network, while the MCA have yet to pay any attention to the village elections in Zhejiang.[33]

These networks have enhanced their capacity to implement village self-governance outside Yanhe Avenue, the site of the MCA.

Wang Zheyao's Superiors
Cui Naifu, Duojicarang, Lian Yin, Yan Mingfu, and Li Xueju were Wang Zhenyao's successive superiors. Cui Naifu and Duojicarang, two former ministers of MCA, were very supportive of village self-governance, while Lian Yin, Yan Mingfu, and Li Xueju were the highest officials in charge of village self-governance from 1988 to 1991, 1993–97, 1998–02, respectively, and Duojicarang was charged of this work in 1992 as well as deputy vice minister. They were not involved in the detailed affairs but played an important role in constructing and democracy in rural China: breeding an environment to implement village self-governance and develop grassroots. Li Xueju, currently minister of Civil Affairs, however, was called the "pilot of the grassroots democracy experimental field."

Wang's Colleagues
Shi Tianjian found that there were protagonists in the MCA responsible for implementing the Organic Law of the Villagers' Committee.[34] These protagonists were subordinate to the Department of Basic-Level Governance and Community Development established in 1988. The first director was Li Xueju from 1988 to 1993, and in 1994 Bei Yihua became the director and Wang Zhenyao the deputy director till 1997, while Wang was the chief operator of village self-governance affair. Ms. Ning Lihua, Mr. Wang Shihao, Mr. Tang Jinsu, Mr. Guo Zhengwen, Mr. Bai Guangzhao, Mr. Zhang Shifeng, and Ms. Fang Yu were Wang Zhenyao's assistants during Wang's term over village self-governance. In 1998, Wang Zhenyao was promoted to director of Department of Relief for Natural Disasters and Social Relief. As eprotagonists of village self-governance, these officials consisted the core of Wang's elite network.

Zhan Chenfu: Wang Zhenyao's Successor

In one report, the IRI expressed a worry about whether village elections would continue to be effectively implemented after Wang's transfer from the department of Basic-Level Governance and Community Development. However, Zhan Chenfu's succession can remove this worry. Replacing Wang Zhenyao in 1998, Zhan Chenfu became deputy director of the Department of Grassroots Administration. Since then he has been the leading player in village self-governance affair. If Wang Zhenyao has been a chief architect of village self-governance during the first stage, as Wang's successor, Zan Chenfu is currently the chief craftman in deepening and consolidating village democracy.

Zhan's contribution to village democracy mainly focuses on promoting villagers' committee election's standardization, institutionalization, and proceduralization. He has several capable assistants, such as Wang Jinhua and Fan Yu, who are currently in charge of the Section on Rural Grassroots Governance.

ENGINEERING RURAL DEMOCRACY

Obviously, many studies on village elections have taken note of the role of the MCA of China and its elites during the past two decades. Shi Tianjian particularly analyzes MCAs elites' tactics by which they crafted village self-governance.[35] Jean C. Oi regards the MCA as the "most visible promoter of democratic village self-rule and the government bureau responsible for village self-governance."[36]

Why did MCA succeed in promoting village elections, while the opponents, in particular, the Organizational Department of the CCP Central Committee (an organ more powerful than the MCA), failed to thwart implementing village self-governance, besides their networks mentioned above? This question draws our attention to the officials' driving force and resources, and the strategies they have adopted.

Empowerment by Central Government and Top Leader's Supports

Since the 1950s, MCA, at that time called as the Ministry of Internal Affairs, has been responsible for basic level governance. [1986] No. 22 Central Party and State Council' Document empowered the Civil Affairs system to shoulder the responsibility of basic-level governments' construction, and establish the elections' leading body; namely, the leading organs of election work, which were set up at national, local and village levels respectively. The elections' leading body at national level is now located in the Division of Rural Work, the Department of Basic-level Governance and Community Development at MCA.

Through empowerment, MCA has been granted organizational power recourse such as bureaucratic rank, personnel, and even access to top leaders. For example, MCA established the Department of Grassroots Governments in 1988 to further strengthen leadership to village self-governance across the country, and promote the status of the leadership at bureaucratic rank. This department is currently the highest official organ in charge of village self-governance.

The support from top national leaders is important as well. Top national leaders' power resources in China include ideology, financial and propaganda apparatuses, meetings and document systems, personnel systems, policy-making, and implementation networks. These resources were vital particularly in the initial stage of village self-governance, which, to a certain extent, decided whether village elections and self-governance could be launched and then implemented smoothly.

Empowerment itself constitutes a parameter within which the officials at MCA can effectively act with perfect assurance. MCA could utilize this empowerment and top leaders' support to extend their influence and space to craft village democracy within the existing institution system.

Expectation and Pressure from the Peasants

Some of the reformers who advocated implementing village self-governance in rural China were initially skeptical as to whether peasants would be enthusiastic about it. The reality was that the village election progress received the peasants' enthusiastic welcome and support. An MCA report cited data, showing that in 1991 peasants from Lishu County of Jilin Province put forward 51,913 policy proposals for village elections.[37] The peasants' enthusiasm encouraged officials at MCA to further promote village elections. In the meantime this provided a good opportunity for them to detect some procedural infrastructure and push for further reform.

On the other hand, during the process of conducting village elections, and particularly the initial stage of village self-governance, many township leaders and village leaders (particularly village party branch secretaries) opposed elections or attempted to manipulate elections. Peasants bravely struggled against various kinds of illegal interference in village elections by boycotting manipulated elections, appealing to higher governments and the media for help. The peasants' resistance brought pressure to bear on local leaders, while this resistance became exactly the MCA's "card," a "peasants' card." The officials at MCA forced local leaders to legally implement the Organic Law through playing the "peasants' card."

MCA does make use of grassroots pressures and the peasants' enthusiasm to force the Organization Department of the CCP Central Committee to reach a compromise on village self-governance, while the latter is much more powerful than the former in political system.[38] Li Xueju has pointed out, "All my experience comes from the grassroots and the invention of people,"[39] which obviously is a strategic explanation. The stronger the villagers' demands become, the easier it is for officials at the central government to transform this pressure into local political reform.

Additionally, officials make use of peasant' initiatives in innovating and developing new political participation mechanisms to further perfect the law and institutions of self-governance, and improve the democratic quality of village elections. The MCA fully affirmed the important role peasants played in implementing village self-governance: "The peasants' active participation and strenuous creation are the fundamental source of village self-governance and grassroots democracy."[40]

Bureaucratic Interests

In analyzing officials at the MAC, Shi Tianjian did not rule out the bureaucratic interest of the ministry and career considerations in several elements to motivate Wang Zhenyao and his colleagues in the MAC to implement the Organic Law.[41] Wang Zhenyao's speech made in Hebei typically revealed the Civil Affairs system's bureaucratic interests pursuit. After briefly reviewing the MCAs power change, Wang thinks that the village election affair is an opportunity for the Civil Affairs system to change its weakness in the governmental hierarchy and then increase its position. He said, "If we have done villagers' committee elections well, the governments at different levels can feel that Civil Affairs system plays a more and more important role."[42] In a simple way, the MCAs pursuit of its mission and interests is in structuring organizational position. Of course, that should not be reviewed as a denial of their democratic ideas.

Actors, particularly political elites or political leaders perform multiple roles in democratization. For example, they formulate the rules and structures of liberal democracy, while those in office play a crucial part in setting up the government and determining the course of policy direction and performance which have a formative influence on public attitudes and hence affect prospects for democracy. In other words, political elites perform top-down functions of control and direction and embrace bottom-up pressures and demands. The main function of the political elites at national level is to fuel village democracy. This study focuses on four aspects.

At the national level, it is important is to build sound circumstances for implementing and promoting village democracy. Top leaders affirmed village elections would be greatly beneficial to the village self-governance development because the reformers' voices could at last prevail over the voice of the opposition by this affirmation. We do not need to take much notice of whether or not these top leaders heartily promote Chinese democracy, while it is important that some top leaders' speeches and actions are objectively helpful to build a sound atmosphere for village self-governance.

As a department responsible for the work of village self-governance, MCA used propaganda to put psychological pressure to make local leaders comply. MCA and relevant governmental agencies use various media and propaganda means to disseminate knowledge of the objectives, signification, and other methods on related issues so local leaders and villagers will be mentally prepared for village elections.

Due to central government and in particularly MCAs endeavors, the environment of the village elections location has improved greatly. Actually building a circumstance is also a process of remaking political ideology and discourse, which not only gives direction to rural policies and influences the state's institutional design, but also and more importantly serves as a tool of the MCA officials' crafting village democracy.

Although democracy is not reducible to law, rules and procedures, and institutions, that is, in its formal aspects, these are indeed especially important for rural democratization in China, because the rule of law and institutionalization are two of the weakest aspects in the process of economic and political modernization.

At the national level, there is a three-tiered structure of laws, rules and regulations of village election, consisting of the Constitution, the Organic Law, and Departmental rules and regulations (table 6.1). The top one is the 1982 Chinese Constitution, Article 111 which stipulates that neighborhood committees and villagers' committees established in residential areas in cities and villages in rural areas respectively are self-governing organizations at the grassroots level, while the chairman and vice chairman are elected by local residents. A basic function of a constitution is its authorizing function. The 1982 constitution grants village elections as a legal guarantee.

Table 6.1   MCAs rules and regulations on village elections and self-governance[43]

Time	Title
26/09/1990	Circular of launching village self-governance demonstration activity through the country
08/02/1994	The guiding program for the national village self-governance demonstration activity
13/12/1994	The suggestions of management of naming village self-governance demonstration units
27/02/1995	Circular of strengthening village committee construction
08/02/1996	Circular of doing our best at village committee elections
10/09/1996	Summary of conversation of the national village committee elections' experiences
02/01/1997	Circular of carrying out the sprint of conversation of rural grassroots organization construction, strengthening village committee construction
05/08/1997	Circular of further perfecting village affairs transparency, deepening village self-governance work
06/01/1998	Circular of doing our best at 1998' village committee election work
06/12/1998	Circular of learning, propagandizing, and carrying out <Organic Law of Village Committee> (With Central Ministry of Organization, Central Ministry of propaganda, the Ministry of justice, legal office of the State Council)
18/12/1998	Additional circular of carrying out <Organic Law of Village Committee>
30/07/1999	Suggestions of taking great effort to guarantee the female's number in village committee
11/07/2000	Circular of establishing institution of report forms of village election
07/2000	Institution of report forms of village election

The second level is the Organic Law of the Villages' Committee. The law was enacted in 1987 at the fifth Session of the Standing Committee of the 6th NPC. However, the 1987 law was experimental, meaning local levels were encouraged but not required to implement it. Ten years later the law was officially approved at a Session of the Standing Committee of the 9th NPC in 1998, requiring nationwide implementation of the institution of village elections, having a significant effect on village governance; most of its provisions were in accord with internationally accepted democratic procedures and were also more explicit. This law granted villagers the most important and complete legal guarantee in village self-governance and political participation.

The third level is the departmental rules and regulations made by the MCA. The passage of a law does not mean the end of the policy-making process. Rather it needs to further draft implementation regulations and then implement, while drafting the implementation regulations involves turning a law into a clearer set of guidelines. As the Organic Law is concerned, the power to formulate the method for implementing the Organic Law at national level reverts to the MCA. From 1990 to 2000, for example, MCA formulated or circled a total of approximately 14 important department rules and regulations on village elections and self-governance (see the following table), which have contributed to the development of village democracy. These circulars and documents bear the imprints of directions' work, and are favorable to the normalization and institutionalization of village elections and self-governance.[44]

J. March and J. Olsen think that political democracy depends on not only social and economic conditions but also the design of political institutions.[45] Whereas Gary Wekkin et al. say, "At the heart of democratization is the task of institutionalizing the democratic impulse in the form of domestic political structures and processes capable of meeting popular demands,"[46] Geoffrey Pridham argues that "decisions on institutional design are usually the most central issues facing transition forms actors in the early years of democratization."[47] The institutional design has been called "political and institutional engineering" by A. Lijphart.[48] S. Huntington thinks that institutionalization is beneficial to acquire value and stability for organization and procedures.[49] Establishing institutions and laws can make a new regime legitimate.

Establishment of village elections and self-government institution and the legislation and enactment of "Organic law" has indeed legitimated the rural democracy and set it out to normalize, whereas institution-building is another engine for launching and promoting village democracy. Among institutional constructions, the village self-governance demonstration model is an important one with salient achievements. The Department of Basic-Level Government in the MCA has been steadily and methodically working to establish model sites for village self-governance in every province, cultivating close ties with local authorities who were receptive to the program and attempting to win over those who were not.

The MCA knew the importance of institutional construction very well. Just after the passage of the provisional Organic Law, the first thing the MCA did was to select "demonstration sites" and sum up the experiences, attempting to extend village self-governance in wider areas and let the law officially pass. The MCA designated some locations as "demonstration sites," giving them special care and guidance. The criteria for setting up demonstration villages for village elections included: high voter turnout in village committee election; a high level of economic development; effective implementation of state policies in the village. Overall China has had 587; 14,067; 265,730 self-governance demonstration villages at county/city, township/town, and village levels respectively by 2000 (see table 6.2).

It is necessary to point out that the elites from MCA have actively summed up and improved local experiences and tried to institutionalize them too. Probably the most well known cases are the introductions of "sea-election" (haixuan) and the villagers' representative assembly system, the process of experimentation leading to the standardization contained in the new Organic Law, passed in 1998.

The institution of village elections and self-governance is the one main task or area of the political elites' crafting at a national level.

To act upon political reform with any degree of success, the officials at MCA knew they had to find a new basis of solidarity, cohesion, and identification,

Table 6.2   Basic data on villager's committee numbers and village self-governance demonstration units

Regions	Villagers committee's numbers	Village self-governance demonstration units		
		Counties/cities	Townships/town	Villages
Total	731,659	587	14,067	265,730
Anhui	29,735	21	728	11,697
Beijing	4,039	4	77	1,354
Fujian	14,834	22	493	9,986
Guangdong	21,942	23	339	2,799
Guangxi	14,750	31	397	3,923
Guizhou	25,696	9	657	12,627
Hainan	2,568	4	44	509
Hebei	49,433	52	1,172	24,524
Heilongjiang	17,285	36	445	6,814
Henan	48,206	23	939	23,341
Hubei	32,001	21	569	14,251
Hunan	47,525	24	636	13,328
Inner Monolia	13,498	34	598	5,753
Jiangsu	32,573	39	834	19,219
Jiangxi	20,518	16	540	4,717
Jilin	10,054	14	424	4,295
Liaoning	15,924	19	440	7,151
Ningxia	2,718	3	159	1,102
Qinghai	18,034	13	526	6,327
Sha'anxi	32,253	29	456	6,126
Shandong	87,504	27	723	31,380
Shanghai	2,771	5	60	1,407
Shanxi	31,355	4	321	3,518
Sichuan	54,996	19	1,412	25,611
Tianjin	3,834	4	70	1,126
Tibet	6,354	54	76	795
Xinjiang	9,556	9	133	2,209
Yunnan	14,968	6	79	795
Zhejiang	42,037	18	325	11,322

Source: Editorial Board of Yearbook of Democratic and Political Grassroots Construction in China, 2001' Yearbook of Democratic and Political Grassroots Construction in China (Beijing: China Society Press, 2002), p. 560.

and a new organizational form—something that could bring a large group of leaders to act together in performing the task of crafting and implementing village elections and responding to the demands of the times in a more productive and effective manner.

Established in 1989, the China Council for the Promotion of Basic-Level Governments and Mass Organizations (CCPBGMO), a semiofficial organization under the MCAs leadership, was an organizational basis for the ministry to unite relevant officials to promote self-governance. Its aim is "unit scholars who study on grassroots power construction, local leaders, and prevalent governmental agencies and institutions" to promote China's grassroots power construction. The ministry tried to construct a working network, which can communicate between the higher and lower levels, contact crosswise.

CCPBGMO has also contributed to rural democratic construction. In November 1995, MCA established the China Society for the Development of Townships and Towns (CSDTT) based on CCPBGMO. In 1998, CSDTT merged the China Council for the Promotion of Development of Urban Communities, which was under the China Social Work Association.

The Council has been an organizational basis of MCA, particularly Wang's network, while many of its members became the core of this network. Wang Zhenyao once said he had many local friends who gave him assistances with his work.[50] These members became MCAs human resource to implement village self-governance, while local leaders embedded in his network can get resources such as information, than those embedded in the network (CCPBGMO) more probably because of the village self-governance demonstration units.

Although macro-circumstance, law and institutions are important, the talented operators are indispensable too. According to Alexis De Tocqueville, the American democratic model is deeply ingrained in the American psyche, which means democracy is a natural state of affairs, people will naturally set up an electoral system like their own if they are given one choice. China did not have a democratic tradition, however. The past experiences show that the details of village election procedures must be taught, learned, and supervised. The village self-governance could not effectively be implemented without relevantly qualified election officials. Hence, training is the main way to achieve this goal. The MCA brings provincial, county, township levels' officials and even village leaders together for workshops and training classes, through which they can learn from the advanced or successful experiments of other areas on village elections and self-governance. However, training is one of the major challenges currently facing the MCA. According to the MCA, around 1.5 million township-level officials need to be trained in order to better implement village democracy nationwide. For this, the MCA has opened one training centre in Beijing and cooperated with foreigners to carry out three projects focusing on training.

The China Rural Official Training Center (CROTC) is a project jointly approved by the United Nations Development Programme and the Chinese Government. The recipient agency is the MCA. The original duration is three years (1996–99). With additional funding from the Government of Finland since 1998, the Project was able to extend the funding to the end of 2000.

The goal is to promote Chinese rural democracy by providing training in villager's self-governance. In this project, the trainees include officials with provincial to county Bureaus of Civil Affairs who are in charge of promoting villagers self-governance, chief leaders of township/town governments, and part of elected villagers' committee members. From 1996 to 2000, CROTC had run total 17 classes in Beijing, Hebei, Fujian, Yunnan, Hunan, Liaoning, Jiangsu, and Jilin respectively, with over two thousand being trained.

The EU-China Training Program on Village Governance is an intergovernmental project between the European Union and the People's Republic of China. On May 22, 2001, the Commission of the European Union and the Chinese Ministry of Foreign Trade and Economic Cooperation, acting on behalf of the Government of the People's Republic of China, started this project by signing a program-financing agreement. The agreement provided for a contribution from the European Union of more than 10.6 million euros. A contribution in cash and kind from the Chinese Government was set for an amount totaling more than 4 million euros. The program is expected to run for five years, ending on May 28, 2006. The MCA is responsible for implementing the program on the Chinese side.

On March 14, 1998, the Carter Center and the MCA signed a Memorandum of Understanding, officially launching The Carter Center's China Village Elections Project. On April 26, 2000, both sides signed "The Cooperative Agreement between The Ministry of Civil Affairs and The Carter Center to Standardize Villager Committee Election Procedures." This agreement is designed to develop model and replicable electoral practices through the following activities: (1) establish a complete data collection system in Fujian and Jilin provinces and in one third of the counties in Sha'anxi province; (2) conduct academic research on standardizing election procedures; (3) print and distribute voter education materials; (4) train provincial and county level election officials in electoral laws, procedures and information delivery techniques; (5) continue dialogues, share experiences and publicize village level election information, and (6) conduct bilateral exchanges between the MCA and The Carter Center.[51]

CONCLUSION

The trials of establishing villagers' committee and elections were first practiced in some villages in Luocheng County of the Guangxi Autonomous Region beginning in 1980 with approval from some top national leaders, particularly Peng Zhen, whereas reform-oriented officials at MCA were empowered to administer village elections and self-governance worked under the support of top national leaders. Among them, Wang Zhenyao and his colleagues in MCA have played a crucial role.

This study illustrates the importance of strategies. Three kinds of resources these elites employed have been identified and analyzed: empowerment and top leaders' support, the expectation and pressures from peasants, and the pursuit of their own interests, through which they can and have effectively constructed a sound environment, formulated the law, rules and regulations, and policies, built institutions, and trained executors for village elections and self-governance. All in all, these elites have fully used various means, methods, and strategies to build up a momentum for village self-governance, and then forced the issue onto the local agencies.

NOTES

1. Refer to Giuseppe Did Palma, *To Craft Democracies: an Essay on Democratic Transitions* (Berkeley: University of California Press, 1990); Robert D. Grey,

Democratic Theory and Post-Communist Change (Prentice Hall, 1997); Gorge Sorensen, *Democracy and Democratization: Process and Prospects in a Changing World* (Westview Press, 1998).

2. Party Literature Research Centre of the CCP Central Committee, *Selected Important Literature from since the Third Plenum of the 11ᵗʰ CCP Central Committee* (Beijing: the People's Press, 1982), p. 1061.
3. Deng Xiaoping, *Selected Works from Deng Xiaoping*, Volume 2 (Beijing: the People's Press, 1984), pp. 144 and 146.
4. Mr. Wang Zhenyao, interview by author, Beijing, China, September of 2001.
5. Mr. Yan Minfu, interview by He Baogang, Beijing, China, July of 1998.
6. Amy B. Epstein, "Village Elections in China: Experimenting with Democracy," in E. Bliney, ed., *Crisis and Reform in China* (Nova Science Publishers, Inc., 1997), p. 152.
7. Gerardo L. Munck, "Game Theory and Comparative Politics: New Perspective and Old Concerns," *World Politics*, vol. 53 (January 2001), p. 192.
8. Shi Tianjian, "Village Committee Elections in China: Institutionalist Tactics for Democracy," *World Politics*, vol. 51 (April 1999), pp. 389, 394.
9. Shi Tianjian, "Village Committee Elections in China: Institutionalist Tactics for Democracy," *World Politics*, vol. 51 (April 1999), p. 411.
10. Guangdong, Guangxi, and Yunnan provinces had not conducted village elections until 1998. However, we cannot equate the appointments employed by these provinces with ones of the Maoist era.
11. Robert Thomson, Frans Stokman, and Rene Torenviled, "Models of Collective Decision-Making: Introduction," *Rationality and Society*, vol. 15, no. 1 (2003), p. 7.
12. Ma Mingjie, "Cui Naifu on China's Village Committees Elections," The *Youth Daily*, June 19, 1998.
13. Ibid., p. 408.
14. Bai Yanhua described the process of the birth of the Organic Law. See Bai Yanhua, *The Reform and Exploration of China's Grassroots Power*, Volume 1 (Beijing: China Society Press, 1995), pp. 282–309.
15. Wang Zheyao, "Chinese Village Self-government and Path to Democratic Development," *Strategy and Management*, no. 2 (2000), p. 100.
16. People's Daily, December 2nd, 1998.
17. Adam Przeworski, "Democracy as a Contingent Outcome of Conflict," in John Elster and Rune Slagstad, eds., *Constitutionalism and Democracy*, (Cambridge University Press, 1988), pp. 59–81.
18. Larry Diamond, ed., *Political Culture and Democracy in Developing Countries* (Lynne Rienner Publishers, Inc., 1993), p. 151.
19. "Swing man" is a figure in a key position at the right time that succeeds in helping to transform the state of affairs and to bring about a solution at a decisive moment in transition. See Geoffrey Pridham, *The Dynamics of Democratization: A Comparative Approach* (London, New York: Continuum, 2000), p. 142.
20. The question is why Marxist "fundamentalists" became "swing men" in village elections? Why did several party elders and particularly Peng Zhen champion the Organic Law in the face of widespread opposition? Some Scholars have offered some reasons. First, Peng Zhen's personal experience in the elections of the Jin Cha Ji Border Region and the CR pushed him to recognize

the importance of the rule of law and democracy, while those experiences were naturally important for Peng to support the implementation of village elections and self-governance. Regarding this point, see Pitman B. Potter, *From Leninist Discipline to Socialist Legalism: Peng Zhen on Law and political Authority in the PRC*, USC Seminar No. 10 of The Chinese University of Hong Kong, 1995, p. 14. Second, the first generation revolutionist of the CCP such as Mao Zedong had firm faith and thirst for the national independence, glory, and democracy. Peng Zhen had ideas and faith in legalization, democratization, the mass line of the CCP, and a real sense of the people's being the master of their own country. Regarding this point, refer to the interview with Mr. Yan Minfu by He Baogang, Beijing of China, in July of 1998. Third, Peng Zhen took a commitment to village elections and self-governance for strengthening the existing political position of CCP in rural China. Regarding this point, see Shi Tianjian, "Village Committee Elections in China: Institutionalist Tactics for Democracy," *World Politics*, vol. 51 (April 1999), p. 392; Li Lianjiang and Kevin J. O'Brien, "The Struggle over Village Elections," in Merle Goldman and Roderick MacFarquhar, eds., *The Paradox of China's Post-Mao Reforms* (Harvard University Press, 1999), p. 131; Tyrene White, "Village Elections: Democracy from the Bottom up?," *Current History*, vol. 97 (September 1998), p. 264; Pitman B. Potter, *From Leninist Discipline to Socialist Legalism: Peng Zhen on Law and political Authority in the PRC*. USC Seminar No. 10 (The Chinese University of Hong Kong, 1995), p. 16. Finally, as the Chairman of the Standing Committee of the National People's Congress (NPC), Peng Zhen needed to increase his own power in Chinese politics. Regarding this point, see Shi Tianjian, "Village Committee Elections in China: Institutionalist Tactics for Democracy," *World Politics*, vol. 51 (April 1999), p. 392; Pitman B. Potter, *From Leninist Discipline to Socialist Legalism: Peng Zhen on Law and political Authority in the PRC*, USC Seminar No. 10 of The Chinese University of Hong Kong, 1995, p. 12.

21. Larry Diamond, "Beyond Authoritarianism and Totalitarianism: Strategies for Democratization," *Washington Quarterly* (Winter 1989), p. 151.
22. Shi Tianjian, "Village Committee Elections in China: Institutionalist Tactics for Democrcay," *World Politics*, vol. 51 (April 1999), pp. 389, 393.
23. Mr. Wang Zhenyao, interview by author, Beijing, China, September of 2001.
24. See Bai Yanhua, *The Reform and Exploration of China's Grassroots Power*, Volume 1 (Beijing: China Society Press, 1995), pp. 282–309.
25. Ma Mingjie, "Cui Naifu on China's Village Committees Elections," *The Youth Daily*, June 19, 1998.
26. Ma Mingjie, "Cui Naifu on China's Village Committees Elections," *The Youth Daily*, June 19, 1998.
27. Li Lianjiang and Kevin J. O'Brien, "The Struggle over Village Elections," in Merle Goldman and Roderick MacFarquhar, eds., *The Paradox of China's Post-Mao Reforms* (Harvard University Press, 1999), p. 133.
28. Ibid., p. 133.
29. Paul Grove, "Challenges and Obstacles to Village Elections in China," IRIs report, February 29, 1999.
30. Anne F. Thurston, *Muddling toward Democracy: Political Changes in Grassroots China*. United States Institute of Peace, Peaceworks 23, 1998, p. 13.

31. Paul C. Grove, "The Roles of Foreign Non-governmental Organizations in the Development and Promotion of Village Elections in China," *American Asian Review*, vol. XVIII, no. 3 (Fall 2000), p. 111.

32. During the interview with the author, when asked how to form his network, Wang Zhenyao said he preferred the word of "cluster" to "network." In this study, the term of personal network is similar to the term of a cluster.

33. The author was told that the leading officials at MCA in charge of village elections and self-governance such as Wang Zhenyao, Zhan Chenfu had not come to Zhejiang to observe village elections, showing they supported Zhejiang Department of Civil Affairs to implement village elections. Mr. He Zhiquan, Former Head of Division of Grassroots Governance of Zhejiang Department of Civil Affairs, interview by author, Hangzhou of Zhejiang Province, China, July of 2002.

34. Shi Tianjian, "Village Committee Elections in China. Institutional Tactics for Democracy," *World Politics*, vol. 51, no. 3 (April 1999), p. 390.

35. Shi Tianjian, "Village Committee Elections in China: Institutionalist Tactics for Democracy," *World Politics*, vol. 51 (1999), pp. 385–412.

36. Jean C. Oi, "Economic Development, Stability and Democratic Village Self-governance," in Maurice Brosseau, Suzanne Pepper, and Tsang Shu-ki, eds., *China Review 1996* (Hong Kong: The Chinese University Press, 1996), p. 131.

37. Chinese Research Society of Basic-Level Governance and Research Group on the System of Village Self-governance in China, *Study on the Election of Villagers' Committees in Rural China* (Beijing: Chinese Society Publishing House, 1994), p. 9.

38. Wang Jinhua, interview by author, East Asian Institute, National University of Singapore, February 15, 2003.

39. "Li Xueju: Contributor to China's Grassroots Democracy," *People's Daily* (Internet version), December 28, 2000.

40. Chinese Research Society of Basic-Level Governance and Research Group on the System of Village Self-governance in China, *The Report on the Villagers' Representative Assemblies* (Beijing: Chinese Society Publishing House, 1995), p. IV.

41. Shi Tianjian, "Village Committee Elections in China: Institutionalist Tactics for Democracy," *World Politics*, vol. 51 (April 1999), p. 391.

42. Wang Zhenyao, "The Speech on 1996' Village Elections in Hebei Province," lecture given in 1996 at Shijiazhuang, <http://www.chinarural.org/zlk.asp?booktime=1996>, accessed March 22, 2003.

43. The author edited this table based on the source from *2001 Yearbook of Grassroots Democratic and Political Construction in China* (Beijing: China Society Press, 2002), pp. 197–235.

44. Additionally, it is commonly known that in China, sometimes a party circle or document is more important and effective than a departmental regulation and even a law. In October 1983, the Central Party Committee and the State Council issued "Circular of Separation of Party and Government, Establishing Township Government," declaring the end of the People's Commune system, which paved the way for the emergency of villagers' committee and soon afterwards village elections. In September 1986, the Central Party Committee and the State Council issued "Circular of Strengthening Grassroots Regime Construction in Rural China," prescribing villagers'

committee construction in detail, encouraging the masses to go on self-management, self-education, and self-service, and instructing the MCA to be responsible to the routine businesses of villagers' committee construction. These circulars have been indeed helpful to the development of village democracy.

45. J. March and J. Olsen, "The New Institutionalism: Organizational Factors in Political Life," *American Political Science Review*, vol. 27 (September 1984), p. 738.

46. Gary D. Wekkin, Donald E. Whistler, Michael A. Kelley, and Michael A. Maggiotto, "The Democratic Impulse and the Movement Toward Democracy: An Introduction," in Gary D. Wekkin, Donald E. Whistler, Michael A. Kelley, and Michael A. Maggiotto, eds., *Building Democracy in One-Party Systems: theoretical Problems and Cross-national Experiences* (Westport, CT: Praeger Publishers,1993), p. 9.

47. Geoffrey Pridham, *The Dynamics of Democratization: a Comparative Approach* (London, New York: Continuum, 2000), p. 93.

48. A. Lijphart, "The Southern European Examples of Democratization: Six Lessons for Latin America," *Government and Opposition*, vol. 27 (Winter 1990), p. 72.

49. S.Huntington, "Political Development and Political Decay," *World Politics*, vol. 18 (April 1965), p. 394.

50. Interview with Wang Zhenyao, Beijing, China, September 2001.

51. Editorial Board of Yearbook of Democratic and Political Grassroots Construction in China, *2001' Yearbook of Democratic and Political Grassroots Construction in China* (Beijing: China Society Press, 2002), p. 543. See also, the Carter Center, "Project Chronology of 26/04/2000," the Carter Center Web site, <http://www.cartercenter.com/peaceprograms/chinashowstaticdoc.asp?docname=chinachronology&submenu=peaceprograms>.

PART III

LEADERSHIP CHANGE AND NEW FOREIGN POLICY ORIENTATION

CHAPTER 7

THE 16TH NATIONAL CONGRESS OF THE CHINESE COMMUNIST PARTY AND CHINA'S FOREIGN POLICY

Shulong Chu

The 16th Chinese Communist Party (CCP) Congress held on November 2003 in the arena of foreign policy is significant for China in the new century. The Party Congress did make a major or rather a fundamental change. The fundamental position and attitude of the Chinese foreign policy is moving from "opposing hegemony" in the past decade to "maintaining international peace and promoting common development," in a more positive direction. Such a change has already affected China's foreign policies toward the international system, including the G-8, and on specific issues in international relations, such as Iraq and North Korean nuclear issues. Therefore, the change is real.

The rationale leading in China's foreign policy have a lot to do with more than 20 years of reform and opening-up, rising economic power and the confidence of the Chinese people, recent victories in its foreign relations agendas, and the integration with the international system and communities.

The change looks like it is setting a somewhat new direction in China's foreign policy for the early twenty-first century. It provides possibilities for a more cooperative, moderate approach in Chinese foreign relations, more stable relations with the United States and other major powers and more multilateral approaches in international and regional affairs. However, the shift of fundamental position and attitudes of Chinese foreign policy has made little impact on the Taiwanese policy, because, to the Chinese, Taiwan is an internal issue and has lot to do with culture, tradition, and public opinion of the Chinese people that government can change little.

A MAJOR SHIFT OF CHINA'S FOREIGN POLICY

When someone reads the report given by Mr. Jiang Zemin, the then general secretary of the CCP Central Committee, to the delegates of the 16th Party Congress on November 8 of 2002, she/he may not notice many changes in Chinese foreign policy. Most statements are almost similar with the 15th Party Congress and those statements made by the Chinese leaders and officials in the past few years.

However, there is one major shift in the statement of the Chinese foreign policy, and this is the *Zongzhi* (the fundamental principle) change.

The Foreign Policy Zongzhi and Goal

Mr Jiang Zemin's report at the 16th Party Congress states that:

> No matter how the international situation changes, we will, as always, pursue the independent foreign policy of peace. The purpose of China's foreign policy is to maintain world peace and promote common development. We are ready to work with all nations to advance the lofty cause of world peace and development.[1]

This statement on the fundamental principle and goal of the Chinese foreign policy is significant change because it is different from past statements.

The previous statements made at the 15th, 14th, 13th, and the 12th party congresses since 1982 always put "opposing hegemonism and maintaining international peace" as the fundamental principle and goal of China's foreign policy.[2] The 16th Party Congress is the first time in 20 years that the Chinese leadership states (at the most important occasion) that the Chinese foreign policy goal and the fundamental principle is no longer "opposing hegemonism" or someone but "maintaining world peace and promoting mutual development."[3]

Looking back, we may find such a shift is not the only fundamental change in the past 20 years, but also a major change in more than 50 years since the foundation of the Peoples' Republic of China (PRC). It opposed American imperialism in the 1950s and fought a hot war against America in Korea from 1950 to 1953. It opposed both imperialism and "revisionism" or "social imperialism" led by the Soviet Union in 1960s and 1970s. China supported the Vietnamese fighting against the Americans during the Vietnam War and had a number of serious border clashes with the Soviet Union in the 1960s. China engaged in strategic cooperation with the United States in opposing "the most dangerous superpower," the Soviet Union, in the 1970s and 1980s. And after the June 4th Tiananmen Event in 1989 band collapse of the Soviet Union in 1991, China's foreign policy against "hegemonism" became retargeting the United States.

It looks like the "Fan Culture" or "opposing culture" had been the strategic culture in China's foreign policy and foreign relations for a long time since the foundation of the PRC until the 16th Party Congress in November

2002. The change of the "Zongzhi" and fundamental goals in China's foreign policy also means the shift of China's strategic culture in its foreign policy and foreign relations. Therefore, it is really a fundamental change.

Is the shift a real change? The answer should be yes when we see the changing Chinese policies on major international relation issues today.

China's Policy on Iraq

The Iraqi issue is not new to China. It has been around the international community for more than a decade, when Iraq invaded and occupied Kuwait. In the past 12 years, the Chinese position on the Iraqi issue has changed somewhat. The government of China stood against Iraq's invasion of Kuwait and demanded Iraq withdraw its troops from Kuwait and restore the sovereignty of the nation. But China voted to abstain when the United Nations passed the resolution to authorize the use of force against Iraq in 1990.

After the first Gulf War in 1991 and until recently, the Chinese position became critical of the American military action in Iraq. China opposed setting up of the "no-fly zones" in northern and southern Iraq, and condemned American and British bombing against Iraq in 1996 and 1998. China supported the lift of sanctions against Iraq before the second 2003 Iraqi war when inspections and investigations on weapons for mass destruction (WMD) had made progress. Chinese sympathy seemed to be shifting to Iraq side after the first Gulf War.

However, when the new Iraqi crisis developed in early 2002, the Chinese government position took another turn. This time the Chinese government neither supported nor opposed U.S./U.K.-sponsored resolution against Iraq and the long planned operation attacking Iraq. China's position seems to be neutral. It repeatedly states its two-sided position on the Iraqi issue before the second Iraq war in March and April 2003. On the one side, the Chinese said that Iraq must comply with the UN resolutions, which required Iraq to give up its WMD program, Iraq must accept and cooperate with the UN inspection teams in Iraq to ensure the country did not develop these weapon systems. At the same time, the other side of the Chinese position is the United Nations should lift its sanctions against Iraq when the inspection had made progress, Iraq's sovereignty should be respected, and the Iraqi issue should be resolved by peaceful means only and within the framework of the United Nations.[4] This is to say that China does not support the American plan or using force against Iraq.

The Chinese two-sided position is not new. What is new is that China did not oppose American/British military action in Iraq this time in the spring of 2003. Many countries, including the American alliance of France, Germany, and Russia stood against military action in Iraq. But China, a non-alliance and a nonfriend of the United States, did not say no to military action before, during, or after the war.

The Chinese position of not opposing American military action against other countries is something new in the past decade since 1991. No more than a decade ago, China stood against almost all American military actions against other countries except Afghanistan. China condemned American action in Panama, Bosnia, Libya, and Kosovo. The only exception was the military action in Afghanistan after 9/11. The Chinese government not only did not oppose but even supported American action in Afghanistan because this was the war against terrorism. On all other occasions, China opposed the United States using military forces against other countries.

China's changing position on American military action this time is hard evidence that Chinese foreign policy has changed, the change stated by the 16th Party Congress. That is, China is no longer taking a position against hegemonism as the central theme of the Chinese foreign policy. China may not like and does not support American military action in Iraq, but the Chinese did not feel that they should oppose the Americans because opposing someone was no longer playing a central role in Chinese foreign policy, the principle set by the 16th Party Congress.

China's Policy on Korean Nuclear Issue

Besides Iraq, another piece of hard evidence indicates a major shift in China's foreign policy on Korea set by the 16th Party Congress.

In more than five decades since the foundation of the PRC in 1949 until very recently, the stated Chinese position on anything of North Korea had been clearly and consistent. The Chinese government always stated its support and sympathy with the Democratic People's Republic of Korea (DPRK). China never criticized North Korea in its public statements given by its leaders, officials, and official news media. China might remain silent toward anything that North Korea did that the Chinese did not like.

However, this is no longer the case since the new Korean nuclear crisis broke out in October 2002, when North Korean leaders told visiting U.S. Assistant Secretary Mr. James Kelly that the country was developing nuclear weapons. The Chinese government changed its position on Korean issues. This time, since October 2002 until now, the Chinese government does not support North Korea, nor keep silence on the actions that North Korea is taking and the Chinese do not like.

All Chinese leaders since October 2002, old and new, and Chinese Foreign Ministry officials have repeatedly stated: China supports non-nuclearization of the Korean Peninsula, the Korean Peninsula should not have nuclear weapons; all relevant parties should honor the agreements, clearly refer to the 1994 U.S.–DPRK Framework Agreement and NPT (Non-Proliferation Treaty) that North Korea has joined. The Chinese leaders and officials even go far to state that China opposes development of nuclear weapons on the Korean Peninsula. This may be the first time in more than half a century that China publicly states that they are opposing something North Korea is doing, although at the same time the Chinese government states that North Korea's security concerns should also be addressed, and China does not support military actions and sanctions against North Korea.[5]

The new Chinese position on North Korea has a number of rationales, and one of them is because of the change of the fundamental theme in China's foreign policy. Because that policy is no longer opposing hegemonism, the then nuclear issue between the DPRK and the United States, and other issues between the United States and other countries are no longer viewed as something between hegemony action and the suffering party of hegemonism. Thus China does not need and should not automatically oppose American position in international affairs, because American positions are no longer viewed as hegemonism through the Chinese eyes. And even if there are hegemony actions, the Chinese need not always oppose them because opposing hegemonism is no longer the major task of Chinese foreign policy.

THE RATIONALES OF CHINA'S FOREIGN POLICY CHANGE

If the above argument that there was major foreign policy changes at the 16th Party Congress is the real case, then the question following was why there was this change?

To be sure, the change in Chinese foreign policy is not incidental. It is accumulated and inevitable action caused by the development in China and the world in the past 20 years.

The Would-be Outcome of the Reform, Openness, and Integration

China has engaged in reform and openness for more than 20 years since 1978, when a session of the CCP Central Committee held in December 1978 made the decision to reform China. Since then, according to Chinese leadership and government, what China has done are basically two things: reform and open-up to the outside world.

Reform is basically something internal. China has undertaken fundamental approaches in the past two decades to reform its economic, political, social, and educational systems. The planning economy is gone, and a market system is taking root in China, as well as fundamental changes. There is much more freedom in residence, migration, occupation, education, marriage, living styles, and cultural habits. Although political reform has not been as dramatic as the economic and social parts, there are major changes in political ideology, governmental structure, governance, the role of law in the Chinese politics and society.

The other major part of Chinese practice in the past two decades is the opening up to the outside world. China became the fifth largest trade power in the world, and it has been one of the biggest receptors of foreign investments. It has joined almost all 3,000 international organizations including the United Nations and the World Trade Organization (WTO). It has become an active player in globalization, international and regional affairs.

The more than 20 years' experience in reform and openness in China has changed China fundamentally in both internal and external policies. One key result is making China part international system, part global political, security, trade, and finally environmental systems. China is now an insider, no longer an outsider in the international system.

Before China fully joined the international system, it was China's nature to stay out of the system and oppose the "hegemony" of the system, and the central part of the system—American hegemonism. And now, when China is within the system and even becomes a major part of the system, it is no longer logical nor reasonable for China to continue opposing the system, and the major part of the system—the United States.

The reform, openness, and integration with the international community also change the Chinese value systems and attitudes toward the outside world. With the growing value systems, a sense and system of the rule of law, honesty, credibility, and responsibility in the market system develops inside Chinese economy and society; the Chinese people and government then share more of those in their foreign relations and international affairs. Inside and outside China, the country becomes a place where people have an increasing care about the rule of law, regulation, honesty, credibility, and responsibility. The Chinese are increasingly emphasizing that laws and regulations should be the guide for behavior inside and outside China; agreements, treaties, and contracts should be followed; and countries and peoples should be honest, reliable, accountable, and responsible in their actions inside and outside their countries. Therefore, any nation, government, and individual who does not follow international law, UN resolution, accepted rules and norms of the international community become negative to the Chinese people and government. Any nation, government, and individual who does not carry out nor honor the agreements and treaties they have signed or joined becomes unpopular among the Chinese. Leaders and governments who do not treat their people democratically become a problem to the increasing number of Chinese people who can get information through the Internet when they cannot get that through officially controlled news media.

In sum, the reform, openness, and integration over the past decades have made the Chinese move closer to some concepts, values, norms of most other parts of the world, and has alienated the Chinese further from those nations, governments, and individuals who are not part of the integrated international mainstream.

The National Psychology Change after Major Foreign Relations' Victories

China is a historical country, with a longer history than most of other countries in the world. History has played a heavier role in past in the Chinese way of thinking, understanding their culture, and their internal as well as external policies.

In the foreign relations arena, the Chinese have had a "national victim psychology" for more than a century. That is the interpretation of the

Chinese people about their relations with the outside world for the past 110 years (since the 1840 Sino-British War) until the foundation of the PRC in 1949, the modern era of China. The Chinese official and popular understanding and interpretation of modern history is that China has been the victim in its relations with the outside world, especially with Great Britain, France, Germany, Russia, Japan, the United States, and other major powers. To the Chinese, the history of those hundred years is the history of imperialists' invasion, occupation, and exploitation over China and the Chinese people in their relationships. That history is a history of humiliation.

And the Chinese people do not see that the history was ended in 1949 when the People's Republic was founded. In the past five decades until very recently, the Chinese people and government tended to believe that the United States, most European countries, Japan, or those Western countries who invaded and bullied China in history intended to continue that history. Therefore, each time during the past 50 years when China had conflicts, incidents, problems, difficulties with those and other countries, the Chinese government and its people tended to see those countries wanting to continue to cause the suffering of China and humiliation of the Chinese people.

Such a "victim national psychology" also applied to the Chinese understanding on international affairs not directly related to them until very recently, when the Chinese saw American action in Korea, Vietnam, Bosnia, Panama, Iraq, and all other parts of the developing world, they saw similarities between what Americans do now with what the imperialists did toward China in the past. Therefore, the Chinese would automatically support or sympathize with those countries who were attacked by Americans or other Western powers, no matter who those regimes were of those developing countries and what they had done internally and externally. Such a "victim national psychology" is the mental and emotional root of China's antihegemonism foreign policy in the past decades.

That psychology has started to change recently, and the forces of change are the series of victories of China's foreign relations in the past years. By winning the bid for holding the 2008 Olympics in 2000, entering the WTO in 2001, plus joining the United Nations in the early 1970s, the Chinese finally found that the world treated them fairly. China has got a fair place in the political, economic, cultural, or symbolic world. Therefore, the "victim national psychology" started to fade, if not totally disappear. Then the Chinese people and government became much more "normal" in understanding and conducting their relations with the outside world, and adopted much more normal attitudes and policies toward international issues. China's foreign policy becomes less emotionally driven, and gets closer to the reality of the real world. China's foreign policy becomes more "seeking the truth from the facts," less seeking truth from emotion, from history, and from its national psychology.

Therefore China now is able to see America, Iraq, North Korea, and other members of international community through a normal and non- or less-biased eyes. Thus it is no longer relevant to stand against hegemony or someone as a basic line of China's foreign policy. The basic line now is facts, and now China would like to take its position on international and foreign affairs according to the facts of the issues, according to the rights and wrongs of the concerning parties.

The Rising Economic Confidence

The change in the Chinese foreign policy certainly does not only come from the psychological revolution of the Chinese people but also from the material revolution over the past 20 years: the rapid economic development and so-called "rise of China."

What has been the logical result of 20 years of economic growth on Chinese foreign policy and foreign relations is the growing confidence of the Chinese people and government over their relations with others in the world, and such a growing confidence changes the Chinese understanding, perception, attitudes, positions, and policies toward foreign and international affairs.

This growing confidence enables the Chinese people and government to take a relatively more normal, relaxed attitude toward foreign and international issues, and become less sensitive and less emotional, especially toward difficulties and differences within Chinese foreign relations and in international affairs.

Because of the uneasy feeling about China's past and its relationship with the outside world, the Chinese people and government used to be very sensitive about anything American, Japanese, and other foreigners would say about China, their relations and policies with or toward China. They were also quite sensitive about American actions in other parts of weak and developing nations, and tried to implicate those American actions in other parts of the world. In other words, the Chinese always tried to find negative and dangerous relations between what Americans' doing somewhere now and what they would do to China sometime in the future.

Therefore, the Chinese used to have great suspicions about foreign powers such as the United States, Japan, European, and other Western countries. When American-led coalition troops attacked Iraq in 1991 and NATOs operation in Kosovo in 1999, the Chinese thought similar cases would apply to China in the future. Many Chinese were afraid that Western powers may use "human rights over sovereignty" as an excuse to interfere in Tibet, Xingjiang in future. And in the spring of 2003, when American/British troops attacked Iraq, some Chinese asked "who is the next" target of American action, and in this list people saw Iran, North Korea, and eventually China.

Even American military action against terrorists in Afghanistan is seen by many Chinese, including some strategists, officials, experts, and officers, as some strategic movement for encircling China from the Western front of China. For those people, action against terrorism in Afghanistan is just a secondary goal for America, the first and most important goal of the American action is using this opportunity to put forces in Central Asia to establish military presence in the region against China and Russia.

The high sensitivity and great suspicions about foreign powers always caused strong Chinese reaction about those incidents between China and foreign countries (such as the embassy bombing in Belgrade in 1999 and the EP-3 incident over the Hainan Islands in 2001). Because of this, most Chinese tended to believe those incidents intentional; thus they became more emotional than usual, and demanded a stronger position from the Chinese government because the Americans intended to attack and cause the tragic death of Chinese people and soldiers.

The logical outcome of the Chinese sensitivity and suspicion about foreign powers, especially the United States, Japan, and countries with whom China had a war with in recent history, is the negative reaction of China over foreign and international issues. That is another major reason why the Chinese stood against the American actions in Panama, Yugoslavia, Bosnia, and Kosovo, and why most Chinese did not support American actions against Iraq in 1991 and 2003, and why even a great number of Chinese were not sympathetic when America was attacked by the terrorists. The reason is fear. Many Chinese fear that what Americans do to other weak and developing countries might be something similar that Americans would do to China in the future. That is why the Chinese sympathy always went to nations being attacked by Americans, and the Chinese government always stood with others than the United States in international conflicts.

This stand is changing. The fear is not completely gone, but the Chinese are becoming more confident. Now more and more Chinese leaders, officials, and experts have become less sensitive toward what the Americans, Europeans, or Japanese are doing. When Chinese saw the Americans attacking Iraq in 2003, and the Japanese sending naval ships to the Indian Ocean in 2001 in supporting the American war against terrorism, many Chinese this time did not worry too much nor fear those movements. Those Chinese would say "so what" to China? Does that mean Americans or Japanese would do similar things to the Chinese in future? Perhaps not. Because China is becoming stronger, and more and more Chinese do not believe that foreign powers would dare to attack China as they did to other countries in the developing world. Thus, in recent years, the Chinese people and government have increasingly taken a relatively relaxed attitude toward American and Japanese actions which the Chinese seem not to like.

With the economic, social, cultural developments inside China and more and more opportunities in the country, there seems to be a tendency for the Chinese people in general to become more self-oriented. That means more and more Chinese are paying less attention to the outside world because they are so busy catching their opportunities or enjoying a better life inside China that they do not have time to think about others in the world. One positive side of such inward looking is less sensitivity about foreign countries' behavior and international affairs, thus weakening the demand for governmental reactions toward those international issues. So the Chinese government, together with its people, is able to care less about what Americans and Japanese are doing in the world and thus easying the tensions between China and other countries on their differences over international affairs.

U.S.–China Policy after the 9/11

There is also an international environment for the change in Chinese foreign policy: the major part of that environment is the United States and its relations with China.

The Sino-U.S. relations have gone through an up-again, down-again pattern in the past decade since the end of the Cold War in the early 1990s. The U.S.–China policy and the situation of the Sino-U.S. relations have had a great impact on the Chinese viewpoint about the world and its foreign policies and foreign relations. The ups and downs till summer 2001 caused great suspicion and uneasy attitudes of the Chinese on their understanding about the world and practices in their foreign relations.

However, since the summer of 2001, the Sino-U.S. relations have come out of the cloud of the EP-3 incident in April 2001. The visit by Secretary State of Colin Powell to Beijing in July put the relationship back on a normal track. One significant development during the visit is the statement by the Bush Administration that the U.S. side would drop its definition on U.S.–China relations as "strategic competition."

The terrorist attack to the World Trade Center in New York and Pentagon in the Washington area since July 2001 stabilizes the positive trend in China policy of the United States and Sino-U.S. relations. Since then, American foreign policy has been focusing on terrorist threats, not the so-called "China threat." The Bush Administration needs cooperation from other countries, including China, in its war on terrorism. And counter-terrorism is the common interest of almost all the nations in the world. Therefore, the United States and China share something in common strategically for the first time since the end of the Cold War in the early 1990s. When leaders of the two countries talk, they tend to focus on something they have common language and interests. This makes the relationship stable and positive in the 2 years since the summer of 2001.

The stable and positive Sino-U.S. relations help the Chinese take a normal and relaxed view about the international environment and global affairs. It weakens the force of anti-Americanism among Chinese general public and officials, thus improving the Chinese view about the United States, especially its foreign policy. The Chinese people and their government view American foreign policy less negatively because American China policy and U.S.–China relations become less negative. Therefore China does not need a general foreign policy against "hegemony" because the hegemonic power seems not so bad to the Chinese now, compared with 2 years ago.

TRENDS AND IMPLICATIONS

The change of Chinese foreign policy "zhongzi" is just starting, and it is going to be a long-term trend rather then a temporary development. Therefore the change in foreign policy principle will have great influence on China's foreign policy and foreign relations in every major respect and area.

Change and Continuities

The change is significant because the driving forces behind the change are so fundamental and significant. It is an economic, social, cultural, and a systemic change inside China in the past two decades of development.

The forces are strong in China, and therefore the change will be stabilized. The Chinese economy is likely to keep rapid growth for another decade or two, mainly because of the consumers' revolution and the strong domestic demand. Although the Chinese economy has many difficulties and problems (such as unemployment, agriculture, state enterprises, and bad loans), those difficulties are not new and they did not prevent China from rapid development in the past 20 years, and they may not prevent China from future development over another 20 years.

What is more significant to the Chinese foreign policy is not just its economic basis. The most important factor affecting China's foreign policy is the changing mind-set and thinking of the Chinese people, including their leaders.

The revolutionary generation has gone, and so have the Soviet-trained generation (Jiang Zemin, Li Peng, and Li Lanqing). The people who are in charge in China now at all the levels are the generation who grew up during the past 20 years of reform and openness. This generation knows little about revolution and the Soviet model of socialism. What they know is the reform and openness that they have experienced during the past 20 years.

The new generation comes to power with new thinking. They are better educated with modern natural and social sciences. They know more about today's world than their parents' generation. They are much more open, flexible, and democratic than the old generation of Chinese people, especially the old leadership of Jiang Zemin. Although the new leadership has been in power for only eight months, it has showed many differences from its previous one. Their new thinking and way of governance can be seen from China's news media coverage about the Iraq War, their management on SARS, and their foreign trips recently.

These positive trends will be continuing because the Chinese people and society are new. No one likes the old ways, old thinking about personal life, community, country, and the world. People are better educated, have access to more information about the world, have become more well-off, care more about individual rights and freedom, and share more common values with the international community. The country and society have become more developed, market oriented, and rule of law.

Those are the fundamental forces which drive China's international and external policies and actions. The general trend of China is that the country becomes more integrated with the other parts of the world, including with the common values. China is getting closer and closer with the international community, and has become a more responsible and powerful player in the world.

The change will continue but will not be made overnight. The change will be long term and gradual. Most of the old thinking about the world and China's foreign policy stays with ordinary Chinese, rather than Chinese leaders, foreign policy officials, and expert community. The Chinese general public has little opportunity to know the real outside world. Their knowledge and view about the world, about major powers such as the United States, Japan, European countries, are still very much old stories. Therefore, the anti-Americanism, anti-Japanese, hard-line attitude is still strong and common among Chinese general public. Such public opinion will continue to exercise some influence upon Chinese foreign policy. It puts pressure on the government and restrains governmental actions in foreign and international relations, especially during crises when emotion is strong.

A Stable and Constructive Sino-U.S. Relationship?

The changing Chinese foreign policy principle is a positive factor in today's and future Sino-U.S. relations, because China no longer puts antihegemony as its major foreign policy theme. This means China's foreign policy will be less anti-American or even be less focused on the United States.

However, the nature and future of Sino-U.S. relations remains uncertain because the relationship is a two-sided story: it not only depends on the Chinese side. The positive change in Chinese foreign policy does not automatically lead to more positive bilateral relations between China and the United States. The relationship also, and even much more depends on the American–China policy and overall American foreign policy today and in the future.

On the U.S. side, the development does not look quite positive. While there have been clear and strong evidences that Chinese foreign policy is changing into a more constructive direction, there has been little evidence that the American China policy and American foreign policy has been moving into a positive direction.

In fact, there is hardly anything really or substantially new in U.S. China policy since "9/11." There have been changes in agendas, topics, formats, and tactics in the American relationships with China and other countries. In the past 2 years since 9/11, Americans have emphasized antiterrorism in its relations with China and other countries. It demands and needs the cooperation with China and other countries in its war against terrorism. And the result is a common language and interests have become mainstream in U.S. foreign relations with China and other countries in the past 2 years.

However, those are tactical, not strategic, change. American leaders and officials have made this very clear in the past 2 years. In many statements given by the President, Vice President, Secretaries of Defense, States, National Security Adviser, and other high level officials, American side have made clear that the new priority of counter-terrorism does not mean the American view, strategy, and policy toward the outside world has changed very much. As far as China is concerned, the American view about China, policy goal toward China, positions on major issues with China such as Taiwan, human rights, nonproliferation, remain same or similar today as they were 2 years ago.

Therefore, the change of Chinese foreign policy principle is not strong enough to ensure a better relationship between China and the United States today and in the future. Long-term Sino-U.S. relations remain uncertain because the American China policy remains uncertain, if not remaining basically negative and hostile.

Taiwan Issue and China's Foreign Policy

There is also something unchanged on the Chinese side too. Neither the Chinese people nor their government have changed on Taiwan. Taiwan's independence is still unacceptable to the Chinese people and their leaders, and national reunification remains a grand dream and a national goal of the Chinese.

To the Chinese people and their government, Taiwan is an internal issue. However, it is also an important issue in China's relations with the United States, Japan, and other countries in Asia and the world. The Taiwan issue remains a fundamental part on which China judges American China strategy and policy. And the Chinese people and government remain determined to fight with Americans in every front of such a foundation of national sovereignty, security, and reunification issue. This position certainly will not always lead to a better and positive relationship with the outside world, especially with the United States on Chinese foreign relations and policies.

NOTES

1. "Jiang Defines Theme of CPC Congress," *China Daily*, November 9, 2002, p. 3.
2. See Hu Yaobang's report at the 12th, Zhao Zhiyang's report on the international situation and foreign policy section at the 13th, Jiang Zemin's report at the 14th and 15th CCP party congresses, documents published by Renmin (Peoples') Press in Beijing: 1982, 1987, 1992, 1997.
3. Ibid., p. 1.
4. The Chinese positions are stated with the following states: Zhao Huanxin: "Political solution Urged for Iraq Issue," *China Daily*, January 31, 2003, p. 1; "Tang Reiterates Position on Iraq Issue," *China Daily*, February 5, 2003, p. 1; "Jiang: UN Role Vital," *China Daily*, February 12, 2003, p. 1; "Weapons Probes Must Go On: Tang," *China Daily*, February 15, 2003, p. 1; "China Opposes New UN resolution on Iraq," *China Daily*, March 10, 2003; and "Top Legislators and Advisers Urge: 'Stop the Iraq War'," *China Daily*, March 22, 2003.

5. The official Chinese statements on North Korean nuclear issues since October 2002 can be seen from the following reports: Meng Yan: "Tang, Powell Talk about DPRK Issue," *China Daily*, January 10, 2003, p. 1; Guo Nei: "China Backs Non-Nuclearization of Peninsula," *China Daily*, January 16, 2003, p. 1; Hu Qihua: "Hopes for Peace Still Exist," *China Daily*, February 28, 2003, p. 1; and "Restraint Called for after DPRK Missile Test," *China Daily*, March 12, 2003, p. 1.

CHAPTER 8

THE IMPACT OF DOMESTIC POLITICS ON CHINESE FOREIGN POLICY

Xinning Song

THE KEY ELEMENT IN CHINESE DOMESTIC POLITICS

China has been an authoritarian state for hundreds of years. The Chinese Communist Party (CCP) does not change the basic nature of the state even though it has carried out domestic reform and opening-up policy in the last 24 years. Since 1978 when Deng Xiaoping started the economic reform and opening-up policy, great changes have been taking place in China. Economically, the market economy mechanism has come into existence, but politically there is still a single party system. There are hardliners and liberals in China who greatly dispute on China's domestic and foreign policies. But there is one point they always agree on: to maintain the ruling position of the CCP. When we look at the domestic politics of China, the rule of the Communist Party is the most important element. And it is this matter that directs the tendency and development of China's foreign policy.

Problem of the Legitimacy of Communist Party

Many Chinese believe that the major challenge to the CCP nowadays is the legitimacy of its ruling position. In the first 40 years of the People's Republic of China (PRC), the basis of the legitimacy of the CCP was neither public participation nor the social or economic welfare, but the charisma of the personal leadership (such as Mao Zedong and Deng Xiaoping), the ideology of Communism plus nationalism, and the centralized political system.

After the beginning of domestic reform and opening up to the outside world, the ideology of Communism has lost its base. Very few people in China care about the Communist future. Nationalism still works because of the Sino-US disputes in various issues. But it is also a challenge to the current leadership. Along with the market economy system, decentralization has become the common demand from the local levels. Mr. Jiang Zemin came into power on a very special occasion. He had no choice but to follow the direction of Deng Xiaoping, because his reputation as a Chinese leader is so popular among the ordinary Chinese people.

Although the Chinese Communist leadership is facing big challenges, most Chinese still believe that no other political forces can or should replace its ruling position, because it was the Communist Party of China who started the process of reform and open-up policy and has provided a better living standard to the Chinese people. It also means that the only legitimacy of the .CCP is the economic welfare. For the Communist Party of China, the only way to keep its ruling position is to keep the Chinese economy developing constantly.

Measures to Maintain the Legitimacy of the CPC

In order to maintain and intensify the legitimacy of the CCP, China's Communist leadership has put forward the so-called "Socialism with Chinese Characteristics."[1] The major feature of this slogan is to put economic development instead of class struggle as to priority for the CCP. Essentially Deng's theory is that everything should revolve around the economic development. After Deng Xiaoping, Jiang Zemin continues this strategy and goes even further. He put forward the so-called "Three Representations" and made some very important changes during the 16th Party Congress in November 2002.

First, the Communist Party of China is never a single class, but a party of the Chinese. In the Constitution of the CPC the nature of the Communist Party has been changed from the *pioneer of the working class to the pioneer of both the working class and the Chinese people, as well as the Chinese nation* (zhonghua minzu).[2]

Second, Communism is not the direct goal of the CCP. "Communism which is the highest idea can only be achieved on the basis of a fully and advanced developed Socialist society. The development and improvement of the Socialist system is a long-term historical process."[3] "China is in the premier stage of Socialism and will stay in this stage for a long time."[4] The CCPs major goal for the next 50 years is basic modernization, not advanced socialism.[5]

Third, economic development is still the priority of the Communist Party. The major goal of the CPC is to keep economic growth and construct a well-off society (xiaokang shehui) in China.

For Chinese leadership, foreign policy is a domestic politics continuation. It is determined by domestic politics and should serve the domestic politics and economics. Because of the legitimacy problem of the Communist Party in China, political stability is regarded as the most important issue in China. But how to maintain the political stability is questionable. To strengthen the so-called People's Democratic Dictatorship or go through economic development and economic welfare? The answer is the latter. Economic development is not only a matter of strengthening China's national capabilities, but also a matter of maintaining the ruling position of the Communist Party. That is the most basic issue of China's domestic position. Chinese foreign policy's major task is to construct a peaceful international environment for China's economic development.

OTHER ELEMENTS OF CHINA'S DOMESTIC POLITICS

Besides the legitimacy issue, there are other elements of domestic politics that impact China's foreign policy.

The Imbalance Between Economic Reform and Political Reform

The Chinese, including government leaders, realize that the political system in China does not adapt to the requirement of the market economy. But political reform is very difficult due to various reasons. It may exacerbate the legitimacy crisis of the CCP. There is very strong opposition from the left-wing and local officials, or certain interest groups. Although the 16th National Congress of the CCP restresses political reform and puts forward nine major tasks (such as upholding and improving the systems of socialist democracy; improving the socialist legal system; reforming and improving the Party's style of leadership and governance; reforming and improving the decision-making mechanism; deepening administrative restructuring; promoting reform of the judicial system; deepening the reform of the cadre and personnel system; tightening the restraint on and supervision over the use of powers, and maintaining social stability[6]), political reform in China will still be a slow and gradual process.

The Pluralist Tendency and Social Divergence in China

Because of the economic reform and introducing the market economy, there are more social divergences that have made China more pluralist than ever before. Nowadays there are at least three groups of people that have more influence on China's domestic politics.

First, private and public entrepreneurs. Many of them are already Communist Party members and have leading position in the national and local People's Congress or Political Consultant Conference. Some of them are representatives of the 16th Party Congress and became a major interviewing target of the medias.

Second, liberal intellectuals. Because of flexibility of the ideological control, Chinese scholars now have more freedom to express their ideas and have more chances to be involved in the policymaking procedures. They are more and more active in the process of economic and political reform process.

Third, the media. Although there is no real freedom of the press, the media have become more powerful and influential in Chinese domestic and international affairs. Some newspapers and TV programmes are very popular because of their discussion about the hot topics of economic and social issues (especially corruptions of the governmental officials).

These social groups have not intervened in China's political process directly but they have a strong social base and good connections with the governmental institutions. They could not be regarded as interests groups as such in the West but their functions have more and more political dimensions. Referring to foreign affairs, liberal intellectuals play the most important role. It is not only because they are involved in the policymaking process more and more directly but also because their nonideological thinking are changing the paradigms of foreign policymakers.

NONIDEOLOGICAL RETHINKING OF CHINESE FOREIGN POLICY

Since the late 1990s, the CCP has changed its priority to develop a tighter relationship with other developed countries, especially the United States and the European Union, due to China's dependency upon trade with the West and the foreign direct investments from the West. Chinese intellectuals in international studies are able to access the foreign policymaking process and have more freedom to do their research and express their views of foreign affairs. According to a few publications and many academic conferences and seminars in China and abroad, we can find the existence of a new nonideological rethinking from Chinese intellectuals. The new thinking refers to the following main topics:

Globalization

The Chinese government always stresses economic globalization and fears talking about political aspects of globalization. For intellectuals, globalization has to have economic, political, and cultural dimensions. The political dimension of globalization has three aspects:

First, globalization is either global capitalization or capitalist globalization. The political implication is that, the current historical *Era* is still Capitalist.[7] Capitalism will still be the dominant form of production and will last for a long period of time.[8]

Second, the globalization of the nation-state system. Many developing countries received the status of sovereign state just after World War II and the Western countries gradually entered into the post-sovereign stage. That is why there are such different views on sovereignty between developed and developing countries.

Third, the tendency of domestic reform to adapt the world capitalist market economy system. Political globalization is not necessary for every country to carry out the Western style liberal democracy. The main goal of the reform is to find a way that suits the reality or characteristics of the country and at the same time adapt the world market economy, to become a normal member of the international community.

Multipolarization

Multipolarization has been a slogan for Chinese leadership for many years. But what is its real meaning? There is no clear answer. Although Chinese leaders are still talking about "multipolarization," most of Chinese intellectuals realize that it is not the case for today and the near future. Some scholars argue that the so-called multipolarization is theoretically wrong and almost harmful. Economic globalization means the world is more and more interdependent rather than conflicted. In practice the emphasis on multipolarization will put China on an opposite position to the United States and its allies.

Chinese realize that the United States will remain the only global hegemonic power for decades to come. The Chinese policy analysts have few illusions about the feasibility of formulating a lasting international coalition that could serve the counterforce to U.S. power. China has neither the capability nor the desire to take the lead to formulate such a coalition, let alone confront the American hegemony by itself.

Contradiction and Cooperation

One of the traditional strategies of Chinese foreign policy is to find contradictions among others and make use of the contradiction for serving China's national interests. During the Cold War, there was contradiction between the United States and Soviet Union. The Chinese policy was to make use of the contradiction between two superpowers and played the game of so-called Great Triangular. A good example is the Three Worlds theory by Mao Zedong.

After the cold war many senior officials and scholars started to find a new major contradiction. Their conclusion was that after the collapse of the Soviet Union the major contradiction in the world would be the conflict between developed countries. That was the so-called North–North Contradiction. China should make use of it to crush down economic and political sanction upon China after Tiananmen in 1989. This strategy was strongly criticized by many liberal intellectuals.

The argument is that, the development of economic globalization and the further development of Capitalism in the world has made developed countries more interdependent and closer. In order to maintain economic growth and domestic social stability, China has to have a good relationship and cooperation with developed countries. China's major strategy in dealing with the West was not to find contradiction among others but to find common interests between China and other Western country, Sino-US, Sino-European or Sino-Japanese.[9]

International Institutions and World Community

How to deal with the international institutions or international regimes is one of the major issues for China's open-up policy. During the later 1980s,

China had a big debate on whether or not China should get into the greater circulation of the world economy. It had great impact on China's application process for entering into the GATT and later the WTO. The question was that whether China should integrate or be integrated into the Capitalist world economy.

Since the later 1990s cooperation with the international institutions, especially the international economic organizations, has been the major choice for China. Related to the issues mentioned before, Chinese intellectuals and policy analysts emphasize that if China wants to keep economic growth and maintain domestic stability we have to keep a good relationship with the developed countries and the international institutions that are dominated by the West.

Another domestic political issue is that if China would like to speed up its domestic political reform, working with international institutions and introducing international regulation into China is a good way. That is to make use of the external pressure to serve the domestic political demand. A good example is China's accession to the World Trade Organization (WTO). Many Chinese higher rank officials recognized that one of the benefits for China to join the WTO is to speed up the restructuring of China's governmental, administrative and legal system. For many Chinese intellectuals, the political implication accession to the WTO is much more important than the economic benefits.

Perspective on Chinese Foreign Policy

As mentioned before, the key issue of China's domestic politics is the legitimacy of the Communist Party in China. The way to result or maintain the legitimacy of the CPC is to keep economic growth and to provide more economic and social welfare to the Chinese people. The major task of Chinese foreign policy is to serve China's largest political.

Another impact of domestic change on Chinese foreign policy is the social pluralization within China. But the main forces that can affect Chinese foreign policymaking are intellectuals and intellectual governmental officials due to the personnel change of Chinese governmental institutions. The Chinese foreign policy will go toward a more cooperative and constructive direction.

Cooperation with the West as the Priority

One of the big changes in the 16th Party Congress was to put the relationship and cooperation with the developed countries as the first priority instead of the last one, as in the 15th Party Congress. The major reason for this change is because of China's tight economic connection with the West instead of the South. Currently more than half of the Chinese foreign trade is with the developed countries, especially exporting. Nowadays, the United States is first and the European Union is second exporting market to China.

More and more foreign direct investments and governmental loans are coming from the West.

Another element of China's priority toward the West is the relationship with the major international institutions. China realizes that we must participate and work with the international institutions and also that most international institutions, especially major international economic institutions such as the WTO, IMF, and World Bank are dominated by the West. Without good relationship with the West it is impossible for China to get more benefits from the world economy.

Referring to economic globalization, this tendency is to enlarge the gaps between developed and developing countries. China would not like to be marginalized in the process of globalization but rather closer to the centre of the world economy. Although China still criticizes the old and unfair international order and proposes to establish a new one, China recognizes and accepts the current world order and would like to keep it stable.

Among the developed countries, the most important relationship for China is still the United States. The United States has not only the biggest economic partnership with China and is regarded as the major potential threat to China because of the Taiwan issues. China recognizes the American hegemonic power in world political economy and would not like to have confrontation with it.

The European Union will be the second priority for China's foreign relations. The EU–China relationship is the best bilateral relations China has with the outside world. It is not just because of the common economic and strategic interests but also some very special political interests for China's domestic politics. It may include: (1) The political system, especially the party system and pattern in Europe are more acceptable for the Chinese. That is one of the major reasons why there are no strong negative reactions from the Chinese side to the EU efforts of promoting democracy, human rights, civil society, and rule of law in China. The same efforts by the Americans are always criticized by the Chinese as an intervention in domestic affairs of China. (2) The EU integration model has more relevance to China for solving its own domestic problem, such as the regional gap between the eastern and western parts of China. (3) The social welfare reform in Europe can be followed by China to establish its own social security system. In sum, many Chinese have such consensus that there are lot of things which the Chinese can learn and benefit from the European experiences.

Good Neighborly Relationship and Partnership with Neighboring Countries with the Priority of Regional Cooperation

In the 15th Party Congress, the Chinese government placed the Good-neighboring policy at first priority. During the 16th Party Congress it became the second. But there is one new element: to step up regional cooperation and bring our exchanges and cooperation with our surrounding countries to a new height. That means China will try its best to develop its relationship with neighboring countries by way of regional cooperation. China is now more active than ever before on regional cooperation in East Asia. China participates in ARF and ASEAN plus three other consecutively. China makes a big effort to reinforce the Shanghai Cooperation Organization. China has made obvious progress on the ASEAN–China free trade area.

Political Cooperation and Economic Competition with the Third World Countries

China has gradually changed its policy toward developing countries since the 1997 15th Party Congress: since then, China has never emphasized relationships with Third World countries as a standing base. One of the major debates for China's foreign relations, after accession into the WTO, is China's relationship with Third World countries. China has a dilemma in dealing with the developing countries: politically, China needs their support, especially Taiwan and on Human Rights issues; economically China has inevitably competition with them, especially in the American and European markets.

The basic policy toward Third World countries would be political cooperation and economic cooperation plus competition. Jiang Zemin speech in his political Report to the 16th Party Congress mentioned this: "We will continue to enhance our solidarity and cooperation with other Third World countries, increase mutual understanding and trust and strengthen mutual help and support. We will enlarge areas of cooperation and make it more fruitful."

APPENDIX I

Table AI.1 Terminology changes from the 15th Party Congress to the 16th Party Congress

	The 15th Party Congress	*The 16th Party Congress*
Nature of the Communist Party of China	The CPC is the pioneer of the Chinese working class.	The CPC is the pioneer of the Chinese working class, and at the same time it is the pioneer of the Chinese people and Chinese nation.
Ultimate goal of CPC	The ultimate goal of the CPC is to achieve the Communist social system.	The ultimate goal of the CPC is to achieve Communism.
The tendency of Socialism replaces Capitalism	Socialism is bound to replace Capitalism. It is an unchangeable tendency of social history development.	No mention.
Development stage of Socialism in China	We are in the primary stage of Socialism. It will take hundreds of years.	We are in, and will stay in for a long period of time, the primary stage of Socialism. It will take hundreds of years.

Table AI.1 Continued

	The 15th Party Congress	The 16th Party Congress
Civilization buildings	Material civilization. Spirit of civilization.	Material civilization. Political civilization (democracy and rule by law). Spirit of civilization.
The World War	It is possible to avoid a new world war in certain long periods of time.	The new world war will not occur in the foreseeable future.
Multipolarization	The tendency of multipolarization has a new development in politics and economics, either globally or regionally.	The trends toward world multipolarization and economic globalization are developing amidst twists and turns. The growing trends toward world multipolarization and economic globalization have brought with them opportunities and favorable conditions for world peace and development.
Hegemony and power politics	The cold war thinking remains. The hegemony and power politics is still the major origin of the threats to world peace and stability.	Hegemonism and power politics have new manifestations.
Anti-hegemony and power politics	We must oppose hegemony and assert world peace. No one could use force and threats to use force, or intervene in another country's internal affairs for any reason, or invade, oppress, and subvert others. We will not force others to accept our social system and ideology. We will not allow others to force us to accept their social system and ideology.	We stand for going along with the historical tide and safeguarding the common interests of mankind. We are ready to work with the international community to boost world multipolarization, promote a harmonious coexistence of diverse forces and maintain stability in the international community. We would like to work with the world community to promote the world multipolarity, to push the harmonic coexistence of different powers and keep world society stable. We will promote development of economic globalization in a direction conducive to common prosperity, draw on its advantages and avoid its disadvantages so that all countries, particularly developing countries, can benefit from the process.
The new world order	The current unfair world order is damaging the interests of the developing countries.	The old international political and economic order, which is unfair and irrational, has yet to be changed fundamentally. Uncertainties affecting peace and development are on

Table AI.1   Continued

	The 15th Party Congress	The 16th Party Congress
		the rise. The elements of traditional and nontraditional threats to security are intertwined, and the scourge of terrorism is more acutely felt.
Intervention of internal affairs	No one could intervene in another country's internal affairs in any reason, or invade, oppress for, and subvert others.	Politically all countries should respect and consult one another and should not seek to impose their will on others. Economically they should complement one another and pursue common development and should not create a polarization of wealth. Culturally they should learn from one another and work for common prosperity and should not exclude cultures of other nations.
Priority of Chinese foreign relations	1. Keep good relationships with the neighboring countries. 2. Strengthen unity and cooperation with developing countries. 3. Continue to improve and system develop relationships with the developed countries under the basis of the Five Principles Peaceful Co-existence	1. Continue to improve and develop the relationship with the developed countries. Put the fundamental interests of each country as first priority, no matter how different their social and ideology. 2. Continue to cement friendly ties with our neighbors and persist in building a of good-neighbor relationship and partnership with them. 3. Continue to enhance our solidarity and cooperation with other third world countries.
China and Hegemony	The development of China will not be a threat to any country. After China is developed in the future, it will never seek hegemony.	We oppose all forms of hegemonism and power politics. China will never seek hegemony and never go in for expansion.

Appendix II: Build a Well-off Society in an All-Round Way and Create a New Situation in Building Socialism with Chinese Characteristics

Mr. Jiang Zemin's Political Report at the 16th Party Congress

The theme of the congress is to hold high the great banner of Deng Xiaoping Theory, fully act on the important thought of Three Represents, carry forward our cause into the future, keep pace with the times, build a well-off society in an all-round way, speed up socialist modernization, and work hard to create a new situation in building socialism with Chinese characteristics.

As human society entered the twenty-first century, we started a new phase of development for building a well-off society in an all-round way and speeding up socialist modernization. The international situation is undergoing profound changes. The trends toward world multipolarization and economic globalization are developing amidst twists and turns. Science and technology are advancing rapidly. Competition in overall national strength is becoming increasingly fierce. Given this pressing situation, we must move forward, or we will fall behind. Our Party must stand firm in the forefront of the times and unite with and lead the Chinese people of all ethnic groups in accomplishing the three major historical tasks: to propel the modernization drive, to achieve national reunification and to safeguard world peace and promote common development, and in bringing about the great rejuvenation of the Chinese nation on its road to socialism with Chinese characteristics. This is a grand mission history and the era have entrusted to our Party.

Implement the Important Thought of Three Represents in an All-Round Way

To open up new prospects for the cause of socialism with Chinese characteristics, we must hold high the great banner of Deng Xiaoping Theory and implement the important thought of Three Represents. As a continuation and development of Marxism–Leninism, Mao Zedong Thought and Deng Xiaoping Theory, this important thought reflects new requirements for the work of the Party and state arising from the changes in China and other parts of the world today. It is a powerful theoretical weapon for strengthening and improving Party building and promoting self-improvement and development of socialism in China. It is the crystallization of the Party's collective wisdom and a guiding ideology the Party must follow for a long time to come. Persistent implementation of the "Three Represents" is the foundation for building our Party, the cornerstone for its governance, and the source of its strength.

The important thought of Three Represents has been put forward on the basis of a scientific judgment of the Party's historical position. Having gone through the revolution, reconstruction, and reform, our Party has evolved from a party that led the people in fighting for state power to a party that has led the people in exercising the power and has long remained in power. It has developed from a party that led national reconstruction under external blockade and a planned economy to a party that is leading national development while the country is opening to the outside world and developing a socialist market economy. Keeping in mind the past, present, and future of China and other parts of the world, we must accurately comprehend the characteristics of the times and the Party's tasks, scientifically formulate and correctly implement the Party's line, principles and policies, and study and settle questions concerning the promotion of China's social progress and the improvement of Party building. We should neither approach questions out of their historical context nor lose our bearings, and we should neither fall behind the times nor skip the stages, so as to ensure that our cause will advance from victory to victory.

The implementation of the important thought of Three Represents is, in essence, to keep pace with the times, maintain the Party's progressiveness and exercise the state power in the interest of the people. All Party members must be keenly aware of this basic requirement and become more conscious and determined in implementing this important thought.

1. To carry out the important thought of Three Represents, the whole Party must maintain the spirit of keeping pace with the times and blaze new trails for the development of the Marxist theory.
2. To carry out the important thought of Three Represents, it is essential for the Party to give top priority to development in governing and rejuvenating the country and open up new prospects for the modernization drive. A Marxist ruling party must attach great importance to the liberation and development of the productive forces. Without development, it would be impossible to maintain the progressiveness of the Party, give play to the superiority of the socialist system, and make the people rich and the country strong.

   In China, a large developing country with a backward economy and culture, where our Party is leading the people in the modernization drive, a good solution to the problem of development has a direct bearing on the trend of popular sentiment and the success of our cause. Shouldering the historical responsibility to propel the Chinese society, the Party must always keep a firm grip on development— the top priority for its governance and rejuvenation of the country.

   Development requires that we always concentrate on economic growth, base ourselves on China's realities, conform to the trend of the times and continue to explore new ways to promote the progress of the advanced productive forces and culture. Development requires that we uphold and deepen the reform.
3. To carry out the important thought of Three Represents, it is essential to bring all positive factors into full play and bring new forces to the great cause of rejuvenating the Chinese nation.
4. To carry out the important thought of Three Represents, it is essential to push forward Party building in a spirit of reform and instill new vitality in the Party.

Objectives of Building a Well-off Society in an All-Round Way

An overview of the situation shows that for our country, the first two decades of the twenty-first century are a period of important strategic opportunities, which we must seize tightly and which offers bright prospects. In accordance with the development objectives up to 2010, the centenary of the Party and that of New China, as proposed at the 15th National Congress, we need to concentrate on building a well-off society of a higher standard in an all-round way to the benefit of well over one billion people in this period. We will further develop the economy, improve democracy, advance science and education, enrich culture, foster social harmony, and upgrade the texture of life for the people. The two decades of development will serve as an inevitable connecting link for attaining the third-step strategic objectives for our modernization drive as well as a key stage for improving the socialist market economy and opening wider to the outside world. Building on what is achieved at this stage and continuing to work for several more decades, we will have in the main accomplished the modernization program and turned China into a strong, prosperous, democratic, and culturally advanced socialist country by the middle of this century.

The objectives of building a well-off society in an all-round way
—On the basis of optimized structure and better economic returns, efforts will be made to quadruple the GDP of the year 2000 by 2020, and China's overall national

strength and international competitiveness will increase markedly. We will in the main achieve industrialization and establish a full-fledged socialist market economy and a more open and viable economic system. The proportion of urban population will go up considerably and the trend of widening differences between industry and agriculture, between urban and rural areas, and between regions will be reversed step by step. We will have a fairly sound social security system. There will be a higher rate of employment. People will have more family property and lead a more prosperous life.

—Socialist democracy and the legal system will be further improved. The basic principle of ruling the country by law will be implemented completely. The political, economic and cultural rights, and interests of the people will be respected, and guaranteed in real earnest. Democracy at the grassroots level will be better practiced. People will enjoy a sound public order and live and work in peace and contentment.

—The ideological and ethical standards, the scientific and cultural qualities, and the health of the whole people will be enhanced notably. A sound modern national educational system, scientific, technological, and cultural innovation systems as well as nationwide fitness and medical and health systems will take shape. People will have access to better education. We will make senior secondary education basically universal in the country and eliminate illiteracy. A learning society in which all the people will learn or even pursue life-long education will emerge to boost their all-round development.

—The capability of sustainable development will be steadily enhanced. The ecological environment will be improved. The efficiency of using resources will be increased significantly. We will enhance harmony between man and nature to push the whole society onto a path to civilized development featuring the growth of production, an affluent life and a sound ecosystem.

Economic Development and Restructuring

1. Take a new road to industrialization and implement the strategy of rejuvenating the country through science and education and that of sustainable development.
2. Make the rural economy flourish and speed up urbanization.
3. Advance the development of the western region and bring about a coordinated development of regional economies.
4. Stick to and improve the basic economic system and deepen the reform of the state property management system.
5. Improve the modern market system and tighten and improve macroeconomic control.
6. Deepen the reform of the income distribution system and improve the social security system.
7. Do a better job in opening up by "bringing in" and "going out."
8. Do everything possible to create more jobs and improve the people's lives.

Political Development and Restructuring

Developing socialist democracy and establishing a socialist political civilization are an important goal for building a well-off society in an all-round way. Adhering to the Four Cardinal Principles, we must go on steadily and surely with political restructuring, extend socialist democracy, and improve the socialist legal system in order to build a socialist country under the rule of law and consolidate and develop the political situation characterized by democracy, solidarity, liveliness, stability, and harmony.

Our Party has always deemed it its duty to realize and develop people's democracy. Since the beginning of reform and opening up, we have pressed on with political restructuring and improved socialist democracy. The key to developing socialist democracy is to combine the need to uphold the Party's leadership and to ensure that the people are the masters of the country with the need to rule the country by law. Leadership by the Party is the fundamental guarantee that the people are the masters of the country and that the country is ruled by law. The people being the masters of the country constitutes the essential requirement of socialist democracy. Ruling the country by law is the basic principle the Party pursues while it leads the people in running the country. The CPC is the core of leadership for the cause of socialism with Chinese characteristics. Governance by the Communist Party means that it leads and supports the people in acting as the masters of the country and mobilizes and organizes them on a most extensive scale to manage state and social affairs and economic and cultural undertakings according to law, safeguarding and realizing their fundamental interests. The Constitution and other laws embody the unity of the Party's views and the people's will. All organizations and individuals must act in strict accordance with the law, and none of them are allowed to have the privilege to overstep the Constitution and other laws.

Political restructuring is the self-improvement and development of the socialist political system. It must help enhance the vitality of the Party and state, demonstrate the features and advantages of the socialist system, give full scope to the initiative and creativity of the people, safeguard national unity, ethnic solidarity and social stability, and promote economic development and social progress. We must always proceed from our national conditions, review our experience gained in practice and at the same time learn from the achievements of political civilization of mankind. We should never copy any models of the political system of the West. We must concentrate on institutional improvement and ensure that socialist democracy is institutionalized and standardized and has its procedures.

Uphold and improve the systems of socialist democracy. It is essential to improve the systems of democracy, develop diverse forms of democracy, expand citizens' participation in political affairs in an orderly way, and ensure that the people go in for democratic elections and decision-making, exercise democratic management and supervision according to law and enjoy extensive rights and freedoms, and that human rights are respected and guaranteed. We should uphold and improve the system of people's congresses and ensure that the congresses and their standing committees exercise their functions according to law and that their legislation and policy decisions better embody the people's will. We should optimize the composition of the standing committees. We should uphold and improve the system of multiparty cooperation and political consultation under the leadership of the Communist Party. We should uphold the principle of "long-term coexistence, mutual supervision, treating each other with all sincerity and sharing weal and woe," step up our cooperation with the democratic parties and better display the features and advantages of the Chinese socialist system of political parties. We will ensure that the Chinese People's Political Consultative Conference (CPPCC) plays its role in political consultation, democratic supervision, and participation in and deliberation of state affairs. We will consolidate and develop the broadest possible patriotic united front. We will fully implement the Party's policy toward ethnic minorities, uphold and improve the system of regional ethnic autonomy, consolidate and enhance socialist ethnic relations of equality, solidarity, and mutual assistance, and promote common prosperity and progress for all our ethnic groups. We will implement the Party's policy toward the freedom of religious belief, handle religious affairs according to law, encourage the adaptability of religions to the socialist society and uphold the principle of self-administration and running religious affairs independently. We will conscientiously carry out the Party's policy toward overseas Chinese affairs.

Extending democracy at the grassroots level is the groundwork for developing socialist democracy. We will improve grassroots self-governing organizations, their democratic management system and the system of keeping the public informed of matters being handled, and ensure that the people directly exercise their democratic rights according to law, manage grassroots public affairs and programs for public good and exercise democratic supervision over the cadres. We will improve self-governance among villagers and foster a mechanism of their self-governance full of vitality under the leadership of village Party organizations. We will improve self-governance among urban residents and build new-type and well-managed communities featuring civility and harmony. We will uphold and improve the system of workers' conferences and other democratic management systems in enterprises and institutions and protect the legitimate rights and interests of workers.

Improve the socialist legal system. We must see to it that there are laws to go by, the laws are observed and strictly enforced, and law-breakers are prosecuted. To adapt to the new situation characterized by the development of a socialist market economy, all-round social progress and China's accession to the WTO, we will strengthen legislation and improve its quality and will have formulated a socialist system of laws with Chinese characteristics by the year 2010. We must see to it that all people are equal before the law. We should tighten supervision over law enforcement, promote the exercise of administrative functions according to law, safeguard judicial justice and raise the level of law enforcement so that laws are strictly implemented. We must safeguard the uniformity and sanctity of the legal system and prevent or overcome local and departmental protectionism. We will extend and standardize legal services and provide effective legal aid. We should give more publicity to the legal system so that the people are better educated in law. In particular, we will enhance the public servants' awareness of law and their ability to perform their official duties according to law. Party members and cadres, especially leading cadres, should play an exemplary role in abiding by the Constitution and other laws.

Reform and improve the Party's style of leadership and governance. This is a matter of overall significance to improving socialist democracy. Leadership by the Party mainly refers to its political, ideological, and organizational leadership. The Party exercises leadership over the state and society by formulating major principles and policies, making suggestions on legislation, recommending cadres for important positions, conducting ideological publicity, giving play to the role of Party organizations and members, and persisting in exercising state power according to law. Party committees, playing the role as the core of leadership among all other organizations at corresponding levels, should concentrate on handling important matters and support those organizations in assuming their responsibilities independently and making concerted efforts in their work. We will further reform and improve the Party's working organs and mechanisms. Acting on the principle that the Party commands the overall situation and coordinates the efforts of all quarters, we will standardize relations between Party committees on the one hand and people's congresses, governments,

CPPCC committees, and mass organizations on the other. We will support people's congresses in performing their functions as organs of state power according to law, in ensuring that the Party's views become the will of the state and that candidates recommended by Party organizations become leading cadres of the organs of state power through legal procedures, and in exercising supervision over them. We will support the government in fulfilling its legal functions and performing its official duties according to law. We will support CPPCC committees in performing their functions by centering on the two major subjects of unity and democracy. We will strengthen the Party's leadership over trade unions, the Communist Youth League organizations, women's federations, and other mass organizations and support them in working according to law and their own constitutions and acting as a bridge between the Party and the people.

Reform and improve the decision-making mechanism. Correct decision-making is an important prerequisite for success in all work. We will improve the decision-making mechanism by which decision-makers will go deep among the people and get to know how they are faring, reflect their will, pool their wisdom and value their resources, putting decision-making on a more scientific and democratic basis. Decision-making organs at all levels should improve the rules and procedures for taking major policy decisions, establish a system of reporting social conditions and public opinion, a system of keeping the public informed and a system of public hearings on major issues closely related to the interests of the people, perfect the expert consulting system and implement a verification system and a responsibility system in making policy decisions with a view to preventing arbitrary decision-making.

Deepen administrative restructuring. We should further change the functions of the government, improve the methods of management, introduce e-government, uplift administrative efficiency, and reduce costs so as to form an administrative system featuring standardized behaviors, coordinated operation, fairness and transparency, honesty and high efficiency. We should standardize the functions and powers of the Central government and local authorities according to law and properly handle relations between the departments directly under the Central government and the local governments. Following the principle of simplification, uniformity, and efficiency and meeting the requirements of coordination in decision-making, execution, and supervision, we will continue to promote the restructuring of government departments, standardize their functions in a scientific manner, rationalize their setups, and optimize their composition in order to delimit the structures and sizes statutorily and solve the problems of too many levels, overlapping functions, overstaffing, divorce between powers and responsibilities, and duplicate law enforcement. We will reform the management system of institutions in accordance with the principle of separating the functions of government from those of institutions.

Promote the reform of the judicial system. A socialist judicial system must guarantee fairness and justice in the whole society. In accordance with the requirements of judicial justice and strict law enforcement, we should improve the setups of judicial organs, the delimitation of their functions and powers and their management systems so as to form a sound judicial system featuring clearly specified powers and responsibilities, mutual coordination and restraint, and highly efficient operation. We should institutionally ensure that the judicial and procuratorial organs are in a position to exercise adjudicative and procuratorial powers independently and impartially according to law. We should improve judicial proceedings and protect the legitimate rights and interests of citizens and legal persons. We should solve the problem of difficult enforcement of judgments. We should reform the working mechanisms of judicial organs and the management system of their human, financial, and material resources and gradually separate their judicial adjudication and procuratorial work from their administrative affairs. We will tighten supervision over the judicial work and punish corruption in this field. We will build up a contingent of judicial personnel who are politically steadfast and professionally competent, have a fine style of work and enforce laws impartially.

Deepen the reform of the cadre and personnel system. Efforts should be made to form a vigorous personnel mechanism under which we can gather large numbers of talented people, put them to the best use and get them prepared for both promotion and demotion, calling them to the service of the Party and state. In reforming and perfecting the cadre and personnel system and improving the system of public servants, we should focus on establishing a sound mechanism of selection, appointment, management, and supervision, with a view to making it scientific, democratic, and institutionalized. In the matter of cadre selection and appointment, Party members and ordinary people should have more right to know, to participate, to choose, and to supervise. With regard to leading cadres of the Party and government, it is necessary to implement the system of fixed tenures, the system of rezignation and the system of accountability for neglect of supervisory duty or the use of the wrong person. It is necessary to improve the system of giving cadres both positions and ranks and establish an incentive and guarantee mechanism for them. We should explore and improve the system of classified management of cadres and personnel in Party and government organs, institutions and enterprises. We should reform and improve the system of dual control over cadres. We should break with the notions and practices of overstressing seniority in the matter of selection and appointment, encourage the rational flow of trained people and create a sound environment which makes it possible for outstanding people to come to the fore in all fields.

Tighten the restraint on and supervision over the use of power. We should establish a mechanism for the exercise of power featuring reasonable structure, scientific distribution, rigorous procedures, and effective restraint so as to tighten supervision over power in terms of decision-making, execution, and other links and ensure that the power entrusted to us by the people is truly exercised for their benefits. We should focus on tightening supervision over leading cadres and especially principal ones, stepping up supervision over the management and use of human, financial, and material resources. We should tighten internal supervision of leading groups and improve the procedures for deciding on important matters and the appointment or dismissal of cadres in important positions. We should reform and improve the system of Party discipline inspection and introduce and improve the system of inspection tours. We should give play to the role of judicial, administrative supervision and auditing organs, and other functional departments. We should implement the system under which leading cadres report in various ways on their work and their efforts to perform their duties honestly, and improve the systems of reporting on important matters, of making inquiries and of democratic appraisal. We should conscientiously implement the system of making government affairs known to the public. We should tighten organizational and democratic supervision and give play to the supervisory function of the media.

Maintain social stability. To accomplish the heavy tasks of reform and development, we must have a harmonious and stable social climate for a long time to come. Party committees and governments at all levels should enthusiastically help the people solve practical problems they may confront in their work and life. They must carry out in-depth investigations and study, strengthen ideological and political work in light of different cases, and employ economic, administrative, and legal means to handle the contradictions among the people properly, those involving their immediate interests in particular, so as to maintain stability and unity. It is essential to improve procuratorial, judicial, and public security work, cracking down on criminal activities according to law, guarding against and punishing crimes committed by evil cult gangs and eliminating social evils so as to ensure the safety of the lives and property of the people. We must combine punishment and prevention, with emphasis on the latter, take comprehensive measures to maintain law and order, and improve social management so as to keep public order. We must strengthen state security, keeping vigilance against infiltrative, subversive, and separatist activities by hostile forces at home and abroad.

Socialist democracy enjoys strong vitality and superiority. The CPC and the Chinese people have full confidence in the road to political development they have chosen and will press ahead with political development under socialism with Chinese characteristics.

National Defense and Army Building

Strengthening our national defense is a strategic task in our modernization drive and an important guarantee for safeguarding our national security and unity and building a well-off society in an all-round way. We must uphold the principle of coordinated development of national defense and the economy and push forward the modernization of national defense and the army on the basis of economic growth.

"One Country, Two Systems" and Complete National Reunification

To achieve complete reunification of the motherland is a common aspiration of all sons and daughters of the Chinese nation both at home and abroad. We have successfully resolved the questions of Hong Kong and Macao and are striving for an early settlement of the question of Taiwan and for the accomplishment of the great cause of national reunification.

We will adhere to the basic principles of "peaceful reunification" and "one country, two systems" and the eight-point proposal on developing cross-Straits relations and advancing the process of peaceful national reunification at the present stage.

Adherence to the one-China principle is the basis for the development of cross-Straits relations and the realization of peaceful reunification.

We place our hopes on the people in Taiwan for the settlement of the Taiwan question and the realization of the complete reunification of China.

"One country, two systems" is the best way for the reunification between the two sides.

The 23 million Taiwan compatriots are our brothers and sisters of the same blood. No one is more eager than we are to resolve the Taiwan question through peaceful means. We will continue to implement the basic principles of "peaceful reunification" and "one country, two systems" and act on the eight-point proposal. We will work in utmost sincerity and do all we can to strive for a peaceful reunification. Our position of never undertaking to renounce the use of force is not directed at our Taiwan compatriots. It is aimed at the foreign forces' attempts to interfere in China's reunification and the Taiwan separatist forces' schemes for "Taiwan independence." To safeguard national unity bears on the fundamental interests of the Chinese nation. We Chinese people will safeguard our state sovereignty and territorial integrity with firm resolve. We will never allow anyone to separate Taiwan from China in any way.

China will be reunified, and the Chinese nation will be rejuvenated. The Taiwan question must not be allowed to drag on indefinitely. We are convinced that with the concerted efforts of all sons and daughters of the Chinese nation, the complete reunification of the motherland will be achieved at an early date.

The International Situation and Our External Work

Peace and development remain the themes of our era. To preserve peace and promote development bears on the well-being of all nations and represents the common aspirations of all peoples. It is an irresistible trend of history. The growing trends toward world multipolarization and economic globalization have brought with them opportunities and favorable conditions for world peace and development. A new world war is unlikely in the foreseeable future. It is realistic to bring about a fairly long period of peace in the world and a favorable climate in areas around China.

However, the old international political and economic order, which is unfair and irrational, has yet to be changed fundamentally. Uncertainties affecting peace and development are on the rise. The elements of traditional and nontraditional threats to security are intertwined, and the scourge of terrorism is more acutely felt. Hegemonism and power politics have new manifestations. Local conflicts triggered by ethnic or religious contradictions and border or territorial disputes have cropped up from time to time. The North–South gap is widening. The world is far from being tranquil and mankind is faced with many grave challenges.

No matter how the international situation changes, we will, as always, pursue the independent foreign policy of peace. The purpose of China's foreign policy is to maintain world peace and promote common development. We are ready to work with all nations to advance the lofty cause of world peace and development.

We stand for going along with the historical tide and safeguarding the common interests of mankind. We are ready to work with the international community to boost world multipolarization, promote a harmonious coexistence of diverse forces and maintain stability in the international community. We will promote the development of economic globalization in a direction conducive to common prosperity, draw on its advantages and avoid its disadvantages so that all countries, particularly developing countries, can benefit from the process.

We stand for establishing a new international political and economic order that is fair and rational. Politically all countries should respect and consult one another and should not seek to impose their will on others. Economically they should complement one another and pursue common development and should not create a polarization of wealth. Culturally they should learn from one another and work for common prosperity and should not exclude cultures of other nations. In the area of security, countries should trust one another and work together to maintain security, foster a new security concept featuring mutual trust, mutual benefit, equality and coordination, and settle their disputes through dialogue and cooperation and should not resort to the use or threat of force. We oppose all forms of hegemonism and power politics. China will never seek hegemony and never go in for expansion.

We stand for maintaining the diversity of the world and are in favor of promoting democracy in international relations and diversifying development models. Ours is a colorful world. Countries having different civilizations and social systems and taking different roads to development should respect one another and draw upon one another's strong points through competition and comparison and should develop side by side by seeking common ground while shelving differences. The affairs of each country should be left to the people of that country to decide. World affairs should be determined by all countries concerned through consultations on the basis of equality.

We stand for fighting against terrorism of all forms. It is imperative to strengthen international cooperation in this regard, address both the symptoms and root causes of terrorism, prevent and combat terrorist activities, and work hard to eliminate terrorism at root.

We will continue to improve and develop relations with the developed countries. Proceeding from the fundamental interests of the people of all countries concerned, we will broaden the converging points of common interests and properly settle differences on the basis of the Five Principles of Peaceful Coexistence, notwithstanding the differences in social system and ideology.

We will continue to cement our friendly ties with our neighbors and persist in building a good-neighborly relationship and partnership with them. We will step up regional cooperation and bring our exchanges and cooperation with our surrounding countries to a new height.

We will continue to enhance our solidarity and cooperation with other Third World countries, increase mutual understanding and trust, and strengthen mutual help and support. We will enlarge areas of cooperation and make it more fruitful.

We will continue to take an active part in multilateral diplomatic activities and play our role in the United Nations and other international or regional organizations. We will support other developing countries in their efforts to safeguard their legitimate rights and interests.

We will continue to develop exchanges and cooperation with political parties and organizations of all countries and regions on the principles of independence, complete equality, mutual respect, and noninterference in each other's internal affairs.

We will continue to carry out extensive people-to-people diplomacy, expand cultural exchanges with the outside world, enhance the friendship between peoples, and propel the development of state-to-state relations.

The world is marching toward brightness and progress. The road is tortuous, but the future is bright. The forces for peace, justice, and progress are invincible after all.

NOTES

1. Many Chinese define the Socialism with Chinese Characteristics as the Capitalism lead by the Communist Party, or Capitalism in economics (market economy) and Socialism in politics (one party system).
2. *Constitution of the Chinese Communist Party* (Beijing: The People's Press, 2002), p. 1.
3. Ibid.
4. *Jiang Zemin's Report at the 16th National Congress of the Chinese Communist Party* (Beijing: The People's Press, 2002), p. 18.
5. *Constitution of the Chinese Communist Party* (Beijing: The People's Press, 2002), p. 4.
6. During the 15th Party Congress, the CCP mentioned only five tasks of political reform, which included improving democratic system; promoting institutional reform; improving democratic supervision mechanism; and maintaining stability and unity.

7. Chinese always talk about the ERA of historical development. There were big debates on the issues during 1980s and continuous discussion before the 16th Party Congress. In the Political Report of Jiang Zemin on the 16th Party Congress, he mentioned only the main theme of the ERA are peace and development. But he did not answer what is the ERA.
8. Both the Political Report of Jiang Zemin on the 16th Party Congress and the new Party Constitution do not mention the inevitable tendency of the replacement of Socialism on Capitalism, but emphasize that, "We are in and will stay in for a long period of time the primary stage of the Socialism. It will take hundreds of years."
9. In the 16th Party Congress, the Chinese government has put the good relationship and cooperation with developed countries as the first priority.

C H A P T E R   9

LEADERSHIP TRANSITION AND NEW FOREIGN POLICY ORIENTATION

Guoli Liu

Leadership transition often leads to new foreign policy orientation. Following Deng Xiaoping's emergence as the top leader of China in 1978, Chinese foreign policy experienced a series of fundamental changes in principle and substance. The rise of Mikhail Gorbachev in 1985 with his "new political thinking" led to radical restructuring of Soviet foreign policy. When George W. Bush became the President of the United States in 2001, neorealism and unilateralism quickly replaced Bill Clinton's neoliberalism and multilateralism. Political scientist Robert Putnam examined close links between domestic politics and foreign relations.[1] In almost all the countries regardless of their regime types, foreign policies tend to be affected by changeover of the national leadership.

In 2002–03, China experienced a significant leadership transition. By carefully examining leadership transition and new policy development, this research expects to demonstrate change and continuity in Chinese foreign policy. Social scientists are puzzled by the intriguing yet critical links between leadership transition and foreign policy restructuring.[2] There is no definitive theory about under what conditions leadership transition will lead to fundamental change in foreign policy. It is reasonable to argue that a smooth power transition may result in more continuity than change in foreign policy. Over the long run, however, new leaders are most likely to change with times and make their marks on foreign policy. Keeping in mind the challenge of predicting any fundamental change in China's foreign policy orientation, this case study is designed to deepen our understanding of the connections between leadership transition and foreign policy change.

LEADERSHIP TRANSITION IN 2002–03

In 2002–03, China experienced a significant yet incomplete transition of power from the third generation of leaders to the fourth generation.[3] The rise of a new generation of leaders is the most significant development of the 16th Communist Party of China (CPC) National Congress held in November 2002 and the 10th National People's Congress (NPC) held in March 2003. In a significant changeover of leadership, the delegates to CPC congress elected 198 members and 158 alternate members to the new CPC Central Committee. The 356-member new CPC Central Committee features 180 new faces, with an average age of 55.4 years, almost 5 years younger than their predecessors when elected in 1997 at the 15th CPC congress. The new leaders are younger, better educated, and more pragmatic and open-minded.

In the first Plenary Session of the sixteenth Central Committee, Hu Jintao was elected as General Secretary of the CPC Central Committee. In fact, among the seven standing committee members of the Politburo of the 15th CPC Central Committee, only the youngest member Hu Jintao remains in the new nine member standing committee of the 16th CPC Central Committee. His six senior colleagues including former General Secretary Jiang Zemin, NPC Chairman Li Peng, and Premier Zhu Rongji all retired from CPC Central Committee. Eight new members—Wu Bangguo, Wen Jiabao, Jia Qinglin, Zeng Qinghong, Huang Ju, Wu Guangzheng, Li Changchun, and Luo Gan—were elected onto the Politburo Standing Committee.

The Politburo Standing Committee is the most important decision making body in China. It makes important decisions regarding both domestic affairs and foreign policy. Hu, Wu Bangguo, Huang, and Wu Guanzheng were all trained as engineers in the prestigious Tsinghua University. Wen, Jia, Zeng, Li, and Luo were also all technocrats. In terms of national leaders' educational background, China today has the most outstanding technocracy in the world.[4]

At the 10th NPC meeting in March 2003, Hu Jintao was elected as the President of China. Zeng Qinghong was elected as the Vice President. Wu Bangguo was elected as the Chairman of the Standing Committee of the National People's Congress. Wen Jiabao was nominated by Hu and elected by the NPC as the new Premier. The line-up of China's new State Council nominated by Premier Wen sailed through the first session of the 10th NPC, with Huang Ju, Wu Yi, Zeng Peiyan, and Hui Liangyu taking up the posts as vice-premiers, Zhou Yongkang, Cao Gangchuan, Tang Jiaxuan, Hua Jianmin, and Chen Zhili as state councilors. Li Zhaoxing became the Minister of Foreign Affairs; Cao Gangchuan was appointed the Minister of National Defense. The new cabinet members are well educated and pragmatic. New Foreign Minister Li Zhaoxing is a professional diplomat who has rich experience including serving as Chinese ambassador to the United Nations and the United States.

One of the most significant factors in the leadership transition is that the 77-year-old Jiang Zemin was reelected the Chairman of the CPC Central Military Commission (CMC) in November 2002. Jiang's position as the head of the Chinese military was reconfirmed at the NPC in March 2003.[5]

Against some speculation that Jiang might step down from his military position soon, it appears that Jiang intends to serve the whole 5-year term of CMC Chairmanship. President Hu is 60 years old and continues to serve as the Vice Chairman of the Central Military Commission. It is uncertain whether power transition in the military will take place in the foreseeable future. As the Chairman of the CPC and State Central Military Commissions (the CPC and State Central Military Commissions are consisted of the same group of people), Jiang will continue to play a significant role in Chinese defense and foreign policy. Due to Jiang's continued prominence in the leadership, the leadership transition is incomplete. It is most likely that Jiang will work hard to ensure some degree of continuity in foreign policy between his and Hu's leadership.[6]

The second important development of the 16th CPC National Congress was the amendment of the Party constitution. The amended Party constitution adopted the theory of "Three Represents." This new theory states that the CPC must always represent the development trend of China's advanced productive forces, the orientation of China's advanced culture, and the fundamental interests of the overwhelming majority of the people. Expanding the Party's previously assumed role as "vanguard of the working class," the amended constitution states that the Party is "also the vanguard of the whole of the Chinese people and the Chinese nation." China's socioeconomic structure has pluralized and more and more people work in the non-State sector.[7]

The party wants to improve the way of leadership to extend its authority to different areas of the society. In particular, private business has mushroomed and boomed. By the end of 2001, the number of private enterprises reached 2.02 million, involving 270 million employees.[8] Redefinition of the Party's representation heralds the welcoming of people from beyond the previously-defined working class, including private entrepreneurs. This fits well the CPCs aim to rally all favorable factors, as well as its new pledge to "advance with the times." According to Hu Jintao, the essence of "Three Represents" is that the Party should dedicate itself to the interests of the public and govern for the benefit of the people. It is clear that the nature of the CPC has changed and the party will continue to evolve in the direction of a party of the people instead of a party for one class. The new Chairman of the Standing Committee of the NPC Wu Bangguo suggests that the Chinese Constitution will also be amended in the same spirit of "advance with the times."

The third significant development of the 16th CPC Congress is the new agenda for economic development. The main tasks of China's economic development and reform in the next 20 years are to improve the market economy, accelerate modernization, maintain a sustained development of the national economy, and steadily uplift the people's living standards. The Party put forward an ambitious goal to quadruple the nation's 2000 gross domestic product and build an all-inclusive better-off society by 2020. Hu Jintao said on November 15, 2002: "The whole Party and people from all ethnic groups will unite more closely and concentrate on construction and development so as to continue pushing forward China's reform, opening-up, and modernization drive."[9]

The fourth significant development of the Party Congress is political reform and the rule of law. High on the list of priorities are undertakings such as Party building and political reforms. After being in power for more than half century, the CPC is faced with the trials of serious problems that have troubled many other veteran ruling parties: divorce from the people; the nurturing of vested interests; abuse of power; and loss of vitality. Widespread corruption seriously threatens the legitimacy of the Party. The CPC has recently been alarmed at many long-standing ruling parties in the world losing power. In order to consolidate its position as a ruling party, the CPC must conduct meaningful political reform and abide by the principle of the rule of law. Recent discussions and debate surrounding the constitution amendment might lead to new political and legal reforms.

One of the first major acts of General Secretary Hu is to emphasize the importance of the current Chinese Constitution, which has been in practice since 1982. All individuals and organizations including the CPC must act within the legal framework of the constitution. No one is above the law. The rule of law and democratic elections should provide new legitimacy to China's leadership in the coming years. When he was elected as President of China in March 2003, Hu also pledged that he would faithfully perform the powers and functions endowed by the Constitution, scrupulously discharge his duties, work hard and industriously, and serve the country and the people with utmost sincerity.

The fifth significant development is the reemphasis on pursuing the independent foreign policy of peace. Jiang emphasized this point in his political report: "No matter how the international situation changes, we will, as always, pursue the independent foreign policy of peace. The purpose of China's foreign policy is to maintain world peace and promote common development."[10]

In the views of Jiang and Chinese new leaders, there are three major historical tasks for China in the twenty-first century: to propel the modernization drive; to achieve national reunification; and to safeguard world peace and promote common development. The full significance of the leadership changeover on Chinese political, socioeconomic, and diplomatic development deserves close examination and critical analysis. Before we examine new foreign policy orientation, it is important to review key theoretical perspectives on Chinese foreign policy. Next section will analyze competing theoretical perspectives.

CONTENDING PERSPECTIVES ON CHINESE FOREIGN POLICY

In order to understand the changing nature of Chinese foreign policy, we should examine contending theories in studying Chinese foreign policy.

Michael Ng-Quinn argues that a coherent and useful theory of Chinese foreign policy must be based on an integration of particulars with regularities in a prioritized fashion, and that particulars are primarily constrained by regularities.[11] It is important to examine the linkages between domestic politics and foreign policy.

The Chinese leaders attach great importance to diplomacy. A commentary by the official Xinhua New Agency points out: "Diplomacy influences the rise or fall of a nation. It is a main battlefield for safeguarding state sovereignty."[12] In conjunction with rapid economic growth and profound social transformation, China's foreign policy is experiencing significant transition.

As China assumes greater prominence in world affairs, the question of how its government will approach key issues in international politics becomes increasingly critical. Thomas Kane identified several fundamental principles that guide Beijing's policy. These principles are a robust approach to sovereignty, a determination to strengthen the ruling faction, and a continuing commitment to ideological distinctiveness.[13]

Some analysts claim that the guiding principle for Chinese foreign policy is Chinese national interest. Yong Deng points out that the pursuit of national interest is the legitimate goal of any state's foreign policy. The conception of national interest lies at the core of the predominant "paradigm" governing the state's foreign policy. Deng argues that the Chinese conception of national interests should not be considered in terms of two mutually exclusive categories—*realpolitik* thinking and liberal values—but rather is best understood in terms of a spectrum. On the one hand, a *realpolitik* perspective will prevail as long as China's international identity is defined in terms of a nationalistic view of modern Chinese history, in which China was brutally victimized in a hostile and threatening world. On the other hand, it is possible that both China's national identity and its interests are open for contestation and redefinition.[14]

In contrast to Yong Deng's view, Thomas J. Christensen argues that Chinese analysts think about China's security like Western scholars of realpolitik such as Hans Morgenthau and Henry Kissinger. Similarly, Alastair Iain Johnston contends that realpolitik thinking in China may have its roots in the dynastic era.[15] Chinese elites' current realpolitik tendencies are infinitely preferable to the messianic versions of Chinese nationalism that might come to the fore if the United States treats Beijing as an enemy.[16]

It is interesting to examine patterns and dynamics of China's international strategic behavior. In the Maoist era, China formed an alliance with the Soviet Union in the 1950s, and engaged in a "pseudo-alliance" with the United States in the 1970s. In the era of Deng Xiaoping, China adopted a foreign policy of independence and peace. "Partnership" is a new concept in Chinese diplomacy in the post–Cold War era. China's foreign policy in the Deng era was mainly aimed at serving the national goal of modernization.[17]

According to Wu Xinbo, Beijing's foreign policy behavior is constantly tested by a set of conflicting variables. China views itself as a major power and wants to play a role accordingly in the world arena, while it always lacks an adequate material basis to do so. The open-door policy requires China to be fully integrated into international society, while strong concern over sovereignty makes it difficult for Beijing to embrace some of the mainstream values. China believes in a set of principles in international affairs, while consideration of its national interests causes Beijing to make a pragmatic compromise from time to time. Beijing has long been accustomed to dealing with others in bilateral settings while the post–Cold War era is witnessing a rise of multilateralism in international politics, which is bring more and more pressure on China's traditional diplomacy. These variables will continue to constrain China's foreign policy behavior while their influence will decline as a result of rapid change in China.[18]

Since the early 1990s, Chinese leaders have strongly endorsed China's involvement in the economic globalization process while pointing out its potential drawbacks. However, this mainstream consensus has not ended the vociferous and emotional debate in China on globalization. In contrast to the mainstream of Chinese officials and researchers who support "peace and development" as well as globalization, the opponents of globalization insist that China should opt out or drastically slow the pace of her integration into the globalization process and return to socialist values and institutions. However, "double-edged sword" views of globalization remain dominant in China, representing the views of most Chinese leaders, officials, economists, and moderate researchers. The new leadership is committed to deepening China's participation in the globalization process. Some Chinese scholars such as Li Shenzhi concluded that China has no alternative to participation in the globalization process if it is to achieve its modernization objectives. If China fails in the face of globalization, it will experience economic decline and social turbulence, which will have negative impact on China's relations with the rest of the world. [19]

Echoing the warning of China's potential failure to meet the challenge of globalization, Richard K. Betts and Thomas J. Christensen suggest: Before one laments the rise of Chinese power, one should consider an even more uncertain alternative: Chinese weakness and collapse. The last time when China was weak and disunited—in the era of warlordism and revolution in the first half of the twentieth century—it was a disaster, not only for China, but also for international peace and stability.[20] Thus, a weaker China might pose more serious problems for the global community than a stronger China. The challenge presented by a rising China is both a theoretical and policy issue.

Among the various components of Chinese national identity, the one that has risen to the forefront in the 1990s is great power identity in a global context. A great power's identity focuses on the country's past, present, and future in international relations, concentrating on its capacity to project power in comparison to other countries with their own ambitions. Gilbert Rozman found that Chinese leaders and analysts are fixated on the balance of powers in various configurations.[21]

According to Robert Ross, what is most striking about Chinese foreign policy is its effort to consolidate regional trends and promote stability. In its policies toward neighboring countries, China has emphasized cooperative measures to consolidate existing relationships rather than forceful measures to promote new patterns of relationships. China is a revisionist power, but for the foreseeable future it will seek to maintain the status quo—and so should the United States.[22]

China's effort to build strong economic ties with other countries has significantly contributed to the dramatic growth of Chinese economy. In the eyes of some analysts, the rise of China will create a huge market that will eventually make substantial contributions to scientific progress. During the process of economic globalization, the rise of China will inevitably stimulate world economic growth by more inventions, investment, and importation. China will increasingly play an important role in global affairs as China's modernization has a major impact on the world.[23] China seeks to establish extensive and intensive linkages with states that have overlapping, competing, and common interests.[24]

Challenging the conventional wisdom on the rise of China, Joseph Nye points out that the "rise of China" is a misnomer: "re-emergence" is more accurate. On the strength of its size and history, China has long been a major power in the Asia-Pacific region. Technologically and economically, China was a world leader (although without a global reach) from 500 to 1500; only in the last 500 years has the West overtaken it. Since 1978, China has achieved extraordinary rapid economic growth.[25] Nye's view coincides with Beijing leaders' call for a revival of Chinese nation and Chinese civilization.

In fact, developing Chinese economy and reviving the Chinese nation are considered as top priority by the current leadership in China. In next section we will analyze transitional Chinese foreign policy.

Foreign Policy and Key Relations in Transition

Since 1978, reform and opening to the outside world have been the driving force for Chinese foreign policy. The PRC has made great strides to join the modern world in the two decades since beginning the process of reform and opening-up in 1978. But China is still in the middle of a vast transformation that has a long way to go. Despite the enormous progress that has been registered, many deep-seated problems remain.[26] The 16th CPC National Congress reaffirmed economic development as the central task for China. If this growth-oriented policy continues to dominate China's political and economic agenda, it is likely that the independent foreign policy of peace will be maintained. Nevertheless, deepening of China's reform and changing international context will certainly lead to changes in Chinese foreign policy. Thus, there are continuity and change in Chinese foreign policy.

According to Quansheng Zhao, three key words, *modernization, nationalism, and regionalism,* can be used to help us better understand the direction of Chinese foreign policy. Modernization refers to China's concentration on economic growth. Nationalism has emerged as a leading ideological current behind China's drive toward modernization and one of the primary forces behind Chinese foreign policy. Regionalism emphasizes that China has remained a regional power, concentrating its political, economic, and military activities primarily in the Asia-Pacific region, despite its global aspirations. The Beijing leadership's interpretation of the internal condition and external environment will continue to play an important role in Chinese foreign policy.[27]

Modernization is a key in understanding Chinese foreign policy. Opening to the outside world has been a key component of modernization strategy since 1978. Few nations have benefited from participation in international trade as much as China has, or in such a brief period of time. In 1978, at the beginning of the reform era, China had about $20 billion of foreign trade; in 2002 that figure had exceeded $600 billion, a 30-fold increase. Foreign direct investment to China reached $53 billion in 2002—nearly one-tenth of the world total.[28]

The new leadership will have to develop foreign policies and strategies to cope with a changing international security environment. The new leadership will have to decide what type of role China will choose to play in the international community of nations. Will China step forward as a leader in international affairs in a manner that comports with the status and respect it demands as a nation of consequence, or will it sit on the sidelines, when convenient, and merely claim to be the world's largest developing nation?[29] How will China manage its relations with the United States, Russia, Japan, and other nations? Different answers to these questions will affect China's future and its role in the world.

President Hu and Premier Wen announced that they would continue to pursue an independent and peaceful foreign policy directed toward peace. The basic objectives of this policy are to safeguard the independence and sovereignty of the country, strive to create a long-standing and favorable international environment for China's reform, opening to the outside world and modernization drive, safeguard world peace, and promote common development. The following major components reflect continuity in Chinese foreign policy:

First, adhering to independence and safeguarding world peace. Beijing leaders decide on their approaches and policies regarding international issues independently. In international affairs, China shall decide its own stand according to its national interests and shall not yield to pressure from any big countries.

Second, establishing friendly and cooperative relations. China is willing to establish and develop good relations with all countries on the basis of the following five principles: mutual respect for sovereignty and territorial integrity, mutual nonaggression, noninterference in each other's internal affairs, equality and mutual benefit, and peaceful coexistence.

Third, developing good-neighborly relations. China actively develops friendly relations with its surrounding countries, safeguards the peace and stability of the region, and promotes economic cooperation at the regional level. China maintains that the disputes concerning borders, territory and territorial waters left over by history should be solved through dialogues and talks so as to seek fair and reasonable solutions. If a dispute cannot be solved right away, it may be put aside for the time being, and common ground be sought while reserving differences. Beijing also pays close attention to building all-round friendly and cooperative relations with the developing countries.

Fourth, opening to the outside world. China opens to developed countries as well as to developing countries. On the basis of equality and mutual benefit, China actively conducts extensive international cooperation to promote common development. As the largest developing country in the world and a permanent member of the UN Security Council, China is willing to make unremitting efforts for world peace and development, and the establishment of a new peaceful, stable, fair and reasonable international political and economic order.[30]

Building a new international political and economic order is an ambitious goal. In reality, Chinese leaders know that they have limited ability in shaping a new international system. In addition to being a permanent member of the UN Security Council, China now is a full member of the World Trade Organization (WTO) and many other international institutions. As an "insider" rather than an outsider, China has a growing stake in the current international system. Beijing's new leaders believe that China can gain more by working inside the international system. In this sense, China can be better understood as a "conservative power" (as described by Robert Ross) rather than a revolutionary power in the global system.

Due to the position of the United States as the only superpower in the post–Cold War world, Chinese analysts have devoted a lot of attention to the United States. Wang Jisi, one of the leading U.S. watchers in Beijing, views the United States as a global and Pacific power in historical, economic, security, and political dimensions. Beijing's attitude towards Washington has its origins in Chinese domestic goals and needs. Despite the negative sentiments toward the United States in recent years, however, the Chinese leadership has a realistic understanding of the United States in international affairs and wants to improve relations with Washington.[31] From Deng Xiaoping on, all top Chinese leaders have been strongly in favor of building a healthy Sino-American relationship.

The terrorist attacks on the United States on September 11, 2001 and the U.S.-led war against terrorism have a great impact on Chinese foreign policy. According to David Shambaugh, China's support for the American war on Al Qaeda and global terrorism has contributed to new stability in the relations, but improvement in bilateral ties was noticeable before September 11. While the Bush administration came to office arguing that China was a "strategic competitor," a coalition of key officials including the President, Secretary of State Colin Powell, and national security adviser Condoleezza Rice soon sought to establish a more stable, cooperative, and enduring relationship with Beijing. The United States and China share a host of interests and concerns that bind the two nations. With nearly $120 billion in two-way annual trade and substantial direct investment, each is of enormous economic importance to the other. If wisely managed by both sides—and if the key sensitivities of each are respected rather than provoked—the new stability in Sino-American relations may endure.[32]

Upon learning of the attacks on the United States in September 2001, Beijing immediately expressed condolences and general support to the U.S. government. President Jiang told President Bush that China opposes all manner of terrorist violence. China has urged the United States to conduct antiterrorism campaign through the United Nations. Support for the war on terrorism is consistent with key goals of the Chinese leadership. China has its own terrorism problem. Combating terrorism and Islamic extremism are among the main purposes of the Shanghai Cooperative Organization.[33] The U.S. Department of State officially defined the East Turkistan Islamic Movement as a terrorist organization. This was a significant step that helped to consolidate U.S.–Chinese joint efforts in fight against terrorism.

In October 2002, President Jiang and President Bush had their third meeting within a year at Bush's Texas ranch. Bush made it clear for the first time that the United States opposes Taiwan independence. The 16th CPC National Congress was postponed to November from its normal September schedule. Part of the reason was to make room for the Jiang–Bush summit. This was an indicator of the great value the Chinese leader attaches to a strong U.S.–China relationship.

The new leaders in Beijing see Sino-U.S. relations as a vital component of Chinese foreign relations. Vice President Hu Jintao's visit to the United States in April 2002 was a success. President Bush and other leaders who met with Hu found him to be a dynamic and pragmatic leader. Although Beijing had reservations about the U.S. war against Iraq, it did not lead opposition against the war. President Hu and President Bush met in Evian, France on June 1, 2003. They agreed to stay in touch and cooperate for the peaceful resolution of the nuclear program of the Democratic People's Republic of Korea (DPRK) through dialogue. China backs the non-nuclearization of the peninsula but also stressed the security concerns of the DPRK should be addressed.

At the Evian meeting, Hu and Bush invited each other to visit their respective countries. Hu urged the United States to honor its commitment to the one-China policy, handle the Taiwan question properly and refrain from sending wrong signals to Taiwan separatist forces. Bush told Hu that his administration would continue its one-China policy, follow the three U.S.–China joint communiqués and oppose "Taiwan independence." This policy has not changed and will not change in the future.[34] The Taiwan question has long been the most sensitive and important question in Sino-U.S. relations. When this question is addressed well, U.S.-China relations will improve. Both President Hu and Premier Wen are coming to visit the United States in late 2003. U.S. Vice President Dick Cheney is scheduled to visit China in the coming months.

China has built a strategic partnership with Russia. From the early 1960 to the early 1980s, China and Russia experienced two decades of rancorous verbal and sometimes lethal dispute. The new strategic partnership reflects a genuine desire on both sides to put the past behind them and forge a more friendly and mutually profitable relationship. The strategic partnership is not yet a clearly conceived design for a coordinated foreign policy toward shared international objectives. It represents, rather, a stable and meaningful commitment to bilateral aid and support. Neither partner has, nor do they share, either an ideology or a coherent international vision beyond their endorsement of multipolarity.[35]

In July 2001, Jiang and Putin signed the Treaty of Good Neighborliness and Friendly Cooperation. The treaty has been hailed by China and Russia as creating a new type of nonalliance, nonconfrontational, and not targeting any third country relationship. Bilateral relations between China and Russia experienced a remarkable upsurge in the past decade, particularly with a relationship of strategic partnership of cooperation. During their meeting in December 2002, Putin and Hu agreed to further promote ties to benefit the fundamental interests of the two peoples, democracy in international relations as well as the regional and world peace.

On May 26, 2003, Hu Jintao left Beijing to visit Russia. Hu Jintao said choosing Russia as the first country he visited following his election as president demonstrated how much importance China attaches to its ties with Russia. The Shanghai Cooperation Organization (SCO) summit was convened in Moscow on May 29, 2003. The SCO was formed by China, Russia, Kazakhstan, Kyrgyzstan, Tajikistan, and Uzbekistan in June 2001. A key goal of the organization is to fight against terrorism, ethnic separatism, extreme nationalism, and transnational crimes including drug trafficking.

According to President Hu, Russia and China support each other when it comes to vital issues dealing with state sovereignty and territorial integrity, and adhere to the principle that they should respect each other's sovereignty and never be at enmity with each other. The two countries had succeeded in raising the volume of bilateral commercial operations from 6.5 billion dollars in the 1990s to 12 billion in 2002. Hu also stressed that China strongly condemned the recent terrorist attacks in Chechnya. In return, Russia has repeatedly stated that it supports China's position on the issue of Taiwan.

China and India have a combined population that accounts for one-third of that of the world, and their shared border runs for 2,000 kilometers. The relationship between the two countries has experienced ups and downs. Though Sino-Indian relations turned sour briefly due to New Delhi's nuclear tests in May 1998, mutual understanding was enhanced and a mechanism for dialogue on security was set up in 1999. President Hu Jintao told Indian Prime Minister Atal Bihari Vajpayee that the aim of Chinese foreign policy is to maintain world peace and promote common development. China does not and will not do anything to threat other countries.[36] On June 23, 2003, China and India signed a declaration that will lay down goals and guidelines for the two countries' relations and provide a blueprint for cooperation. In the declaration, the Indian government has for the first time recognized explicitly the Tibet Autonomous Region as part of China's territory.

Prime Minister Vajpayee called for closer cooperation between the two countries, stressing "combined strength" and "complementarity" of the India-China partnership. "We are both at the forefront of developing and applying the technologies, which drive the knowledge-based economy." "We should focus on the simple truth that there is no objective reason for discord between us, and neither of us is a threat to the other."[37]

Beijing has adopted a more flexible policy toward the Association of Southeast Asian Nations (ASEAN) in recent years. Unity of the ASEAN members will strengthen their bargaining position versus Beijing. However, differences among ASEAN members have aroused skepticism abroad over the organization as an effective regime to address general security problems in East Asia.[38] Since signing a landmark framework agreement with the (ASEAN) in 2002, China has started the process of establishing a China–ASEAN Free Trade Area.

On June 28, 2003, China's top legislature unanimously passed the State Council's motion of joining the Treaty of Amity and Cooperation in Southeast Asia and its two amending protocols. The approval will make China the first to join the treaty among all of the major countries outside of Southeast Asian and it will also further cooperative relations between China and the ASEAN member countries.[39] China is actively building a comprehensive cooperative relationship with other Asian countries.

NEW FOREIGN POLICY ORIENTATION

The above analysis indicates that there are elements of continuity and change in Chinese foreign policy. In the foreseeable future, new foreign policy orientation will emerge as China continues its domestic reforms and adjusts its role in a changing world. China's foreign policy has reached a crossroad and is experiencing new transition. For the last quarter century, the main task of China's foreign policy has been creating a peaceful international environment in order to promote economic development. That policy has served China's national interest well and should be continued as long as possible. However, China's foreign policy will experience new changes due to the following factors.

First, the post–Cold War international environment has been changing rapidly and thus requires all countries to adjust their foreign policy. China has tried very hard to meet the challenges of the post–Cold War world. As the nature of the post–Cold War system continues to change, China must adjust its policy in order to meet new challenges under an evolving international system.

Second, China's reform and opening have achieved great success and are facing new challenges. The transition to a market economy has led to an unprecedented rapid growth in China and increased level of economic interdependence between China and the outside world. After more than a decade of serious efforts, China finally entered the WTO in 2001. As a result, China has increased rights and obligation in the global economic system. China's foreign policy must adept to the opportunities and risks that come with globalization.

Third, September 11 terrorist attack on the United States and the subsequent U.S.-led war against terrorism have a profound impact on the new international system. China has been a partner in the international fight against terrorism. At the same time, however, Chinese leaders have expressed reservation about the war against Iraq because they are deeply concerned about the Bush doctrine of preemptive strike. Chinese foreign policymakers are confronting hard choices regarding the war against terrorism. How does China respond to this challenge will influence its future foreign policy.

Fourth, leadership change will have an impact on foreign policy formulation and implementation. The 16th CPC National Congress held in November 2002 was a milestone in Chinese politics and foreign policy. The congress achieved a significant though incomplete transition of power from the "third generation" to a new generation of leaders.

One way to discover the emerging new foreign policy orientation is to examine the policy statements and actions of the new leaders. From May 26 to June 5, President Hu Jintao paid visits to Russia, Kazakhstan, and Mongolia, and attended the Moscow summit of the Shanghai Cooperation Organization (SCO), the ceremony marking the foundation tri-centenary of the Russian city of St. Petersburg and the South–North leaders' informal dialogue meeting in Evian, France. One of the highlights of Hu's Euro-Asia trip was his participation in the South–North leaders' informal dialogue meeting on June 1 in the French resort of Evian.[40] It is a sign of China's readiness to take a more active part in world affairs. While the world economy has been sliding, China has kept an encouraging growth momentum and improved its position within the world economy. For the first time, the Chinese leader attended a meeting with the Group of Eight (G8). It provides China one more channel for communication and contact with G8.

China's recent diplomacy, such as hosting the talks between itself, the United States and the DPRK, adhering to its stance on the Iraqi issue, responding positively to the invitation to the G8 summit and its protocol reform for the sending-off of Chinese leaders on overseas visits, has demonstrated a more flexible and pragmatic mentality and the progressive style of the new generation of leadership.

In his speech at informal leaders' meeting between North and South held in Evian on June 1, 2003, Hu Jintao said countries should tap their potential for economic development and enhance the adjustment of macroeconomic policies for maintaining normal trade order. Hu stressed the importance of preserving diversity in the world, suggesting that exchanges and competition of various civilizations and development models will inject new vigor into the development of world economy. He also raised the difficulties of developing countries in making full use of the opportunities brought by globalization and asked developed countries to open up their markets, remove trade tariffs and carry out their commitments in increasing funds and technical assistance and reducing debts.[41]

China's new leadership is confronting multiple challenges. One of the toughest challenges for the new leadership is the nuclear crisis in Korean Peninsula. The resurfacing of the nuclear issue of the DPRK was a reminder that the Korean Peninsula remains one of the world's most capricious flash-points. President Bush's designation of the DPRK as part of the "axis of evil" after September 11 as well as potential target of U.S. pre-emptive strikes made the situation more complex. In October 2002, Washington exposed, and Pyongyang acknowledged, the existence of the north's nuclear weapons program. China, Russia, and Japan have all appealed for a peaceful solution, urging the parties to come back to the negotiating table. While Washington prefers a multilateral talk on the North Korean nuclear issue, Pyongyang for a long time insisted on holding a direct talk with the United States. Specifically, the North Korean government demands for a nonaggression pact with the United States and economic assistance.

Unless this nuclear crisis is resolved, peace on the Korean Peninsula will remain fragile. Both Beijing and Washington are deeply concerned of the frightening consequences of North Korea going nuclear. A North Korea armed with nuclear weapons will be dangerous. If the worst case scenario becomes true, the Japanese leaders might decide to break Japan's constitutional restraint and build nuclear weapons. Right wing Japanese politicians already boasted that Japan could build a lot of nuclear weapons in a short period of time. In terms of technological and economic resources, Japan's nuclear option is certainly viable. The real issue is political and strategic. Due to Japan's militaristic history and past brutal invasion of its neighbors, a Japan with nuclear weapons will become a serious threat to peace. A nuclear arms race in East Asia will certainly disrupt the balance of power in the region and threat global peace and security.

The Bush administration has urged China to exercise its influence on Pyongyang to resolve the crisis. On this critical issue, China prefers to conduct quiet diplomacy. Beijing sponsored a talk of North Korea and the United States in April 2003. With a strong sense of urgency, Chinese envoys frequently visited Pyongyang, Washington, and Moscow in the last several months to search for rational solutions. After Beijing's active shuttle diplomacy, North Korea has finally agreed to a U.S. demand for multilateral negotiation. The six party talks will include the United States, North Korea, China, South Korea, Japan, and Russia. Although uncertainties remain, there is hope for peaceful resolution of the crisis on Korean Peninsula.

Another serious challenge is to deal with new issues facing China after its entry into the WTO. Joseph Fewsmith analyzes the political and social implications of China's accession to the WTO. If WTO membership will enhance the benefits that China has received from participating in the global trade system, it will also reinforce other trends apparent in China's political economy. In particular, it will help weed out inefficient state-owned enterprises, break down the bureaucratic interests that have fostered economic paternalism, erode local protectionisms, and curtail industrial monopolies. China's opening to the outside world has over the course of the past two decades created a variety of economic and political forces in China with an interest in preserving and expanding those relations. Participation in WTO will, over time, have considerable impact on China's political system. Furthermore, China's entry into the WTO may strengthen China's overall relations with the United States and other trading nations.[42]

Since entering the WTO in December 2001, China has made tremendous efforts to implement its commitments. Both the former WTO Director-General Mike Moore and current Director-General Supachai Panitchpakdi agree that China is a responsible member. Since 2001, China has greatly improved transparency in its policy decision making. More government areas are releasing draft regulations for comments from the public before they are finalized. So far, China has cut its average tariff rate from 15.3 percent to 12 percent. According to Christian Murck, chairman of the American Chamber of Commerce in China, the most important thing about China's WTO accession is the indication of the country's resolve to further open its domestic markets. The Chinese Central government has revised or abolished more than 2,300 regulations that conflicted with WTO rules, while local authorities have corrected or done away with tens of thousands of administrative regulations for the same reason. These efforts are of far-reaching significance to the country's transition from a centrally planned economy to a market economy with Chinese characteristics.[43] WTO accession has improved China's market environment and will pave the way for foreigners to implement long-term investment strategies.

According to Chinese State councilor and former Foreign Minister Tang Jiaxuan, the global situation will be favorable to China for a long period in the future. China's diplomacy should abide by and serve its strategic goal of building a well-off society in an all-round way. Despite fruitful worldwide antiterrorism cooperation, terrorism still runs rampant, which will surely have a profound impact on international politics, economy, and security.[44]

Chinese foreign policy is in transition as a result of leadership change and domestic and international development. The world situation is complicated and full of risks and opportunity. The speech given by Hu Jintao after he was elected President of China summarized his views on international and domestic priorities. Thus, it is worthwhile to highlight here what Hu said to the NPC delegates. Hu declared that "China's development is at a new historical starting point, we should emancipate our minds, seek truth from facts, advance with the times, and take full advantage of the strategic opportunity period in the first two decades of the twenty-first century to focus on construction and development, push forward reform and opening-up in a big way, promote a coordinated development of socialist material, political and ideological civilizations, and advance firmly toward the grand goal of building a well-off society in an all-round way." In regard to foreign policy, Hu said that "China is a peace-loving nation. We shall continue the independent foreign policy of peace, maintain and develop friendly and cooperative relations with all other countries and, together with the people of all countries, work for a fair and rational international political and economic order and ceaselessly promote the lofty cause of peace and development of mankind."[45]

Chinese analysts believe that multipolarization has become an irreversible trend in the wake of the end of the Cold War. However, the path to a multipolar world has never been smooth. The inability to prevent the U.S.-led war with Iraq is an indication of other countries' currently limited influence over a determined U.S. President.

The main task of Chinese foreign policy is to work for a peaceful world that will be conducive for sustaining economic growth and enhancing people's living standards. So far China has benefited significantly from its increased participating in the world economy. However, there is no guarantee for sustainable economic growth and favorable international environment. China's new leaders are facing tremendous socioeconomic problems, political uncertainty, and international development.[46]

In addition to numerous traditional problems, China is also facing nontraditional threats. There are many issues of nontraditional security. Typical cases include ecological pollution, financial crisis, transnational Internet hacking, international terrorist attacks and the spread of fatal diseases like AIDS and severe acute respiratory syndrome (SARS). Nontraditional security threats are often more destructive than traditional wars. Such threats have many new features. First, they are destructive, and their forms, range and regularity are hard to define. Second, compared with traditional national security threats, their forms and ranges are more complicated. Third, nontraditional security threats usually take place within a country. Among all the security issues, human security is the core issue and social security is the basis for national security and international cooperation.[47] The rise of nontraditional security threats has affected Chinese thinking and foreign policy.

Careful analysis can reveal development in style and substance of Beijing's foreign policy. In March 2003, the low-profile President Hu and Premier Wen proposed reductions in the entourage accompanying leaders on their overseas visits and simplification of the corresponding ceremonies to send off and welcome back leaders. Their antipathy toward and endeavors to get rid of vain behavior could not but win them favorable public opinion.[48] Hu's first trip overseas as China's president took pace between May 26 and June 5. He visited Russia, Kazakhstan, Mongolia, and France on what was the first trip in decades by a senior Chinese leader without any official formalities to send him off or welcome him back.

Following his election as the president of China, Hu Jintao vowed to "use my power for the people, link my feelings to the people, and focus my heart on the pursuit of public welfare." When confronted with the SARS epidemic crisis in Spring 2003, President Hu and Premier Wen decided to break away from the traditional secrecy in handling a matter of public interest. The true picture of the SARS epidemic had not been made available to the public until April 20 because of a fear of instability. The political and economic stakes were especially high, given the broad consensus that China cannot afford to lose its hard-won economic fruit. The new leadership's decision to share information with the public was a major boost for the global efforts to contain the spread of the life-threatening disease. The decision honored the country's promise to be a responsible member of the international community. The dismissals of the former Beijing mayor and health minister demonstrated the new leadership's resolve to act differently. They fitted in well with the new leadership's appeal to take on a new look. The cohesion the new leaders have forged with the people in a time of crisis will prove a precious asset on the way ahead.[49]

In sum, a new orientation of Chinese foreign policy is emerging. For analyzing the new orientation, the following points deserve special attention. First, the fundamental goal of Chinese foreign policy is to create a peaceful environment in service of building a "well-off society in all round way." The objectives of China's modernization are to quadruple the GDP of 2000 by 2020 (reaching US$4 trillion based on 2000 exchange rate), and to become a mid-level developed country by 2050. For this purpose, development and peace are inseparable. Beijing's new leaders perceive the first two decades of the twenty-first century as a "strategic opportunity" for China to develop its economy. In addition to the discussion of building material and spiritual civilizations, President Hu and his colleagues started talking about "political civilization" in 2002. Political civilization should include more democratic governance, the rule of law, and a more open and transparent foreign policy.

Second, China's leaders are more realistic about China's strengths and limitations. Both President Hu Jintao and Premier Wen Jiabao worked for many years at local and provincial levels in less developed areas of China. They have an urgent sense of addressing issues of disparity inside China. On the other hand, they have fully participated in the reform and opening which led to rapid economic development. As a result, the new leaders are likely to be more modest yet confident when dealing with international economic issues. Hopefully the *pingmin* (common people) background of leaders such as Hu and Wen will enable them to better understand people's needs and more effectively manage relations with foreign leaders on an equal footing.[50] In order to consolidate their authority, the new leaders must be able to demonstrate that they are able to manage a more balanced and sustainable economic growth at home and act as responsible and respectable statesmen on the world stage.

Third, the new leaders must take bold new initiatives in foreign policy as a result of China's entry into the WTO. Although it is premature to assess the full impact of China's WTO membership, it is reasonable to say that China's comprehensive integration into the global economy will have profound impact on the Chinese economy and society. A more open China in the world community must develop new foreign policies that will facilitate China's better cooperation with other nations and international organizations.

Fourth, Chinese new leaders are standing for going alone with historical tide and safeguarding the common interests of all mankind. In the previous eras of Chinese foreign policy, Beijing leaders tend to emphasize "anti-imperialism (anti-U.S.)," "antirevisionism (anti-USSR)," and then "antihegemonism (anti-Soviet and sometimes also anti-U.S.)." For the new leaders, China's foreign policy is aimed at building "peace and development," rather than opposing to someone or something. Of course, this fundamental shift actually started with Deng Xiaoping's opening and reform. But Deng still emphasized "antihegemonism" as a key component of Chinese foreign policy in the 1980s. The new leaders in Beijing today are the first generation of post-"anti . . . ism" leadership. *Bu shu di* [do not seek enemy] has become an essential part of China's new foreign policy. [51]

Fifth, pragmatism and professionalism are likely to become key features of Chinese foreign policy. Pragmatism includes a new concept of security featuring mutual trust, mutual benefit, equality, and coordination.[52] Ideology is playing a less and less significant role in China's relations with foreign countries. For instance, China has developed a much closer economic relations with South Korea than with North Korea.[53] Chinese diplomats are becoming more professional.[54] A stronger sense of pragmatism and a higher level of efficiency should contribute to more meaningful participation of China in world affairs. Chinese diplomacy will project a more confident and open image.

Finally, China's new leaders are facing unprecedented domestic and international challenges. The lines between domestic and foreign issues are diminishing. China is undergoing marketization, urbanization, and potentially democratization in the context of globalization. It is also going through a communication revolution. There are increasing economic disparity, social tensions, and political risks. A rising China is still searching for its proper role in a world full of economic troubles, political instability, and security threats. Policymakers in Beijing will face more and more complex challenges including the following issues: serving the needs of sustainable economic development, fighting against terrorism and ethnic separatism, dealing with the war against terrorism and crisis in North Korea, managing the issue of Taiwan and seeking for national unification, and maintaining regional stability and global peace in the long term. Indeed, China is confronting serious challenges on many fronts.[55]

In addressing such multiple challenges, there is no doubt that Chinese foreign policy will continue to experience significant transition. Understanding Chinese foreign policy is an increasingly important and challenging task. In fact, policymakers and scholars both inside and outside of China are engaging in a serious learning process.[56] It is fitting and appropriate to conclude this chapter with a Chinese saying: *Renzhong daoyuan*—the burden is heavy and the road is long.

NOTES

1. See Robert Putnam, "Diplomacy and Domestic Politics: The Logic of Two Level Games," *International Organization*, vol. 42 (1988), pp. 427–60.
2. For a theoretical analysis of foreign policy restructuring, see Jerel A. Rosati, Joe Hagan, and Martin W. Sampson, eds., *Foreign Policy Restructuring: How*

Governments Respond to Global Change (Columbia: University of South Carolina Press, 1994).

3. The Chinese leadership can be divided into five generations: The first generation was led by Mao Zedong who dominated Chinese politics from 1949 until his death in 1976. At the core of the second generation was Deng Xiaoping who was the supreme leader of China from 1978 to the early 1990s. The third generation was headed by Jiang Zemin who became the General Secretary of the CPC in 1989. Jiang remains the Chairman of the Central Military Commission today. Hu Jintao is the leading figure of the fourth generation, but he has not been officially called the "core" of the fourth generation. The emerging young leaders will be the fifth generation. For recent studies of Chinese leadership, see Chen Li, *China's Leaders: The New Generation* (Lanham: Rowman & Littlefield, 2001); David M. Finkelstein and Maryanne Kivlehan, eds., *China's Leadership in the 21st. Century: The Rise of the Fourth Generation* (Armonk: M.E. Sharpe, 2003); and Andrew J. Nathan and Bruce Gilley, *China's New Rulers: The Secret Files* (New York: New York Review Books, 2002). For an in-depth analysis of the rise of Hu Jintao, see Richard Daniel Ewing, "Hu Jintao: The Making of a Chinese General Secretary," *China Quarterly*, vol. 173 (March 2003), pp. 18–34.

4. In fact, the transition to the technocracy was achieved in the third generation. The emergence of Jiang Zemin and his colleagues at the center of political power represents a transition of Chinese political leadership from a generation of revolutionary politicians to a generation of technocratic politicians. This new group is characterized by its lack of any absolute authority based on charisma and prestige established through decades of wars and construction and by its relatively narrow power base. No single leader can command unquestioned authority simultaneously in the three major systems of China's political power—the party, the government, and the military. This has led to a collective decision-making process, with checks and balances reflected in the structure and composition of the Politburo Standing Committee, which has begun to represent more bureaucratic and regional interests. See Lu Ning, *The Dynamics of Foreign-Policy Decisionmaking in China* (Boulder: Westview Press, 1997).

5. Joseph Fewsmith provides an insightful analysis of Jiang's continued dominance in Chinese politics. See Fewsmith, "The Sixteenth National Party Congress: The Succession that Didn't Happen," *China Quarterly*, vol. 173 (March 2003), pp. 1–16.

6. The role of the military in Chinese politics is complex. Mao Zedong observed that "political power flows from the barrel of a gun." As China's highest-level military organ, the CPCs Central Military Commission (CMC) is responsible for the making and coordination of defense policy. It also wields potent political influence, and it is an unwritten but general rule of Chinese politics that the country's paramount leader must also be in charge of the CMC. Whether this is still true remains to be seen.

7. The Sociology Institute of the Chinese Academy of Social Sciences published a *Research Report on Social Strata in Contemporary China* in 2002. From 1952 to 1999, industrial workers jumped from 6.4 percent to 22.6 percent in China's social strata. Peasants declined from 84.21 percent to 44 percent. During the same period, service people in business went up from 3.13 percent to 12 percent. Private enterprises owners increased from 0.18 percent to 0.6

percent. Technical professionals grew from 0.86 percent to 5.1 percent. See *Dangdai Zhongguo shehui jieceng yanjiu baogao (Research Report on Social Strata in Contemporary China* (ed. Lu Xueyi, Beijing: Shehui kexue wenxian chubanshe, 2002), p. 44.

8. *China Daily*, November 14, 2002, p. 4.
9. *China Daily*, November 16, 2002, p. 1.
10. *China Daily*, November 9, 2002, p. 4.
11. Michael Ng-Quinn, "The Analytic Study of Chinese Foreign Policy," *International Studies Quarterly*, vol. 27 (1983), pp. 203–24. For an overview of literature on Chinese foreign policy, see Michael Hunt, "CCP Foreign Relations: A Guide to the Literature," *Cold War International History Program Bulletin*, no. 6–7 (Winter 1995/6), pp. 129, 137–43.
12. Xinhua, "Pushing Peace and Development," *China Daily*, November 15, 2002, p. 4.
13. Thomas Kane, "China's foundations: guiding principles of Chinese foreign policy," *Comparative Strategy*, vol. 20, no. 1 (January–March 2001), pp. 45–55.
14. Yong Deng, "The Chinese Conception of National Interests and International Relations." *China Quarterly*, (June 1998), pp. 308–29. For a critical review of Chinese nationalism and its impact on China's foreign policy in the post-Deng era, see Allen S. Whiting, "Chinese Nationalism and Foreign Policy After Deng," *China Quarterly*, vol. 142 (June 1995), pp. 295–316. For a controversial view of racial nationalism, see Barry Sautman, "Racial Nationalism and China's External Behavior," *World Affairs*, vol. 160, no. 2 (Fall 1997), pp. 78–95.
15. Alastair Iain Johnston, *Cultural Realism: Strategic Cultural and Grand Strategy in Chinese History* (Princeton: Princeton University Press, 1995).
16. Thomas J. Christensen, "Chinese Realpolitik," *Foreign Affairs*, vol. 75, no. 5 (September/October 1996), pp. 37–52.
17. Joseph Y.S. Cheng and Zhang Wankun, "Patterns and Dynamics of China's International Strategic Behaviour," *Journal of Contemporary China*, vol. 11, no. 31 (2001), pp. 235–60.
18. Wu Xinbo, "Four Contradictions Constraining China's Foreign Policy Behavior," *Journal of Contemporary China*, vol. 10 (2001), pp. 293–301.
19. Banning Garrett, "China Faces, Debates, the Contradictions of Globalization," *Asian Survey*, vol. 41, no. 3 (2001), pp. 409–27.
20. Richard K. Betts and Thomas J. Christensen, "China: Getting the Questions Right," *National Interest*, (Winter 2000–01), pp. 17–29.
21. Gilbert Rozman, "China's Quest for Great Power Identity," *Orbis*, vol. 43, no. 3 (1999), pp. 383–402.
22. Robert S. Ross, "Beijing as a Conservative Power," *Foreign Affairs*, vol. 76, no. 2 (March–April 1997), pp. 33–45. For a contrasting view by two journalists, see Richard Bernstein and Ross H. Munro, "The Coming Conflict with America," *Foreign Affairs*, vol. 76, no. 2 (March–April 1997), pp. 18–32.
23. Yan Xuetong, "The Rise of China in Chinese Eyes," *Journal of Contemporary China*, vol. 10 (2001), pp. 33–39.
24. Avery Goldstein, "The Diplomatic Face of China's Grand Strategy: A Rising Power's Emerging Choice," *China Quarterly*, vol. 168 (December 2001), pp. 835–64. Some scholars mainly perceive China as a regional power, see

Samuel S. Kim, "China as a Great Power," *Current History*, vol. 96 (September 1997), pp. 246–51. For the most through analysis on the rise of China, see Samuel S. Kim, "China's Path to Great Power Status in the Globalization Era," *Asian Perspective*, vol. 27, no. 1 (2003), pp. 35–75.

25. Joseph S. Nye, "China's Re-emergence and the Future of the Asia-Pacific," *Survival*, vol. 39, no. 4 (Winter 1997–98), pp. 65–79.

26. Michael Yahuda, "China's Foreign Relations: The Long March, Future Uncertain," *China Quarterly*, vol. 159 (September 1999), pp. 650–59.

27. Quansheng Zhao, "Chinese Foreign Policy in the Post-Cold War Era," *World Affairs*, vol. 159, no. 3 (winter 1997), pp. 114–29. For a related argument, see Quansheng Zhao, "Modernization, Nationalism, and Regionalism in China," in Steven Hook, ed., *Comparative Foreign Policy: Adaptation Strategies of the Great and Emerging Powers* (Upper Saddle River: Prentice Hall, 2002), pp. 66–91.

28. *China Daily*, December 7, 2002

29. David Finkelstein and Maryanne Kivlehan raised many challenging issues. See Finkelstein and Kivlehan, *China's Leadership in the 21st. Century*, p. 5.

30. This list is a summary of Chinese official statements before and after the 16th. CPC Congress. Foreign Minister Tang Jiaxuan provided an interesting official statement on recent development of Chinese foreign policy. See Xinhua News, "Tang Jiaxuan: Unprecedented Rise in China's International Status in the Last Thirteen Years," October 9, 2002.

31. Wang Jisi, "The Role of the United States as a Global and Pacific Power: A View From China," *Pacific Review*, vol. 10, no. 1 (1997), pp. 1–18. See also Yong Deng, "Hegemon on the Offensive: Chinese Perspectives on U.S. Global Strategy," *Political Science Quarterly*, vol. 116, no. 3 (Fall 2001), pp. 343–65; and Robert A. Pastor, "China and the United States: Who Threatens Whom?," *Journal of International Affairs*, vol. 54, no. 2 (Spring 2001), pp. 427–43. For an insightful overview of US–China relations, see Harry Harding, "The Uncertain Future of US–China Relations," *Asia-Pacific Review*, vol. 6, no. 1 (1999), pp. 7–24.

32. David Shambaugh, "Sino-American Relations since September 11: Can the New Stability Last?," *Current History*, vol. 101, no. 656 (September 2002), pp. 243–49. See also Aaron L. Friedberg, "11 September and the Future of Sino-American Relations," *Survival*, vol. 44, no. 1 (Spring 2002), pp. 33–50; and David M. Lampton, "Small Mercies: China and America after 9/11," *The National Interest* (Winter 2001–02), pp. 106–13.

33. Denny Roy, "China and the War on Terrorism," *Orbis*, vol. 46, no. 3 (Summer 2002), pp. 511–21.

34. *China Daily*, June 3, 2003.

35. Lowell Dittmer, "The Sino-Russian Strategic Partnership," *Journal of Contemporary China*, vol. 10, no. 28 (2001), pp. 399–413. For a comprehensive survey, see Lowell Dittmer, *Sino-Soviet Normalization and Its International Implications* (University of Washington Press, 1992). For a Chinese perspective on Sino-Russian relations and an American response, see Li Jingjie, "Pillars of the Sino-Russian Partnership," *Orbis*, vol. 44, no. 4 (2000), pp. 527–39; and a response to Li by Gilbert Rozman. "A New Sino-Russian-American Triangle?" *Orbis*, vol. 44, no. 4 (Fall 2000), pp. 541–55. See also Stephen J. Blank, "The Strategic Context of Russo–Chinese Relations," *Issues and Studies*, vol. 36, no. 4 (July/August 2000), pp. 66–94;

and Elizabeth Wishnick, "Russia and China: Brothers Again?," *Asian Survey*, vol. 41, no. 5 (2001), pp. 797–821.

36. *Renmin Ribao*, June 6, 2003, p. 1.

37. *China Daily*, June 24, 2003, p.1

38. Allen S. Whiting, "ASEAN Eyes China: The Security Dimension," *Asian Survey*, vol. 37, no. 4 (1997), pp. 299–322. See also Rosemary Foot, "China in the Regional Forum: Organizational Process and Domestic Modes of Thought," *Asian Survey*, vol. 38, no. 5 (1998), pp. 425–40.

39. *China Daily*, June 30, 2003, p. 2. The treaty was originally signed by the members of the ASEAN in Indonesia on February 24, 1976. The treaty has been amended twice respectively in 1987 and 1998, making it open to membership for countries outside of Southeast Asia. The treaty says that member parties shall deal with one another by the following fundamental principles: Mutual respect for the independence, sovereignty, equality, territorial integrity, and national identity of all nations; The right of every state to lead its national existence free from external interference, subversion or coercion; noninterference in the internal affairs of one another; settlement of differences or disputes by peaceful means; renunciation of the threat or use of force; effective cooperation among member nations.

40. Hu Jintao made several key foreign policy speeches during the visits. For his speech at the Moscow Institute of International Relations, see *Renmin Ribao* (May 29, 2003), p. 1.

41. *Renmin Ribao* (June 3, 2003), p. 1.

42. Joseph Fewsmith, "The Political and Social Implications of China's Accession to the WTO," *China Quarterly*, vol. 167 (2001), pp. 573–609. See also Greg Mastel, "China, Taiwan, and the World Trade Organization," *Washington Quarterly*, vol. 24, no. 3 (Summer 2001), pp. 45–56; and Zhiqun Zhu, "China, the WTO, and U.S.–China Relations," in Guoli Liu and Weixing Chen, ed., *New Directions in Chinese Politics for the New Millennium* (Lewiston: Edwin Mellen Press, 2002), pp. 249–73.

43. *China Daily*, November 11 and 12, 2002.

44. *China Daily*, December 23, 2002.

45. See Xinhua News Agency, March 18, 2003.

46. For instance, unemployment has become a serious issue without ready solution. According to a recent report by the Ministry of Labor and Social Security, about 14 million urban job seekers will be disappointed this year because too many people are looking for too few jobs. About 24 million people (including 10 million new urban job seekers, 6 million laid-off workers from state-owned enterprises, and 8 million registered jobless) have been swarming into job fairs, but only 10 million openings at the most will be available by the end of 2003. Sources from the Ministry of Education said that more than 2.12 million college students graduated this year, 670,000 more than last year. Only 70 percent of these graduates are likely to find work, while there may not be jobs for the remaining 30 percent, which means about 700,000 graduates. See *China Daily*, June 24, 2003, p. 3.

47. Wang Yizhou, "Rethink Approach to Security Threats," *China Daily* (May 29, 2003), p. 4. Wang is a researcher with the Institute of World Economics and Politics under the Chinese Academy of Social Sciences. He has played a key role in introducing new theories and methodology into China's international studies. See Wang Yizhou, *Xifan Guoji Zhengzhixue: Lishi yu*

Lilun [Western International Politics: History and Theory] (Shanghai: Shanghai renmin chubanshe, 1998).

48. Yan Xizao, "New Leadership Wins Trust," *China Daily*, June 27, 2003, p. 4.

49. *China Daily*, June 27, 2003, p. 4.

50. Several foreign leaders including President Bush who have met with Hu found him to be a reliable and capable partner. Hu, Bush, and Russian President Putin all belong to the same generation.

51. I am grateful to Chu Shulong for pointing this out.

52. "China's Document about the Position on New Security Concept," *Renmin Ribao*, August 2, 2002, p. 3.

53. The President of the Republic of Korea (ROK) Roh Moo-hyun visited China from July 7 to 10, 2003. In 1992, Sino-South Korean trade was $5 billions. The bilateral trade reached $44 billion in 2002. Though China remains a major supplier of food and energy to North Korea, there is no active trading between the two sides. Their bilateral trade is less than $1 billion. Beijing leaders have encouraged North Korean leaders to conduct meaningful economic reforms. So far, North Korea has not conducted any significant economic reform.

54. Xiaohong Liu, *Chinese Ambassadors: The Rise of Diplomatic Professionalism since 1949* (Seattle: University of Washington Press, 2001).

55. China's new leaders have an acute sense of the critical socioeconomic issues. Premier Wen Jiabao pointed out: China has a workforce of over 740 million people, but for the developed economies, European countries and America combined, their workforce stands at 430 million. (One independent research estimated the urban unemployed figure as high as 50 million.) The number of migrant workers who seek job opportunities in cities normally caps around 120 million. More than 30 million farmers are still living under the poverty line. Even for those who have been lifted above the poverty line, their lives are at a low level. Per capita income for them is only 625 yuan (US$75). If we substitute the benchmark for the poverty line with an increase of 200 yuan (US$24), then the total poor population will be 90 million. The gap between China's East and China's West is very wide. The GDP from five to six provinces in the coastal areas accounted for more then half of China's total GDP. *China Daily*, March 19, 2003. For an in-depth analysis of the major issues facing China, see Joseph Y.S. Cheng, *China's Challenges in the Twenty-first Century* (Hong Kong: City Univeristy of Hong Kong Press, 2003).

56. See Lowell Dittmer, *Learning and the Reform of Chinese Foreign Policy* (Singapore: Singapore University Press, 1999).

CHAPTER 10

CROSS-STRAIT RELATIONS AFTER 16TH NATIONAL CONGRESS OF THE CHINESE COMMUNIST PARTY

John Fuh-sheng Hsieh

The relationship between China and Taiwan has remained more or less unchanged since the 1995–96 crisis. On the one hand, political relations have been strained very much ever since, but economic and social ties have been growing quite rapidly. It is interesting to see if the situation will change with the new leadership in Beijing after the 16th National Congress of the Chinese Communist Party (CCP). The purpose of this paper is to look into possible factors which may lead to the changing relationship between the two across the Taiwan Strait.

CHINA'S TAIWAN POLICY

China's Taiwan policy has been quite consistent since Deng Xiaoping emerged in the late 1970s as the paramount leader of China. This policy can be summarized in two parts: (1) peaceful unification under "one country, two systems," and (2) the use of force against Taiwan if it declares independence.

The Standing Committee of the National People's Congress (NPC) issued a letter as early as January 1, 1979 addressed to their "Taiwan compatriots," stating that

> Our national leaders have already expressed their determination to accomplish the great mission of reunifying the motherland by taking into account the real situation. In solving the issue of reunification, we will respect the current situation in Taiwan, and the opinions of the people from all walks of life in Taiwan, by taking appropriate policy and methods so as not to inflict any damages on the people of Taiwan.[1]

A month later, Deng was quoted as saying, "We no longer talk about 'liberating Taiwan.' As long as Taiwan returns to the motherland, we will respect the reality and the current system there."[2] This was reiterated in greater detail in "Ye's nine points" issued by Marshal Ye Jianying on September 30, 1981, and in "Deng's six points" enunciated by Deng himself when he received Winston L.Y. Yang on June 26, 1983, a Chinese–American scholar teaching at Seton Hall University.

Such ideas were later encapsulated into "one country, two systems," meaning that, "after reunification, Taiwan can still enforce its capitalism as the mainland enforces its socialism, but it will be a unified China."[3] Along with the use of force against Taiwan if it declares independence, it has become the cornerstone of China's Taiwan policy.

Deng's successor Jiang Zemin remains faithful to this principle. In the so-called "Jiang's eight points," he stated that

> Since the Standing Committee of the National People's Congress issued "A Letter addressed to the Taiwan Compatriots" in January 1979, we have formulated the basic principle of "peaceful unification, and one country, two systems," . . . firmly establishing the guiding principle for realizing the peaceful unification of the motherland.[4]

At the CCPs 16th National Congress, Hu Jintao succeeded Jiang Zemin as General Secretary of the CCP. He later replaced Jiang to become the new head of the Taiwan Affairs Leading Small Group (TALSG).[5] However, since Jiang remains the all-powerful chairman of the Central Military Commission, and one of his protégés, Jia Qinglin, reportedly serves as Hu's deputy at the TALSG.[6] Clearly, at least in the next few years, China's Taiwan policy will not deviate too much from the current course.

To be sure, we know very little about Hu's views on many issues, including Taiwan affairs. On March 11, 2003, in participating in the discussion of the Taiwan delegation in the 10th NPC, Hu presented his views on Taiwan:

> First, we need to always uphold the one-China principle; second, we need to greatly facilitate the economic and cultural exchanges between the two sides; third, we need to forcefully implement the principle of having confidence in Taiwan people; and fourth, we need to unify our compatriots on both sides to come together to promote the great revival of the Chinese people.[7]

Nothing is really new in this speech. He seems to be very careful not to stir up any controversies. This seems to match many outsiders' impression of him.

Given that China's Taiwan policy has been consistent and not much change can be expected in the foreseeable future, the most important factor that may affect the ups and downs in the cross-Strait relations is how Taiwan formulates and implements its mainland China policy.

TAIWAN'S MAINLAND CHINA POLICY

Taiwan's mainland China policy has been more volatile, in contrast to the consistency of China's Taiwan policy, reflecting, to a large extent, the democratic nature of the Taiwanese polity and the divergent views on the national identity issue on the island. At the outset, when China launched a peace offensive in the late 1970s and early 1980s to allure Taiwan, the Nationalist government in Taiwan insisted on the "three no's policy"—no contact, no negotiation, and no compromise—claiming that China's new gesture was just another united front gimmick.

China's peace offensive came at the same time as the launch of "reform and opening policy." As a result of the change in China, many Taiwanese sneaked into China in violation of Taiwan government's regulations. They went to China to see their relatives or to seek business opportunities. It was estimated in one study that, before 1987, over ten thousand people went to the mainland each year.[8] And indirect trade between Taiwan and the mainland via Hong Kong had increased from US$460 million in 1981 to US$955.5 million in 1986.[9] These figures were quite alarming as far as the Taiwanese government was concerned.

Finally, the Taiwan government (under the leadership of President Chiang Ching-kuo), citing humanitarian reasons, decided to loosen up by allowing the Taiwanese to visit their relatives on the mainland beginning from November 1987. This decision triggered tremendous changes in the relationships between the two sides in the following years.

After Chiang passed away in January 1988, his successor Lee Teng-hui continued to expand the scope of exchanges across the Taiwan Strait. The two sides even gradually engaged in political dialogues. Nonetheless, as Taiwan tried to assert its sovereign status by stepping up efforts to participate in the international community under the rubric of "pragmatic diplomacy" (including its bid for joining the United Nations), the tension between Taiwan and China surged. Moreover, Lee's comments on certain sensitive issues irritated China. He was, for example, interviewed by a Japanese writer, speaking about the sorrow of being Taiwanese. He was quoted as saying that the Kuomintang (Nationalist Party, KMT) regime, like other regimes ruling Taiwan, was externally imposed on the Taiwanese, and the KMT should be changed into a Taiwanese party.[10] Such comments were interpreted by China as evidence showing that his Chinese identity was dubious.

In June 1995, Lee came to the United States to visit his alma mater, Cornell University. China protested against it from the very beginning. It not only suspended many exchange programs between China and Taiwan, but also launched a series of military exercises and missile tests in areas close to Taiwan.

In March 1996, Taiwan held its first direct popular presidential election, and Lee was the KMT candidate. China's military maneuverings before the election was apparently intended to scare Lee's support. However, this backfired. Lee was reelected by winning 54 percent of the vote. The cross-Strait relations remained strained during his whole new term as the president of the Republic of China (ROC) on Taiwan.

In the March 2000 presidential election, Chen Shui-bian, pro-independence Democratic Progressive Party (DPP) candidate, defeated Lien Chan, the

KMT candidate, and James Soong, a KMT-turned independent, to become the new president of the ROC. As expected, China did not trust Chen, given his inclination toward independence, and he was also suspicious of China's moves, fearing that they were intended to shake Taiwan's sovereign status. Even though Chen and his party have advocated the establishment of an independent Taiwan, he has refrained from explicitly pushing for it after taking office. Chinese leaders in Beijing have also taken a wait-and-see attitude toward him. The cross-Strait relations have stagnated.

Politically speaking, the relationship between Taiwan and China has been strained in the past several years, though the economic and social ties across the Strait have not been stalled. Although the Taiwan government still does not allow direct trade and transport links between Taiwan and China except for some special arrangement (e.g. the so-called "mini-three links"), the economic and social exchanges between the two sides have been greatly increased in the past several years. The volume of indirect trade in 2002, for instance, reached US$41 billion.[11] In terms of Taiwanese investment in China, the total contracted amount in 2001 came to US$6.91 billion, and the realized amount reached US$2.98 billion.[12] From January to November 2001, Taiwanese made 3.18 million visits to China.[13]

FACTORS CONTRIBUTING TO THE VOLATILITY OF TAIWAN'S MAINLAND POLICY

As noted above, the major factor contributing to the volatility of Taiwan's mainland China policy is the divergent views on the national identity issue, a controversial issue no one interested in the politics of this democracy would overlook.[14] Indeed, it serves as the major cleavage in the society, underpinning Taiwan's party structure.[15] It has tremendous influence on the making of Taiwan's mainland China policy.

The national identity issue refers to the views on the political association between Taiwan and mainland China. Some people hold the view that Taiwan is part of China, and should eventually be reunified with the mainland. Some disagree and insist that Taiwan and China are different countries, and should be separated for good. There are still others who take a middle position, and are willing to live with the status quo which contains a certain degree of Chineseness (e.g. the official name of the country, the Constitution, the national anthem, and so on) while maintaining de facto independence. Table 10.1 displays the distribution of voters on this issue since 1992.

The figures in table 10.1 are based upon surveys conducted by the Opinion Research Taiwan in 1992, and by the Election Study Center of National Chengchi University in 1994–99. The 2002 data are drawn from the 2001 Taiwan Election and Democratization Studies (TEDS) survey which was actually conducted in early 2002. They are all nationwide surveys except the 1994 survey which excludes Taipei and Kaohsiung Cities. As a result, the 1994 data are not comparable with others. However, since the

Table 10.1 Voters' attitude toward the national identity issue

Issue position (Year)	Independence (%)	Status quo (%)	Reunification (%)	Total (%)
1992	12.4	30.6	56.9	99.9
1994	18.1	45.0	36.9	100.0
1995	15.3	51.1	33.6	100.0
1996	21.4	53.5	25.1	100.0
1999	27.7	43.5	28.8	100.0
2000	21.5	46.1	32.4	100.0
2002	24.0	48.3	27.7	100.0

Note: Cell entries are row percentages that may not sum to 100 due to rounding.

Source: Based upon surveys conducted by the Opinion Research Taiwan in 1992 and the Election Study Center of National Chengchi University in 1994–2000. The 2002 data come from Taiwan Election and Democratization Studies (TEDS) 2001 (actually conducted in early 2002).

trend revealed in 1994 is consistent with other surveys, they are included here, but should be read with more care.

In these surveys, the respondents were asked about their attitudes toward the national identity issue. Often, two or more types of questions are used to tackle the respondents' positions on this issue. The one reported here is the question asking the respondents to locate their own positions on an eleven-point scale ranging from 0 to 10 with 0 standing for independence and 10 for reunification. They were also asked about the major political parties' positions on this issue as they perceive. As is clear in table 10.1, regarding the respondents' own positions, there has been, over the years, a slight increase in the number of people favoring independence (scores 0 to 4), and a decrease, quite drastic at the beginning, in the number of people supporting reunification (scores 6 to 10). Except for the 1992 survey, a majority (or close to a majority) of the respondents took the middle position (score 5) which might be seen as the status quo, neither independence nor reunification.[16]

Among the major political parties, there are two broad camps, the pan-KMT and the pan-DPP camps. The former is seen as more pro-reunification and the latter more pro-independence. Within each camp, there are subtle differences among the parties. In the pan-KMT camp, the KMT stresses the status quo but leans somewhat toward reunification, and the two parties split from the KMT, the People First Party (PFP) and the New Party (NP), particularly the latter, are often seen as more pro-reunification. In the pan-DPP camp, the DPP has been known for its stance on independence; but lately, in order to attract voters in the middle, it modified its position by claiming that Taiwan has already been independent, and its current name is the Republic of China. This shift irritated many of its staunch supporters, some of whom left the party to form the Taiwan Independence Party (TAIP). The Taiwan Solidarity Union (TSU), formed in 2001 with Lee Teng-hui, former ROC president and KMT chairman, as its "spiritual leader," was originally able to attract supporters from both the pan-KMT and pan-DPP camps, but is now often regarded as even more pro-independence than the DPP.

In debates over Taiwan's mainland China policy, national identity is certainly not the only issue involved—though definitely the dominant one. Among other issues which may be brought into the picture, the issue of business interests versus security concerns often looms very large. Yet, in the final analysis, it can be found that even such an issue is closely intertwined with the national identity cleavage.[17]

As noted previously, economic ties between Taiwan and China have expanded a great deal in the past several years. China's cheap and hard-working labor and its huge market have attracted a lot of Taiwanese businessmen to seek business opportunities in China. As a matter of fact, Taiwan has benefitted from its China trade as evidenced by its huge surplus, amounting to $25.11 billion in 2002.[18] Some people also argue that, by moving, for instance, labor-intensive industries from Taiwan to China, Taiwan may be able to upgrade its industrial structure.

But others disagree. Quite a few of them are worried that relying too heavily on the Chinese market may endanger Taiwan's security. After all, China remains hostile toward Taiwan, and Taiwanese businesses may be, in a sense, held hostage by China. As shown in table 10.2, the share of Taiwan's indirect trade with China in Taiwan's total trade has been steadily increasing over the years. Now, China has already become Taiwan's largest export market. Taiwan's trade in 2002 with China accounted for 16.9 percent of its total trade; the export figure reached 25.3 percent. Many people are also concerned about the increasing investment by Taiwanese businessmen in China, especially recent investments in hi-tech industries.[19]

The business interests versus security concerns issue is a very controversial one, which would inevitably affect the government's policy toward mainland China. Nonetheless, if we take a closer look at the debate, it is interesting to note that this issue is closely intertwined with the national identity issue. Generally, those who are in favor of Taiwan independence are especially

Table 10.2 The share of the cross-Strait trade in Taiwan's total foreign trade (%)

Year	Export share	Import share	Total trade share
1991	9.1	1.8	5.8
1992	11.9	1.6	7.1
1993	14.9	1.3	8.5
1994	15.7	2.2	9.3
1995	16.0	3.0	9.8
1996	16.5	3.0	10.2
1997	16.8	3.4	10.3
1998	16.6	3.9	10.4
1999	17.5	4.1	11.1
2000	17.6	4.4	11.2
2001	19.6	5.5	13.0
2002	25.3	7.1	16.9

Source: Estimated by the Board of Foreign Trade, Ministry of Economic Affairs, Republic of China. See <http://www.trade.gov.tw/prc&hk/bi_ch/mo_index.htm>.

concerned about the negative impact of business dealings on Taiwan's security while those supporting reunification tend to see economic exchanges between mainland China and Taiwan in a positive light.

Among the political parties, the TSU is now very much on the independence side, and is fiercely opposed to economic exchanges between Taiwan and China. The DPP is more moderate; since it is now the ruling party, it feels pressures from the business community to loosen up the governmental regulations restricting business dealings with China. But the party as a whole remains suspicious of close economic ties with China. On the other side, the parties in the pan-KMT camp are generally in favor of doing business with China. This is particularly true for the PFP and NP.

However, there are exceptions to this general rule. For example, some businessmen may be in favor of Taiwan independence, but they may well consider business dealings with China necessary. Or many of those working in the security apparatus in Taiwan may be socialized in Chinese nationalism, and may thus favor eventual reunification between Taiwan and mainland China. Yet they are very much concerned about Taiwan's security, and may consequently oppose close economic ties with the mainland under the current circumstances.

Nevertheless, barring exceptions, the national identity issue and the issue of business interests versus security concerns are closely intertwined. Indeed, if our interest is to examine Taiwan's mainland China policy which is made essentially by politicians and the political parties they belong to, we can safely disregard the businessmen and security personnel. As a result, the issue of business interests versus security concerns may be submerged in the national identity issue. To understand the making of Taiwan's mainland China policy, what we need to do is to look at essentially the positions taken by the various political parties on the national identity issue. Then, what type of policy will eventually emerge will be determined by the relative strength of the political parties in the policymaking process. The crucial question is: Who controls the government?

WHO CONTROLS THE GOVERNMENT?

Before we talk about who controls the Taiwan government, we need to clarify the term government in Taiwanese context. Basically the ROC Constitution provides for a parliamentary form of government. According to the Constitution, the highest administrative organ in the country is the Executive Yuan (cabinet), not the president; the Executive Yuan is responsible to the Legislative Yuan (parliament), not to the president; the Legislative Yuan can employ a vote of no confidence against the Executive Yuan although the president or the premier, the head of the Executive Yuan, with the consent of the president, can dissolve the Legislative Yuan after the Legislative Yuan passes the vote of no confidence; and when the president promulgates laws and issues ordinances, he or she should obtain the countersignature of the premier or the countersignatures of the premier and the ministers concerned. All these indicate that the system is essentially parliamentary, and even after the recent constitutional reforms, the basic structure remains intact.[20]

But the ROC presidents have almost always been very powerful in the policymaking process with the exception of Yen Chia-kan in 1975–78. Before democratization gradually took shape in the late 1980s and early 1990s, the presidents' power came from their role as heads of the ruling KMT, which had commanded a comfortable majority in parliament, and, in the cases of the two Chiangs at least, from their firm control of the military as well. Indeed, the power structure within the KMT was so centralized that the leader of the party dominated almost everything. Through the party, Chiang Kai-shek, Chiang Ching-kuo, and Lee Teng-hui could, thus, exert tremendous influence in Taiwan's policymaking process, including the making of Taiwan's mainland China policy.

Even after Taiwan became democratic, President Lee, serving simultaneously as the chairman of the KMT, was able to dictate Taiwan's mainland China policy, particularly after he defeated many of his conservative political enemies in the early 1990s.

With the inauguration of the DPP president, Chen Shui-bian, in 2000, the situation has been different. The KMT remained the majority party in the Legislative Yuan. Chen first appointed a nonpartisan "all-people" government, and a few months later, formed a minority DPP government. Without the majority support in the Legislative Yuan, it could be expected from the outset that there would be a serious stalemate between the executive and legislative branches of government.

In the 2001 Legislative Yuan election, the DPP emerged as the largest parliamentary party; and with the help of the TSU, the position of the DPP in the Legislative Yuan has improved a great deal, but the pan-DPP camp was still short of a majority, and a certain degree of deadlock has persisted. Yet the KMT is now weakened and the pan-KMT camp is further divided. Consequently the DPP government is in a somewhat better position to exploit the situation.

As far as the cross-Strait relations are concerned, this means that, without enough support in the Legislative Yuan, it is very difficult for the current DPP government to, say, move toward establishing an independent Taiwan, not to mention many other internal and external constraints keeping it from moving in that direction.[21] Therefore we can anticipate the continuation of the current policy, at least until the March 2004 presidential election.

Who is going to win in the 2004 election? This is certainly highly speculative. However, if, as it seems to be, the pan-KMT camp can come up with a single ticket, and given the relative strength between the pan-KMT and the pan-DPP camps, the former, under normal circumstance, may defeat the latter in such an election.[22] Of course nothing is absolutely certain. If there was a scandal implicating the pan-KMT candidates, it may change the electoral balance drastically. Or if Chen is able to find a running mate acceptable to many pan-KMT supporters, the situation may change as well.

Of course, which camp is going to win the presidential election and to control the Legislative Yuan will greatly affect Taiwan's mainland China policy. If the pan-KMT camp, as expected, is able to win the presidential race in 2004 and manages to control a majority in the Legislative Yuan, the cross-Strait relations may be more cordial than under the current DPP administration.

CONCLUSION

Ever since the 1995–96 missile crisis, the political relations between China and Taiwan have been strained. Yet the economic and social exchanges across the Taiwan Strait have grown tremendously. Generally, China's policy toward Taiwan has been pretty consistent over the years. Even with the ascendance of the fourth generation leadership led by Hu Jintao, the policy may not deviate too much from the previous course. However, Taiwan's mainland China policy has been much more volatile given the democratic nature of the Taiwanese polity and the divergent views on the future political association between Taiwan and mainland China among the people in Taiwan. Thus, the key to understanding the possible changes in cross-Strait relations may lie in Taiwan's internal political dynamics. In this context, the March 2004 presidential election is definitely an important event to watch. Under normal circumstances, the pan-KMT camp is more likely to win if it can hold together as a single ticket. And if it indeed wins, and is able to maintain its control over the Legislative Yuan, the cross-Strait relations may be very different from what we have witnessed under the DPP administration. But nothing is certain. A number of factors (e.g. scandals) may tilt the balance between the two major camps in the 2004 presidential race. We must just wait and see.[23]

NOTES

1. *People's Daily*, January 1, 1979.
2. *People's Daily*, February 1, 1979.
3. Quoted from Deng's talk to an American delegation on February 22, 1984. See Kuo Li-min (ed.), *Mainland China's Policy Toward Taiwan: Selected Documents (1949–1991)*, Volume 1 [in Chinese] (Taipei, ROC: Yung-yeh, 1992), pp. 588–89.
4. *People's Daily*, January 31, 1995.
5. James Kynge, "Beijing's New Leader Takes Over Key Post," *Financial Times*, June 18, 2003.
6. Ibid.
7. *China Times*, March 12, 2003.
8. See Chu Hai-yuan, Ting Ting-yu, Lin Cheng-I, and Tsai Ming-chang, *The Impact of Visiting Mainland Relatives and Other Visits* [in Chinese] (Taipei, ROC: Institute for National Policy Research, 1989), p. 12.
9. Mainland Affairs Council, *Cross the Historical Gap: Retrospect and Prospect of a Decade of Cross-Strait Exchanges* [in Chinese] (Taipei, ROC: Mainland Affairs Council, Executive Yuan, 1997), p. 371.

10. See Lee Teng-hui, *Managing a Great Taiwan* (Taipei: Yuan-liu, 1995), pp. 469–83. This interview was deleted from the new edition of the book.
11. See <http://www.trade.gov.tw/prc&hk/bi_ch/mo_index.htm>.
12. See <http://tga.moftec.gov.cn/article/200208/20020800035529_1.xml>.
13. See <http://www.chinabiz.org.tw/maz/Eco-Month/home.htm>.
14. See John Fuh-sheng Hsieh and Emerson M.S. Niou, "Issue Voting in the Republic of China on Taiwan's 1992 Legislative Yuan Election," *International Political Science Review*, vol. 17, no. 1 (January 1996), pp. 13–27; idem., "Salient Issues in Taiwan's Electoral Politics," *Electoral Studies*, vol. 15, no. 2 (May 1996), pp. 51–70; and Tse-min Lin, Yun-han Chu, and Melvin J. Hinich, "Conflict Displacement and Regime Transition in Taiwan: A Spatial Analysis," *World Politics*, vol. 48, no. 4 (July 1996), pp. 453–81.
15. See John Fuh-sheng Hsieh, "Continuity and Change in Taiwan's Electoral Politics," in John Fuh-sheng Hsieh and David Newman (eds.), *How Asia Votes* (New York: Chatham House, 2002), pp. 32–49. This makes Taiwan very different from most Western democracies where class, religion, and so on are the major cleavages shaping party structures.
16. It should be noted that the national identity issue is intertwined with ethnic identity. Except for a small group of aborigines, there are three major ethnic groups in Taiwan: Minnan, Hakka, and mainlanders. The first two groups are local Taiwanese whose ancestors came from mainland China to Taiwan several hundred years ago, and the last group, the mainlanders, arrived in Taiwan only in the late 1940s or afterwards. As can be seen from the following table, Minnan Taiwanese are more likely than others to favor Taiwan independence, while the mainlanders are more likely to support reunification. The Hakka Taiwanese are somewhere in between. Nevertheless, a sizeable portion of respondents in each group are in favor of the status quo.
17. See John Fuh-sheng Hsieh, "National Identity and Taiwan's Mainland China Policy," *Journal of Contemporary China* (August).
18. See <http://www.trade.gov.tw/prc&hk/bi_ch/mo_index.htm>.
19. See, for example, Peggy Pei-chen Chang and Tun-jen Cheng, "The Rise of Information Technology Industry on the Mainland China: A Formidable Challenge to Taiwan's Economy," paper presented at the Conference on Taiwan Issues, University of South Carolina, Columbia, South Carolina, April 20–22, 2001.
20. A lot of people argue that since the recent constitutional reform, the president is now directly popularly elected, and can appoint the premier without the need of an investiture vote in the Legislative Yuan, the constitutional form of government is no longer parliamentary. However, this is erroneous because these features appear in many other parliamentary democracies as well. Many people also maintain that the current ROC system resembles the mixed

Position ethnicity	Independence (%)	Status quo (%)	Reunification (%)	Total (%)
Minnan Taiwanese	27.0	48.7	24.3	100.0
Hakka Taiwanese	21.0	50.0	29.0	100.0
Mainlanders	6.5	42.9	50.5	99.9

Note: Cell entries are row percentages that may not sum to 100 due to rounding.

Source: Taiwan Election and Democratization Study 2001 (actually conducted in 2002).

system as exemplified by the French Fifth Republic. But even this comparison is not quite right since the French president can wield a number of important weapons to counteract the parliament while the ROC president simply cannot. See John Fuh-sheng Hsieh, "The 2000 Presidential Election and Its Implications for Taiwan's Domestic Politics," *Issues & Studies*, vol. 37, no. 1 (January/February 2001), pp. 7–9.

21. For a discussion of such constraints, see John Fuh-sheng Hsieh, "How Far Can Taiwan Go?" *Cambridge Review of International Affairs*, vol. 15, no. 1 (April 2002), pp. 105–13.

22. The relative strength of the two major camps has been very much stabilized in the past decade or so. See Hsieh, "Continuity and Change in Taiwan's Electoral Politics."

23. After finishing this article, Taiwan held the presidential election on March 20, 2004. Even though most of the polls indicated that the pan-KMT candidate Lien Chan would defeat the incumbent President Chen Shui-bian, the assassination attempt at Chen on the eve of the election tilted the balance between the two sides, resulting in the victory of President Chen by a slim margin. The pan-KMT camp immediately asked for recount and decided to sue the President and the Central Election Commission for irregularities in the election.

INDEX

Italics indicate table.

16th Congress of the CCP, 4–8, 10,
  15–24, 31, 37, 39–42, 45, 48–50,
  57, 73, 133–134, 136–137,
  148–149, 152–156, 170–171,
  175, 178, 181, 193–194
  ideological preparations for, 26–28
  key personnel arrangements for,
    25–26
  terminology changes from 15th
    Congress, *154–156*

age, as political factor, 7–8, 16–17, 25,
  38–41, 45, 52, 91, 94, 170
ASEAN (Association of Southeast Asian
  Nations), 25, 154, 180

Bunce, Valerie, 3
bureaucracy, 19, 30, 72–73, 75,
  119–120, 182
Bush, George W., 33*n*, 142, 169,
  177–178, 181–182

Cao Gangchuan, 16, 21–22, 40, 170
capitalism, 3, 5, 11, 23, 27–28, 31,
  59–60, 150–152, 154, 194
Carter Center, 126, 130
Central Committee, 7, 17, 21, 40–42,
  47–51, 84–85, 87, 89, 100,
  107–108, 110, 115, 120, 134,
  137, 170
Central Military Commission (CMC),
  21, 171, 187*n*
  see also military
centralism, 8, 38, 47, 49, 51–52, 107
centralization, 5, 7, 51, 62, 64,
  147–148, 200
charisma, 5, 58, 69, 72, 147
Chen Shui-bian, 25, 195, 200
Chiang Ching-kuo, 53, 195, 200

China Council for the Promotion of
  Basic-Level Governments and Mass
  Organization (CCPBGMO),
  124–125
China Society for the Development
  of Townships and Towns
  (CSDTT), 125
Chinese Communist Party (CCP), 3–8,
  10–11, 15, 17, 21, 23, 38, 42,
  46–48, 57–66, 69, 72–73, 82–83,
  86, 89, 106–108, 110, 113,
  115–116, 119–120, 124–125,
  133–134, 137, 145, 147–150,
  193–194
  division of power within, 48–49
  intra-party democracy, 46–52;
    contraints on, 51–52
  introduction of electoral mechanisms,
    49–50
  legitimacy of, 147–149
  power sharing among the Party elite,
    47–48
  transformation of, 58–61
  village branches, 84–86
  see also 16th Congress of the CCP;
    Party Constitution
Chinese People's Political Consultative
  Conference (CPPCC), 160–162
Chinese Rural Official Training Center
  (CROTC), 125
citizens' political petition access, 61–64
clans, 82, 87, 96, 98–99, 116
communes, 62–63, 83, 85–86, 97,
  105–107, 109–110, 113, 129
cooperatives, 83, 85
corruption, 8, 48, 52, 58, 60–61, 69,
  75, 87–88, 93, 95, 97, 150, 163,
  172
crime, 69, 71, 76, 164, 179